Things I Only Did Once

Growing Up Stories

Clark Malcolm Greene

PUBLISH AMERICA

PublishAmerica
Baltimore

First printing

ISBN: 1-4241-7610-7 (softcover)
ISBN: 978-1-4489-2061-7 (hardcover)
PUBLISHED BY PUBLISHAMERICA, LLLP
www.publishamerica.com
Baltimore

Printed in the United States of America

Dedicated to my wife, Paula Jean Matrosic Greene.
You inspire and encourage me.
You take me by the hand when I lose my way.
What else needs be said about love?

Author's email address: cmalcolmg@hotmail.com

Author's web site: clarkmalcolmgreene.com

Thank you so much,
Ellie Jordaan & Carolyn Mathes-McAninch.
Where would this mish-mash be floating without
the keen eyes and red pens of my editors?

For Basil and Carolyn and Pat and Ray.
Who would have thought?

Cover photo by Paula Jean Matrosic Greene.

Excerpt from "Going for Water" and "Stopping by Woods on a Snowy Evening" from THE POETRY OF ROBERT FROST edited by Edward Connery Lathem.
Copyright 1923, 1934, 1969 by Henry Holt and Company.
Copyright 1951, 1962 by Robert Frost. Reprinted by permission of Henry Holt and Company, LLC

Table of Contents

Chapter 1
A Beginning, of Sorts

There is more to a namesake than a name.

There was a time in his life when one of my grandfathers was a gangster. In the 1920s and 1930s quite a few people in Detroit were involved in some sort of questionable activities and my grandpa Clark wasn't one to be left on the sidelines or kept clear of any money making enterprise.

He certainly looked the part of a gangster as a young man, tall and burly, wearing a double breasted suit, hair slicked back, and hat pulled down low over one eye. The eye that is visible in one of his old photos also shows a man you might think twice about speaking to. That caution extended to his family as well.

Family lore had it that during the Depression, when the bulk of the population struggled and scrabbled for every nickel, Grandpa had wads of money secreted in all of his pockets and had a "special" roll kept in a money belt he wore under his clothes. He then drove a big V-12 Lincoln, courtesy of Ford Motor Company. He had been somehow, which was never explained, involved with Henry Ford, wore a huge Masonic diamond ring, and had a shave and a shoe-shine every day at a hotel in downtown Detroit.

Grandpa knew and associated with people like Richard Daly, of Chicago mayoral fame, Jack Dempsey, the heavy-weight champion, and he went on several paid-for hunting excursions to Cuba and Argentina, and played golf with Henry Ford and Orville Hubbard, the mayor of Dearborn. According to my father, Grandpa also knew quite a few people who drove big black cars but were never introduced to the family when they came for a visit.

Of course, some of the money and associations came with a price beyond dollars. My father told of several occasions when he and my uncle Dave were growing up that they slept a few nights with the living room couch as a barrier between them and anyone with a grudge driving by. I don't think Grandpa worried about that. Even when he turned respectable, he carried a pistol in a shoulder holster and continued to do so until his death in the late 1960s. He said it was habit. He also said, "You never know."

Grandpa Clark served several terms as Commissioner of Public Works in Dearborn during the 1940s, and made political friends who proffered plums of opportunity. Grandpa picked those fruits easily enough and he spent money freely when he had it. The good times frequently didn't last and he had to find something else for income. Grandpa Clark gained and lost several fair fortunes during his lifetime, and when he managed to grab one he spent it quickly, before it "disappeared all by itself," he used to laugh. The highs and lows didn't bother Grandpa. He laughed frequently regardless of his finances.

He could make money and his sailboat was proof of that. The boat had a woman's name, "Gracie," after my grandmother. Grandpa bought it and their Stoney Pointe peninsula home when he was in one of his "have money" phases, enjoying the possessions that his good fortune could buy.

The sailboat was a beauty, thirty-five feet long with an enclosed cabin and white hull, a wooden sloop with a blue stripe down her sides. The cabin was all varnished mahogany and teak with a real ship's wheel, no tiller here, and Grandpa loved the boat fiercely. Despite his affection, the boat's namesake would seldom come on board. Grandma Grace would excuse herself through the pretense of her work as a youth psychologist, retreating to the study and busying herself there. She thought it silly that Grandpa had the boat, but that day in July would be different.

While my family still lived in Manchester, my Grandpa and Grandma Greene purchased their beautiful peninsula home looking out over Lake Erie from a high-banked beach lot. The home at "The Pointe" was luxurious by any standards, with four bedrooms, three baths, and servants' quarters, although my grandparents never had any. The house was additional proof of Grandpa's money. Our family often spent weekend time there swimming and playing beach games. My sister, Carole, and I both looked forward to these weekends for both grandparents spoiled us with treats and toys.

On one hot July day, Carole, my mother, and Jere Ellen, my Uncle Dave's new wife, would stay at the house while Grandpa Clark, Uncle Dave, my father and Grandma Grace would be taking 2½-year-old little Clark on his first sail. I was excited as we waded out in the lake to climb the stern ladder on the boat, and ran around and around the cabin as soon as my father set me down from his shoulders, until Grandma grabbed me while the men got the boat ready. Grandpa usually kept the boat in Luna Pier, well south of Monroe, but for the weekends he would sail up and anchor it bow and stern off the beach in front of their house.

Grandpa was a long-time sailor and handled the boat well. He had a willing crew in my father and my uncle, Dad's younger brother, and ordered them about with the dual authority of Captain and Father. Grandma Grace was along just for the ride and to keep me from falling overboard while the men played at sail boating. Everyone was in bathing suits because of the wade out to the boat, but Grandma had carried some shirts and pants perched on her head for me if I got cold. It didn't look like I was going to need the clothes on that July 4th, but she said even hot days could seem cold when the boat skimmed fast over the water.

Grandma had a tight grip on me most of the time, but I kept her busy when I managed to break free and scurry to my father and uncle sitting on the forward deck. I was satisfied with being just like the "big boys" for only a few minutes before I was off again running around the cabin, Grandpa growling and laughing at me every time I passed. We rounded the peninsula and headed south, the lake smooth and sleek before us. We would sail past Luna Pier to Toledo and back again. As with lots of youngsters, I tired out quickly, my energy flowing away like the water speeding past the hull. The boat's motion and the warm sun almost put me to sleep before we had traveled half-way to Toledo and my father carried me down into the cabin where he put me in one of the two forward berths. I usually hated naps but the lure of that one was irresistible.

I woke up because my head smacked the hull with a thud. I started screaming and it took some minutes for Grandma Grace to get to me because she hadn't heard me right away because of other pressing matters. The boat was leaning so badly I couldn't move away from the berth's curved wall. I heard the slurp of water inside as Grandma lurched into the cabin. I was scared to death, actually terrified, and wailing to prove it, but my screams were drowned by the explosions of thunder and wind outside the cabin.

The boat gave a terrible lurch with the sound of wood splintering and there was suddenly lots more water in there with Grandma and me. She was screaming then and I'm sure we were making more noise than the storm, but nobody else came below. The three men were far too busy.

While I had slept, a storm had blown in from the north astern of the boat and Grandpa had noticed it boiling and roiling up as we were still approaching Luna Pier. Grandpa had run the boat well off shore, almost two miles, and my grandmother was worried by the storm. Grandpa *almost* bowed to the wishes of Grandma Grace when she begged to put in to the mooring at Luna Pier, but Grandpa Clark wanted the boat kept at the house for the weekend. He said the storm was going to Canada but he would come about and head back to the Pointe and quit sailing for the day if she was worried. He might have listened but that wasn't the way my grandfather did things. He mostly went 180 degrees from suggestions as a part of his nature, and he wasn't about to go against it this time.

Storms on Lake Erie will shake the water up fast. Erie is a shallow lake and storm driven waves reach eight and ten feet in height quickly. The lake's shallow depth also creates waves without patterns which build and crash into one another as often as on the shore. Coming out of the north, the storm was on Grandpa too quickly to run the boat before it. He sailed in close to the shore, into Brest Bay and the peninsula's lee, hugging the beach in order to reduce the storm's effect if it continued to pick up.

The sky darkened like night when the clouds thickened and the wind picked up to a howl lashing boat and people with huge splats of rain. Lake Erie can create terrible boating conditions even for a boat the size of the Gracie, and the waves threw the boat in many directions at once. When Grandpa rounded the tip of the Pointe, no longer in the lee of the peninsula, the boat took a wave across the stern bad enough to wet the engine compartment and prevent the motor from starting. That wave wet Grandma and me too.

The screaming violence of the wind and waves threw the boat up on the rocks at the peninsula's tip as the lightning flashed bright on the houses.

Although Grandma and Grandpa's house was in sight and we were almost there, nothing could be done once the storm grabbed the boat. Grandpa was a fine sailor despite the miscalculation of the storm. He had managed to keep the boat pointed up in the wind and was struggling to hold it off the beach. It was a fight he couldn't win but that didn't stop his trying.

Grandma and I were tossed and thrown about like puppets on strings inside the cabin. We were both drenched from the water pouring through the hatch. I watched her move in stop action as the lightning lit up the cabin in stutters and flashes. The wave's jumbled violence prevented the boat from making progress away from the shore and the Gracie went stern to onto the rocks. She lodged on the rocky ledge and the bow swung to and fro with every wave as Uncle Dave and Dad stumbled and fell down the ship's ladder.

Grandpa Clark threw life preservers down the hatch and screamed over the booms of thunder, "Get one on the boy! Grace, you get one on too, the boat's gone! She's going down! We've got to get out!"

The thunder and lightning flashed and boomed again and again to punctuate Grandpa's fear. Everyone was scared, but Grandma and I were the only ones screaming.

I watched my Uncle Dave put his hands on Grandma's butt and shove her up the ladder to Grandpa just as a wave swung the Gracie's bow parallel to the shore. Grandma and Grandpa must have both run to the bow of the boat and jumped into the water only thirty or forty feet from the shore because that's where I saw them next. Uncle Dave followed them up on deck and Dad had me securely around the waist as he laced the oversize life preserver on.

I couldn't stop screaming but the noise didn't seem to go

anywhere. The thunder pounded so loud it shook the boat when it cracked and rolled over it. A series of waves rolled the boat over on the port side farther and farther and with each roll the boat's keel walked itself deeper into the sand and rocks. She was really sinking now, so full of water that the undulations slowed down, and she rocked lazily back and forth. The storm seemed to worsen and the sky lit up in long sheets and flashes of lightning. The Gracie had plenty of water inside her, so heavy then she rolled farther over on her side and didn't come back up.

The lurch caused my father to lose his footing and caused Uncle Dave to slide across the deck into the water. Still inside the cabin, Dad had taken a heavy fall, crashing against the hull interior but he had managed to keep hold of me.

"Give him to me, Jerry, give him to me!" Uncle Dave hollered from the water.

Dave had been thrown clear and was steadying himself in about four or five feet of water. Dave disappeared in every wave but fought his way back toward the boat in every trough, and holding himself away from the hull when it rolled. The lightning continued, blinding, crackling and snapping sharp.

Finally, Grandma and Grandpa reached shallower water and were almost to shore. Despite having to brace against the waves, they stood watching as Dad handed me out the hatch to his brother and waves broke over us both. Uncle Dave managed to swing me to his shoulders and let the waves push and carry us to shore, my dad two strokes or steps behind us.

I didn't need any more scaring but the storm apparently thought I did. A series of waves broke over my head and I choked on the water and screamed anew with the fright and shock. Uncle Dave tried to calm me by making it a game but I wasn't having any of that.

I was terrified, and twisted and squirmed and screamed louder once I got rid of the water. Every time the lightning flashed, I could see Grandma and Grandpa and I let go of Dave's neck to hold my hands over my ears when the thunder exploded.

The waves were crashing on the concrete walls that fronted everyone's property and receding, only to gather again. Where the sand was visible, it was all froth and foam, the wind and water changing with each wave that smashed upon it. Both men were exhausted by the time they reached the half-submerged beach.

Grandma took me from my uncle's shoulders and hurried the several hundred yards down the beach to their house. She gave a little screech every time a wave reached her feet or the lightning flashed. We were both crying and shrieking when we finally got to the house.

The three Greene men watched the boat roll back and forth as the Gracie sadly rocked farther onto the rocks and sand.

The next day the Gracie didn't look like much of a sailing ship. Her sails were full of sand and there was a big jagged hole where the rudder should have been. She was rolled all the way over, her cabin partly full of sand from the waves and her mast touching the beach. A crowd of neighbors and curious people gathered to look at the boat. As they walked around the hull, touching and talking about it, Aunt Jere Ellen took pictures. All the grownups, all the neighbors said how lucky we were to have reached shore.

"How lucky...and with that little boy too."

"Everybody was lucky."

"Such a terrible storm."

Grandpa said very little and he didn't look very lucky to me. He just looked sad.

As we viewed the boat, Uncle Dave told me I had been brave but I didn't remember being brave at all. I only remembered being scared.

My Grandpa had to hire a crew of people from Detroit to free and right the boat, so the Gracie was salvaged after the storm's fury, but Grandma made him get rid of her.

Many years later, my father told me he knew the boat was going to the rocky point just as soon at they rounded the Pointe when the wind's violence stopped the boat dead in the water and they took the waves that caused the knock on my head. He said the boat's loss was one of the saddest things he had ever seen.

My Grandpa Clark never again talked to anybody about the tragedy.

Lake Erie held many more surprises in store for me and the rest of the family.

Although most days the lake is a place of pleasure and play, it can be an unpredictable beast at times.

One spring Lake Erie was all turmoil. There had been early and quick warm weather along with several consecutive days of high winds from the east. Water pushed up over the beach and roadways until it filled the first level of Grandpa Clark's garage and house with four feet of still frigid water. School closed because all the beach neighborhoods had low areas and roads became impassable. Mom used the school-closed time to give us Noah and the ark lessons.

On the third straight day of high water, a phone call from Grandpa informed us that the rising water had trapped him and Grandma Grace.

Stoney Pointe Peninsula had one circuitous road running between the houses and the man-made canal. This shallow waterway had been dug around the turn of the century to shelter property owner's pleasure boats from the occasional violence of Lake Erie's storms. In the shape of an inverted "V," the canal was about forty feet wide and was crossed by three bridges, one of them at the entrance from the lake on the southeast bay side of the peninsula.

In order to rescue Grandma and Grandpa, Dad had to park by Eddie Orleans' store at the entrance to Stoney Pointe, a distance of several hundred yards or more from where the beach should have been. The road was covered with about two feet of water, but my father knew it would get deeper before he waded onto Grandpa's street. He had worn knee-boots and so had I, but both of us took them off and put our shoes on again. The water would be much deeper than up to our knees. We were going to be really wet and really cold before this was over. We managed to wade hand in hand to a point adjacent the peninsula entrance despite the waves that were frequently big enough to rock me back on my heels. I got scared as the water crept higher up my thighs and I was quick to tell my dad I wanted to go back to the car or home where it wasn't wet, where it wasn't cold.

He just laughed and asked me, "Whatareyou, afraid of a little water? C'mon, I'll carry you."

Yes, I was afraid of this "little" water. There was nothing but water in the direction we were heading. I could see the water stretched from where I was all the way to a dim horizon. It was late in the evening and turning dark, something that would only add to this five-year-old's fright.

By now I was wet to my belt and my undies were starting to chafe. My father wasn't a tall man, only five-eight, but it was so amazing how my perception of rising water differed from his. I was only three feet tall. Dad laughed again and crouched down a bit so I could clamber to his shoulders. I put my left foot on his thigh and swung my other leg over his neck holding him with both hands under his chin. This was definitely better despite my already soaked condition.

Dad wore his old Navy pea-coat made from thick wool and it was hard to get a grip with my legs but he kept me in place with both of his hands on my wet tennis shoes. He waded to the wooden bus stop shed before the water got much deeper, though from my current position I wasn't concerned about how deep it got now. I knew I was safe. The waves from Lake Erie were much higher and stronger by the bus stop and I could feel my father tense and hesitate as each wave pushed against him. The water was lots deeper here and the waves were getting me wet again. I wondered out loud if Dad's undies bothered him, too. He said, "Yes."

Dad resembled a deep-sea diver as he half-swam, half-walked to Grandpa and Grandma's house, complete-with-Clark-for-a-helmet. He had to continually lean forward against the slow motion, heavy force of the water and I'm sure it exhausted and chilled him badly. He ended up wading about a half mile through freezing water and he had to stop every so often by a jutting tree to rest for a short time. We eventually got to Grandpa's but by then my father had been in the cold water for about an hour and was shivering badly. We stopped long enough to cut the rope holding Grandpa's small rowboat by the canal but we couldn't see the canal's edge and I remember my father feeling carefully with his feet for the invisible edge of the canal's bank. It had grown full dark and the only objects to mark anything were the houses on one side and several trees on the far side of the canal, not much help.

Everything was submerged. Dad had to struggle to get his pocketknife out of his wet jeans and I recall him shuddering violently and uncontrollably from the long immersion. He swung me off his shoulder to put me in the boat and guided it to the back door of

Grandpa and Grandma's house. The first floor of their house was flooded, completely under water, and it took Dad some time to secure the boat and get the door open. He was almost to the point of not functioning from the effects of the water when Grandpa walked down the half covered stairs to help Dad into the house.

Grandpa Clark told me he'd be right back. "Stay there."

No problem, I wasn't going anywhere unless the boat worked free. He was only gone a few moments but it seemed a week. I was shivering, too, when Grandpa gathered me in his arms and climbed the stairs. Dad was standing next to Grandma in front of the fireplace when Grandpa set me down and I scurried over to the crackling fire. Grandpa walked over to his well stocked bar.

We didn't have alcohol at our house because Mom lived there.

So did God. At least we were told He visited "whenever one or more were gathered in His name."

While there was nothing stronger than Kool-Aid (and not much of that) at our house, my grandpa did have liquor and plenty of it. Glittering bottles with silver and red and gold labels lined the mirror base behind his hand-built watering station. They were beautiful, even though they contained alcohol, something Carole and I had already been warned about.

I was pretty surprised when Grandpa gave Dad a glass of something from one of those bottles and even more surprised when my father emptied it in a gulp. I saw Grandpa pour him a refill as soon as he put the glass back on the table. Grandma Grace hustled to wrap first me and then Dad in blankets and threw more wood into the big stone fireplace. It was toasty and warm. It was a good thing the wood had remained dry. Grandpa kept it stacked in the front of the house, an area still out of the floodwaters. Their power had failed on the second day and this was the only warm spot in the house.

Grandma and Grandpa had obviously been sleeping next to the fireplace. Blankets and pillows were folded and stacked up in the corner. Opened tin cans of pork and beans, soup, and Dinty-Moore beef stew were on top of several plates with silverware stuck in a glass. Their kitchen was on the first floor and had been under water for three days. They had been camping out, something I liked a lot. They had run out of food by then; the water-pump wouldn't work due to the power outage, and the lake didn't look like it was going down anytime in the near future. Grandpa said they had been going to the toilet in the lake. Grandma Grace gave him an elbow in the ribs for this. Why she did that I didn't know. I peed in the lake every time I went swimming. I tried to picture them doing it and couldn't quite get an image. It was the first I heard that grandmas and grandpas even went to the bathroom.

After much discussion, it was decided we would all spend another night. The morning would be better with the daylight and the water might start to recede by then. The trip had sucked the energy out of Dad and from me, too, despite the piggyback ride. There were plenty more blankets and pillows for us to wrap up in. I was all for this, a night at Grandma and Grandpa's, something I didn't get too often. Grandma Grace would have had Carole and me over all the time but my Grandpa Clark probably figured he had done his stint as child watcher. While he loved us and showed it lavishly, there usually came a time during our regular visits when he had enough and barricaded himself behind the closed door of his study.

We headed out bright and early in the morning because there wasn't any food left for breakfast. It was a good thing we ate at home before we started out on this rescue. I got hungry just thinking that there wasn't any food.

Grandma shook me gently in the morning. Dad and Grandpa had been stowing a few things in the small boat. If the water was down, it wasn't down much and still filled the stairway. We would all get more than a little wet getting out the door. Another cold swim and wade for my dad because the boat was much too small to hold us all and we didn't have any oars. They had floated out the open garage door when the waters first rose. Grandpa and Grandma were to be the riders in the boat while I was to get another ride on Dad's shoulders to make sure the boat didn't get overloaded.

We managed to get past the bus stop without incident although my father was once again shivering so badly I was jiggling right along with his every vibration. We took a short cut from the road to lessen the time back to the car. We started to cut across the field inside the curve to the beach and my dad lost his footing immediately. I went under with a shriek. After being warm, even though I had been splashed a bit during the return trip, the water was a shock like no other.

I came up flailing and screaming. Grandpa reached over the side of the boat, grabbed my coat collar, and lifted me half out of the water.

"You're okay, boy, you're okay, you're okay. Quiet down now, we're almost there."

Dad laughed despite the soaking and swung me back up in place. We waded back to the submerged roadway where the footing was more certain, but now I was cold, wet clear through, and it wasn't just my underwear that was chafing me now.

It took another twenty more minutes before we got to where the boat wouldn't float any longer with its load of grandparents. As soon as they got out, we could pull the boat farther along the way to the car. The water was going down; we could see more of the road, and soon we heard only little splashes as we walked. Grandma took two blankets out of the boat and put one around me and another around Dad. They didn't help much but we were almost back to the car. We shoved the boat off the side of the road when we couldn't pull it any farther.

"Leave it, I don't care," my grandpa commanded.

We all were cold and miserable, but Dad was the worst off. Those two trips in deep water sucked the energy right out of him and he was physically spent by the time we reached the car. Grandpa Clark demanded Dad's keys from him and said he would drive. My father, who drove everywhere we went, didn't argue.

The trip to the house took only a few minutes, but I was ready to stand in front of our fireplace during the whole ride. Grandpa beeped the horn as we came to a stop in the driveway. Mom was waiting at the door. She began stripping my wet clothes off as soon as I got in the door and by the time I got to the fireplace I was naked. Dad stripped down to his skivvies and grabbed a blanket off the chair. I saw Grandpa and Grandma in their underwear and wasn't shocked. I didn't even care that Carole was there and I slowly turned with arms outstretched to warm myself. It got crowded around our fireplace quickly. Mom rubbed me down with a big towel, put a dry blanket around me and sat me on the small brown chair over the furnace register on the porch.

Grandpa Clark and my father were sitting on the sofa by the doorway into the living room getting dry and warm. I heard my Grandpa Clark tell my father thank you for coming to get them.

Dad said so softly I almost didn't hear, "I'm your son."

It was apparent early in life that I would find trouble no matter how well it was disguised.

I may have been born under a darkling moon or during some mysterious tempest. Later in life, my parents probably wished for a caul that they'd have been slow to remove, but the fact remains that while other children were involved with being sweet and cuddly, I often found myself being caught between the proverbial rock and someplace harder.

My folks quickly recognized a series of sharp u-turns from their planned straight and narrow road and were able to hold back some of the inevitable disasters that could have befallen me. I managed to careen through most of my early years with the simplest of bumps and bruises.

Early for me meant the age of not quite two, and while my family lived in Manchester, Michigan, located on the fringe of the Irish Hills region. My folks had settled there after my father came home from World War II, and it was within easy driving distance of various grandparents, aunts, uncles and cousins. I had a pair of good attentive parents, but often my legs were able to translate their newfound and wondrous abilities into several escapes. One of these rambles certainly contributed to an everlasting shortness of breath in my mother and a vapor-like temper in my father.

We lived in a small, middle-class wood sided house with a big front porch filled with an older sister, Carole, and my parents, Gerald and Dorothee Greene. Manchester was a farming community as well as the home of my maternal grandparents, Teddy and Phoebe Billings. Although our house was within the small city limits, we had a myriad of animals that either supplemented our diet or provided some small distractions which should have kept me from straying too far.

Two blocks away from our house was a small metal stamping plant: a drab, dirty green, cement block building that resonated with thumps, clunks and clangs and smelled of hot oil. Even at this early age, I was fascinated with the talking building, and I would strain to look through the car window as I sat on my mother's lap. The men who worked there and were taking a break outside would wave and say "hello" to us on nice days. Both of my parents thought it was adorable that I was so interested in the secret doings every time we drove past.

Sometimes, when she was busy elsewhere, it was my mother's practice to tie one end of a rope around my waist and fasten the other end to her belt or to the porch railing. She could garden, tend animals, and hang washing out to dry while easy in her mind about little Clark's whereabouts. I had about a twenty foot limit to my freedom, and for a long while I didn't know about the pleasures of being really free. One summer day, while my mother was curling my sister's hair, or feeding the rabbits, or milking the goat, I was tied to the porch but escaped from this tether which normally kept me close at hand. Maybe she didn't tie the rope well or maybe my fingers had figured out how to un-magic the knots. At any rate, during some microsecond of that day, I was free.

I followed my ears, if such a thing can be, and marched right in to an open and temptingly dark doorway.

The shadowy building was everything I'd hoped for and was much louder and stinkier to boot. The door marked an invisible line. Outside was sunlight and blue sky, but the other side was a perpetual cave-like dusk. There were rows of huge machines that went clangbangswoosh and others that went swooshcrankslap in a never-ending boil. An oily mist drifted everywhere and it was no wonder that the doors were kept open. Most of the fans that poked through the walls weren't doing other than looking like big black flowers behind their screen protectors. At each machine stood one or two men feeding thundery sheets of metal into the opening-closing jaws of their stations.

I was enchanted.

I suppose that the grownup men weren't accustomed to looking down that low for someone when they walked through the open doors or maybe they never expected that so small a package would be brave (or stupid) enough to enter such a forbidding place. At any rate, I was able to slip in unnoticed. No one saw me as I meandered though the back side of the huge presses.

In the meantime, my mother discovered the straggling rope end and no Clark. She began hyperventilating, called my father at work, called my grandparents and the sheriff's department, and ran through the immediate neighborhood screaming my name. She'd raised such a hue and cry as she ran past the modest factory that some of the factory workers heard her and came out and assured her no such little guy had been spotted.

I wandered about the clanging machinery for about thirty minutes before I was found out and then only because one of the men had to empty his scrap basket behind one of the stamping machines. I was sitting behind one press next to the wire basket, filthy with dark brown oil, playing with the enticing sharp shapes that had been spat out of the presses during their cycles.

I was gathered up with a shout that brought most of the plant production to a halt as if the quitting time whistle had blown. The overalled man grabbed me and threaded his way around several machines, slowly shaking his head but grinning and telling me that I should come back much, much later if I wanted to work here. He carried me into the office and the clamor those folks set up should have been a warning of things to come. I was immediately set upon by an office full of people. One gray haired woman who sat at the company switchboard pulled out a handkerchief and began to spit daub my face and hands while the man held me outstretched to prevent my soiling her clothing. I was oil-soaked front and back and sides and top and bottom. Another woman ran outside saying she'd find out where I belonged. I was enjoying all the attention although I didn't care much for the spit cleaning. I thought her ministrations were too much like my mother's after I wrestled with the goat.

Something about my mother's face as she rushed through the door caused me to start wailing although until that time I had been perfectly happy and innocent of any wrongdoing. I must have believed my adventure perfectly within my rights as a little man, but those thoughts quickly vanished like a dry leaf in a high wind.

I'd later recall how much the look on my mother's face resembled a female bear as she protects her cubs. She grabbed me in a hard enough hug to strengthen the feeling. The people gathered around me must have noticed the similarity, too. They immediately backed off to a safer distance. A few minutes later my red-faced father slammed through the door and began the timeless duty to indelibly instruct his child, the personification was made whole. He grabbed me and almost had time to pull his gripping hand from my arm before my mother gave it a quick slap. It was a good thing Momma didn't have claws.

"He's had just about enough excitement for one day, Jerry. It won't do for you to add more to it now. We can talk about it when we get home."

"He's got to learn, Dorothee."

"He will, but my way."

Mom made me get undressed on the porch outside while my sister Carole looked out the window and made laughing faces at me. My mother carried me into the bathroom, scrubbed me all over with a brush until the stain and stink went away (which was a long time), toweled me dry, and enveloped me in sun dried pajamas. Still holding me protectively close, she carried me into the bedroom. Although it was still daylight, I didn't mind going to bed. Somehow the excursion had exhausted me. The bath had been accompanied by lots of her "don'ts," but we didn't really talk about my getaway until the next day.

Right after breakfast.

It is the first such behavioral discussion that I remember. My mother told me how lucky I was that I'd not been sliced up by the sharp metal pieces I'd been playing with. She showed me the stained clothing and further impressed their ruin by standing over me while I pitifully scrubbed Fels-Naptha soap over them in an attempt at cleaning. She also took me out in the backyard and made me stand still while I was introduced to Willie Willow Switch.

David Clark Greene was a younger, happier version of my father.

David was six years my father's junior. According to my dad, he'd been largely responsible for David's upbringing during the tempestuous years of their parents' divorce. They were close siblings. Uncle Dave came often for visits, both in Manchester and Monroe. He helped my parents move all their worldly possessions, as well as Carole and me when we left our hometown.

He'd also lived for a year with Mom and Dad when I was two years old, and this early exposure may have explained my great affection for him. Not only was he Dad's younger brother, whenever he came for a visit, he always made time for play. My impression was that he always thought there was time enough and his duty and privilege as an uncle meant taking advantage of the opportunity.

Uncle Dave was in the Marines but had been on inactive duty until 1951. His time away from service was put to good use by his graduating from Michigan State University, and finding his perfect girl, a term he used to describe his wife, Jere Ellen. They often came down for an extended visit either staying at our house or at my grandparents' house at Stoney Pointe Peninsula. He and my father had been responsible for getting me off Grandpa's sinking sailboat when I wasn't yet three.

Then the call to active service came and he came over with Jere Ellen to say goodbye. Uncle Dave was going to report to officer training school in Quantico, Virginia. Jere Ellen went with him to Virginia and that's where my new cousin Wendy Lorraine was born. In between officer training and California, all three came for a visit. I joined right in with everyone's sadness as they went back home before they left for California. After some additional training at Camp Pendleton, he was going to Korea. His wife and daughter would go with him to California but return to their home in New Jersey when he left for overseas duty.

I wrote him two letters while he was in the service, one to Virginia and one to California. While my letters weren't much more than childish scrawl, Uncle Dave wrote back once telling me about all the hard work they were making him do. He said he looked forward to our next game of catch. He didn't get the second letter even though it was forwarded to him overseas in Korea. It came back unopened with his personal effects, sent back to Aunt Jere Ellen. She didn't open it either.

Jere Ellen called Grandpa and Dad to tell them of David's death on July 7, 1952. Dead of a mortar round exploding at his feet, killed by the shrapnel. His company commander wrote Grandpa Clark that 1st Lieutenant David Clark Greene had given his flak jacket to one of his men before the assault by the Chinese began. The letter was complimentary of Uncle Dave's so selflessly thinking of a soldier under his command. It was a costly gift. Grandpa said having a flak jacket probably would have saved his life. I didn't know anything about costly gifts except that the news was devastating to the whole Greene family.

My Grandma I.G., Dad and Uncle Dave's mother, went right to the hospital and when we went over to Grandpa Clark and Grandma Grace's house their front door was draped in a black ribbon that touched the ground. Grandpa and my father both cried openly and Grandpa got "drunk as a lord," as described by my mother. My father had a few drinks, in the face of Mom's disapproving glare, and as I recall his speech was slurred remarkably like my grandpa's. Mom didn't have a "drunk as a..." for my father. All in all Uncle Dave's death was very costly for the family.

I had never seen my grandfather cry and I had never seen him drunk.

I had never seen my father cry either.

My Grandma I.G. had to be hospitalized and heavily medicated all the time she spent in the hospital, more than a month, and wouldn't talk to any of us when we went to visit.

I wasn't feeling real happy myself.

I dreamt of my uncle almost every night for the next few weeks in recurring visions of stormy weather and Grandpa's sailboat. I had a knowledge that we surely weren't going to be playing ball anytime again. I really wanted to go to his funeral but it was in a place called Arlington, much too far away for a little boy. My father and Grandpa were going to go but not me. I was too young. I looked the cemetery up in the encyclopedia and found out that all the heroes had to be buried there. It was a law or something. All of the heroes were there.

My Uncle Dave sure was that. He got me off that sinking sailboat and listened when I'd told him how scared the storm made me feel. He'd told me I was brave even when I wasn't. I was going to miss him for a long time.

Chapter 2
Trouble in Paradise

Parents in the 1950s worried every summer.

Kids thought summer vacation meant play and we had neither responsibility of school or homework. Kids liked summertime.

But summer for parents meant regular and German measles, mumps, scarlet fever, rheumatic fever and a disease of particular dread called polio. Our neighborhood network spread word of who had what and when they got it to each household and was particularly quick during the summer. Parents spoke the words in whispers, as if soft voices wouldn't attract the virus' attention. Also known as infantile paralysis, polio was and is a disease capable of striking at any age but seemed to target the young, the ones who had their lives in front of them. There had been a number of children stricken with the disease among the beaches in the last three years. I knew of three, two little kids who had been in my school as well as an older girl in my neighborhood and I was just six.

One year, a girl named Mary contracted the virus and then spent every moment in a huge contraption in her parents' front room. The big metal cylinder, an iron lung, wheezed as it helped her breathe. Swish and sigh, swish and sigh, in and out, with an electric cord plugged in to the wall. Mary couldn't breathe by herself, couldn't speak, and couldn't even eat without help. She was the same age as my sister Carole and had attended school with her, a classmate and a friend. Her younger brother Pete was a good buddy of mine and we played together all the time. Mary's illness scared the whole neighborhood beyond belief. In 1952, at the very best, the diagnosis of polio meant some form of paralysis, but at the worst, it meant death. There was no cure, no prevention, nothing to do except hope your child would make it through another summer, the time when the disease seemed most prevalent.

Suddenly in the spring of 1953, there was hope. Dr. Jonas Salk had developed a vaccine, a treatment that might prevent the condition. It was untried, but laboratory results were promising and the U.S. government was encouraging parents to sign their children up to participate in the trial. "The newspapers called it an experiment," my father read out loud to us one night.

My mother and father talked about it privately for months before speaking to Carole and me. It was thought to be "chancy," they said, and rumors abounded. There were children who actually fell ill after getting the vaccine but that didn't happen very often. I listened when Mom talked to Grandma Phoebe about the trial and my grandmother was absolutely, positively against it.

"Wait until they try it on other children, Dorothee," Gram said. "Don't let them be the guinea pigs."

But Mary's illness had badly frightened my parents. We visited her even though she couldn't tell us if she wanted us to or not. Her folks seemed grateful, but so sad and broken hearted because their daughter had no hope. The most they could do to make their daughter any better was nothing at all. They could only watch her wither. Mom was even more concerned after each visit. If there was a chance, just a small chance, that polio wouldn't threaten her children, my mother thought the risk acceptable. When she heard about the trial, had talked about it and prayed about it, she signed us up. We were to be "Pioneers," a role I was eager to take. We were going into new territory, undiscovered lands, places where people had never been before.

All I wanted to know was, "Can I wear my coonskin cap?"

On a Saturday in April, the whole family piled into the car to go to Monroe so Carole and I could get the vaccine. I looked just like Davy Crockett although my mother made me leave my tomahawk at home. At a podium, a man gave a speech about the hope this marvelous preventive meant to everyone, an end to the dreaded ailment. There were hundreds of kids there, loud and running around, but we had to stay by Mom and Dad behaving like we should. When the speech over, we had to stand in one line while my parents signed a consent form and were given suggestions for steps to take if there were problems. Once finished there, Carole and I went to stand in another line, waiting for our turn and I was pretty surprised when we got to the front. A lady in a white uniform handed us each a sugar cube. Hey, I had been screwing up my courage in order not to cry when someone gave me a shot. A sugar cube! Great! This was easy.

The family went home jubilant and secure, knowing we had helped the fight against this horrific child crippler. Dad said he was proud of us both. We had to stay inside for a while. We needed to be "watched," but I didn't know why.

That evening when Mom asked if anyone wanted ice cream I said, "I do." But when I tried to get up to help scoop it into dishes, my legs didn't work. Uh, oh. They wouldn't bend, were sticking straight out, and felt kind of funny. Mom thought I was kidding at first but then tried to help me up and saw that I wasn't fooling at all.

"Oh, Jerry," Mom began to cry. "Oh, no! No! It can't be. It just can't be!"

Mom ran to the phone and called Dr. Sisman who gave her a list of things to do. He was coming out to the house and would be right there.

Dad lifted me up and set me on the couch while Mom ran to the bathroom and filled the tub with hot, hot water and added Epsom salts.

"Wrap his legs in a blanket, Jerry," Mom yelled. "Get his pants off but keep his legs warm!"

When the tub was full, my father carried me into the bathroom and laid me gently in the hot water, but I didn't feel the warmth. My legs had completely stiffened by then and would not work. It was like they weren't even there.

Dr. Sisman didn't even knock; he burst through the front door taking my temperature and checking reflexes in arms and legs, but by then I didn't have any reflexes. He said do this, do this, do this some more. Still nothing, just like two pieces of wood. He and Mom and

Dad massaged my legs turn and about, when one or the other tired, for almost four hours. They kept the water hot, and kept right on rubbing until my legs looked like they had been painted rosy pink.

Mom cried the whole time, something I had seldom seen her do. She was usually a stoic woman and took our injuries and illnesses as something to be expected. But this was different. Everybody was worried including me.

Sometime in the night the sensation of feeling very slowly came back in my legs; then I could wiggle my toes, and I finally could move my legs. The doctor said everything was going to be fine. It had been a temporary reaction to the vaccine and probably would have gone away by itself anyhow. Neither parent even suspected temporary when my legs stiffened and I had seen pure terror contort the faces of both mother and father. For an unbearable amount of time, they'd believed their son was falling into the Hell of polio.

Dr. Sisman ordered, "Put him to bed."

My father lifted me out of the tub and dried me off while Mom went somewhere to shed tears and say, "Thank You, Lord." Dad carried me to my bed even though I told him I could walk just fine. He held me to his chest for a long time before he put me in and covered me up.

"Good night, son. See you in the morning."

The next morning I had no residual effects except the memory. It was as if nothing had happened although my mother woke me up several times in the night to make sure I could still move my legs.

Mom checked me out all over again in the morning but I was just fine. It seemed I wasn't going to get polio. Mom and I talked about polio for a long time the next morning. I was sorry for Mary because if that sugar cube would have been passed around just one year sooner, maybe she'd have been okay. I was glad it didn't get me. There was too much left for me and my dog Patch to do.

Mom had convinced the scout leader that despite not having reached the magic age of seven, I was ready to be a Cub Scout.

I had started school early, was big for my age and Mom wanted me to progress with my school chums. She was convincing, and I became a Cub Scout, fully fledged. My friend, Ralph and I were in the same Cub Scout troop and had learned to repeat the motto.

"On my honor I will do my best
To do my duty to God and my country
and to obey the Scout Law and the laws of the Pack;
To help other people at all times;
To keep myself physically strong,
mentally awake, and morally straight."

We had both acquired Cub Scout hatchets in the early spring due in large part to the bake sale our mothers had contributed to at a Scout Rally held in the auditorium at Brest Bay School. Many beach "troops" and their families were there. We were presented with merit badges, had programs to indicate our growth as scouts, and performed Indian dances in homemade regalia accompanied by a tom-tom drum.

The hatchets were delivered about four weeks after the bake sale and scout gathering. Mrs. Meyers had filled out the official order form and sent it to a far off place, Cub Scout Headquarters. We thought the headquarters was a fort with battlements and ramparts, fiercely defended against the communists by boys just like us. I didn't have the vaguest idea what a communist was, but I had heard about them at the dinner table. Our pack's goal was to join that group of staunch and fearless boys. We would do our best for God and Country, and the hatchets were sure to be a requirement before we could report for duty. Hatchets would make us one step closer to Glory.

We were something to see wearing moccasins made from kits, available only through the Scouts, loincloths made from bed linens, tomahawks made with stone heads and heavy branches for the handles. We had a teepee and a fake cooking fire with a pot suspended over it on a stick. We were so in character at the rally it was a wonder that our troop leader, Mrs. Meyers, Jack's mother, could keep us from scalping one another or running amok through the audience. I wondered later in life how anyone had the patience to put up with a group of seven- to ten-year-old boys.

Mrs. Meyers passed the torch to my mother right after the hatchets arrived and Mom also showed amazing restraint as a troop leader. Proof was that everyone was still alive when the meetings ended each week.

The hatchets were our pride, our joy, the first "grown-up" thing we'd ever owned. They were steel and painted blue, and we could really and truly chop stuff. There would be no more homemade stone hatchets for us except in play. These were tools, store-bought, made by someone else just for Cub Scouts and they occupied a special status. They came with a sheath with the Cub Scout emblem branded into it and a loop that we threaded our belts through. I slept with mine, but I had to swear on my oath as a scout I would keep it in the sheath. Dad said he would show me how to file the edge to keep it sharp. We wore them everywhere we went.

We hacked everything. Of course, there were the inevitable rules, as with every new responsibility and progression in our lives. This Cub Scout stuff gave mothers and fathers a distinct new advantage. They began to make us swear our oath to everything they told us. We had to swear to take the garbage out, swear to keep our clothes picked up, swear we had washed our hands before dinner, swear we wiped good. It got pretty ridiculous but it was effective. Parents knew how to keep the upper hand, especially Mom. Regarding the axe, she made me swear an extra lot.

I couldn't chop anything that was living, not one single thing. Mom said she would go around the neighborhood and check tree trunks and I believed her. I could hack at the woodpile we had in the back yard. I could chop up driftwood at the beach, although this was hazardous to the axe because the beaches were rocky. We could swing away at any fallen branch we could find although we were pledged to bring home all resulting fireplace-sized wood.

The more we chopped, the duller the axe, a lesson all in itself.

We gained other insights: dull axes produced glancing blows which were dangerous. I whacked myself in the leg several times but fortunately hit only the flat side of the axe against my shin. I didn't let anybody know about that. I wasn't that stupid even though my father had made statements to the contrary. I needed to learn about this sharpening stuff, but my father hadn't gotten around to the training.

Grandma Phoebe and Grandpa Teddy drove down one weekend

in their 1950 Plymouth. They didn't often come to see us; we mostly went to the farm, but this time they came to our house. Their visit was none too soon as far as I was concerned because my grandpa was a craftsman. He had retired as an engineer, built furniture, fixed water pumps and furnaces, and would certainly know how to sharpen an axe.

Our axes had gotten so dull by now that they were effective bludgeons, good smashers, but wouldn't do much in the way of chopping and cutting without super-human effort. We mostly carried them for show. We still had lots of chopping left in us if we could just get the tools back in shape. Besides, we knew that a dull axe wouldn't pass inspection if we were called to Cub Scout Headquarters, and that was something we expected at any moment.

Despite being short on patience, Grandpa was a good teacher. He said he'd help, and I trailed behind him to the garage where we scrounged around in the workbench drawer until he found a file.

"A flat bastard," he chortled with a hint of glee knowing this was forbidden vocabulary for most boys and especially for me.

I would definitely try those words out later though not in front of my mother. They had such a great sound. Surely there was someone I knew who was "A FLAT BASTARD." Yup, I knew several: Timmy, Gary and Randy. New ways for me to get their attention.

There was a vise attached to the workbench and Grandpa sandwiched the axe between two pieces of wood so it wouldn't slip.

Grandpa showed us how to hold the file, "left hand on top in the front, right hand behind on the handle. Be careful not to push too far, you'll cut your knuckles."

"Push the file forward with pressure down and lift, lift the file on the backstroke."

"Don't drag it backwards; it only dulls the file. Make it a loop at the top motion, boy."

I recall sawing it back and forth and receiving a thump in the back of my head for this rule's disregard several times.

I remember the lesson. Even now, whenever I use a file, I look over my shoulder to make sure Grandpa isn't standing there with hand poised to get my attention. I learned to sharpen my hatchet and advertised this new skill to the rest of the troop at a nickel per hatchet. I showed the method to my dad and he contracted for the lawnmower blades, his long handled, wood splitting axe, and the shovel my mother used to dig in the garden.

I did not get nickels for any of the homegrown work; it became just another of my chores. I didn't charge Ralph either.

One of the first resident grownups I discovered at Pointe aux Peaux was Mr. Miller.

Like Easter egg hunts, finding spring's first crocus, or waiting for the pussy-willows to bud, the anticipation for Mr. Miller's return was part of winter night dreams. Even while snows blew and howled along Lake Erie's shore and we crowded around the fireplace or perched over the heat registers in our home, we expected him any day.

Mr. Miller was a character even before I knew what that meant. He was built like the Pillsbury Dough Boy: A short man, he had the most perfectly round, protruding belly I had ever seen and dressed mostly in checkered polyester pants with suspenders, no belt, white shirt, hat and tie. His belly moved up and down, up and down, when he laughed. He was always manicured, barbered, and neat. I cannot recall ever seeing him any other way although I had burst in one day and caught him with his tie loosened and his pants-legs pulled up due to the heat. He was embarrassed, but not as much as I was.

I recall Mr. Miller's arrivals ever since we moved to the beach. You knew that he would re-open his little realtor's office just outside the stone pillared gates, but just like spring, you just were never quite sure what day it would happen. We were ever in anticipation of his return because shortly after the snows melted and the sun warmed the fields, the open door to his realtor's office would beckon to the children of the subdivision.

Mr. Miller was always addressed as Mr. Miller although he was the only grownup who invariably made time for the kids. Even though he was more like one of the kids, we still used Mr. Miller when we saw him. We called Mr. Edwards, Ken; Mr. Hemry, Bud; and Mr. Terry, Bill. These were people we encountered everyday and the only time they ever gave us anything was when they were giving us the devil. With him it was different mostly because I think he genuinely liked children. We could come and go into his office with

34

few constraints and were always met with a smile. Mr. Miller was always Mr. Miller, emphasis on Mister.

An independent realtor, he handled summer rentals and the occasional sale of beach properties. He was busy during the summer months, dealing with families seeking respite from the dirt and heat of Detroit, located about 50 miles north of Pointe aux Peaux. Those city folks would flock to the beaches of Lake Erie seeking sunburn and relaxation which a summer on the lake provided. After school ended each year, his gravel parking lot was packed with cars jammed-full of parents with kids we just knew we weren't going to like.

But we did like Mr. Miller.

He and his wife spent every winter in Florida. This by itself was pretty neat because it meant he had two homes, something no one around here managed to do. Florida was a far off place to us both geographically and in our minds. We could only imagine it as a treasure trove of sea horses, seaweed, and seashells. Seashells were the evidence Mr. Miller brought back to us every spring. His arrival used to happen about April or May just after we had verified the return of spring by rolling around on the wet grass to determine that the Michigan ground wasn't still frozen. His big car packed with clothes, souvenirs, and shoeboxes of shells rolled back into Pointe aux Peaux with all the regularity of the seasons.

His return preceded the last day of school, and we would pile off the bus with gleeful cries. "Mr. Miller's back; I wonder what he brought us?" We were mindful of laying up treasures on earth disregarding my mother's teachings as far back as the fifties. He never disappointed us and would greet us with all the affection of a long absent uncle or grandfather. We would line up at the door just like waiting for Santa Claus.

This was due in part to a small office but also because Mr. Miller played favorites. Any boy or girl could tell exactly where he or she stood in his esteem. They would get shells and baubles according to how polite they were, how nicely they asked, and how often they bathed, I think. If one of us had been bad the previous year, suspected of soaping his office windows on Halloween, then that one came away with a single periwinkle shell. These were so small they got lost in the lint in your pocket. I also think he handed out the shells separately because he did like some children better, but didn't want to embarrass any child regardless of how much or little he liked them. For those of us who had helped Mr. Miller unload rental records, air out the office last year, and maybe even helped him wash windows, the treasures were stunning.

One year after I had soaped his windows but hadn't been caught, I felt quite guilty. I atoned by helping him unpack his car in the spring and was afterward blessed with a dried sea horse carefully wrapped in tissue paper. I got a large whelk shell as well and was permitted to take handfuls of miscellaneous shells from a Keds shoebox. I was in heaven. I had enough multi-colored shells and curiosities to outlast any swapping spree that would happen that summer. We didn't particularly like many city kids, but we would swap with them because they had to be well off. We didn't go anywhere for summer vacation and they did. If they could go away for the summer, they had to have stuff. Stuff is what we were after.

The only shells normally in Lake Erie were those of fresh water clams. These clams have a nondescript shell on the outside and aren't much better on the inside. In order to liven things up at the beach, we would sometimes "salt" Lake Erie's shores with the shells Mr. Miller brought back. It was easy to drop a few bright shells as we walked along the water's edge. We would then sit up farther on the beach to observe what happened.

I suppose everyone walks beaches the same way the world around looking for shells, pirate treasure, or some other flotsam. Once the summer kids discovered the few beautiful shells we secretly placed, it was easy to swap for most anything. We got a really big kick out of watching kids and adults from the city become absolutely astonished at finding these beautiful mementos. We would offer to provide them with others we'd found in the off-season, in the winter when there were more.

We made up tales of braving storms winter and summer to find these precious shells. We told of winter ice floes gouging out the lakebed and bringing up the shells to shore. We told of having spent our entire lives accumulating the treasures we laid before them. We told them of the shell collection being passed down to us by long-dead relatives or people who lived here long, long ago. Some of the adults were skeptical, but when faced with all the proof, they almost believed. They wanted to anyway. The city kids, well…We had them right in the palm of our hands. We traded shells for baseball mitts, gloves, and bats. We traded shells for bicycles, wagons, and soda pop. We traded shells for comic books (forbidden in my house), whistles, and yo-yos. We named any price for our commodity.

We made out like the bandits we were, and all because of Mr. Miller. It was no wonder we called him Mister.

The lake brought us gifts as well.

My mother had a curious ability to modify rules according to the situation. Her alterations weren't limited to the Laws of the House, but periodically could include God's Commandments as well. Mom would dig up an irresistible plant from someone's garden or take a cutting from some other Eden to bring home for her own. There was no incongruity in these actions because she didn't take all of what there was, only a snippet from the original. She sometimes ignored this aberrant behavior in her children when the treasure glimmered brightly enough.

We learned by the authority vested in Mom. If you leave some behind, it isn't considered stealing. Finders keepers, losers weepers. The rocky shores of our subdivision repeatedly gave us treasures washed up for the finding.

We knew if there was ever anyone righteous enough to challenge God's laws, it was surely my mother.

There was no formula for these discoveries although the wicked storms that sometimes strafed the subdivision offered more opportunity but more didn't mean better. Dorothee's children learned at a young age to bring curiously water-smoothed driftwood pieces home to place in her flower gardens. Our yard was adorned with alligator and dragon shaped pieces carefully placed to guard the roses, tulips, daisies and alyssum she so treasured. We knew that with these special finds her favor could be earned or we might even have some previous crime expunged. The more fantastic the shape the larger the reward might be. We brought home driftwood until our yard looked as if it were filled with the twisted and curious shapes of an Alice in Wonderland setting. In addition to hauling driftwood, we learned to drag home buckets and baskets of stones for the driveway every time we went to the beach.

I used "the waterline rule" when I found items at the lake. If it looked like the water had deposited the treasure on the shore, it belonged to whoever found it. The evidence necessary for proof could be seaweed attached, other floatable items in the vicinity, or just wet from the waves. I had occasionally splashed water on a particularly attractive find when it was worthwhile and nobody else was around. When questioned, I could declare that it had been wet in all truthfulness. Lake Erie *must* have washed it up.

The Lake Erie shoreline was under constant assault. The lake was capable of producing waves big enough to undermine and erode the areas well past whatever riprap the owners put on the shore. The people who lived on the lakeshore also had the breaking up of the ice to contend with. The relentless wind-driven movement of big slabs had cut wide grooves in lawns all over these lake front homes, and I had even seen one house damaged when the ice moved far enough to smash the front porch. The lake was an awesome force when riled, and the homeowners on Sterling Drive had to constantly tend the defenses of stone and broken concrete. Property owners were constantly supplementing the natural shore with truckloads of fill.

Whenever I combed the beach, there was a sure expectation of finding the one item that would make us rich forever. I just knew some pirate's chest would appear freshly uncovered by the waves. As I walked along the beach, one day I saw part of the coastline glittering and shiny from the sun.

"Gold! Jewels! Treasure!"

The face of the beach from the waterline to the lawn was strewn with shiny blue chunks of glass, hundreds of football sized and smaller jagged lumps of blue green, like looking through the ice when the lake was frozen. Bright and glistening, and I couldn't imagine what they were, but I knew I wanted some. The lumps were deep aquamarine in color and sparkling with the sunlight. Amidst other chunks of rocks that were slaggy and rough in nature, I thought the lake had scattered these beautiful big blue jewels just for me.

"Pirates! Treasure!"

I had just finished reading Treasure Island, a favorite of mine, for the second or third time. Jim Hawkins didn't have anything on me! Smart as paint! This was worth a fortune!

As I scrabbled over the rocks, I stayed close to the water knowing the ten or twelve-foot bank would conceal my movements from anyone at the house. People's lawns were off limits, but the lakeshore rocks were another matter. While I really believed I had a right to these huge baubles, I still knew the owner would give me the devil if he caught me taking any. No sense in leaving it up to chance. I took a big chunk that had rolled down the sloping bank into the water. The blue glass was more than pretty. It was also razor sharp.

The large irregular piece shed thin shards at its edges.

My beautiful trophy sliced a gash in my left hand that extended from one side of the palm to the base of my thumb. The edge was scalpel sharp and virtually painless but the blue quickly was covered in red blood. No treasure can be had without cost. I thought about going up and trying to find someone to help but knew better instantly. I might have to surrender my jewel. It would be better just to go home. Mom would love it.

Mom was more than excited when I got home.

I hollered for her to come take a look when I opened the front door. I said she better come out before I went in. As soon as she saw the blood, Mom went back and got the Bag-Balm. First things first. My mother was experienced in repairing boyhood wounds. I had given her so many opportunities to fix mine that the count was lost several years before. I could spend hours telling scar stories.

As she inspected my hand, I responded honestly to her questions.

"Where'd you get it?"

"In the water."

"Where at?"

"Past the boat ramp."

"Where did you get it?"

"Really, Mom, it was in the water, washed up."

My mother really liked the blue treasure I'd brought home, oohing and ahhing over the lovely translucent color, but she had some doubts about the washing up part. When I told her there were more down by the lake, she made me show her the trove. I led her down to the boat ramp, and we could see the glitter from where we stood.

After we scrambled over the rocks, Mom was almost as impressed with the scattered lumps as I was.

"Did you ask if you could have it?"

"It was in the water."

And that was good enough. I gathered as many as I could safely hold. I think Mom saw such a profusion of glass pieces she couldn't imagine anyone having enough zeal to take them all away. Word of my discovery spread to the rest of the neighborhood and before long there was a line of kids hauling pieces of the glass off the beach. Like ants to sweets, the procession extended and I wasn't the only one who got cut that day. So many kids joined in everybody forgot to be stealthy about it, and instead tromped boldly across the lawn. There were probably six or seven kids out there when the homeowner finally noticed and chased us off.

I snuck back after a few days and grabbed another piece. I carried it off just as fast as I dared for the rest of the summer, but the possibility of being caught limited my raids. Mom wasn't too pleased with my foolish handling of something so sharp without taking any precautions, but she put every piece her children brought home in her garden and bandaged every cut those sharp pieces caused and she never got mad about us bringing them home.

We left some.

Chapter 3
Walter

My brother and I spent much of every summer as Indians but never more so than in 1954.

Right down to loincloths made by Mom, Mohawk haircuts, and being allowed to scare passersby with blood curdling war whoops, we were Indians through and through. At the end of the last day of school, we sat squirming on the black kitchen stool while Mom shaved the sides of our heads. She left the winter's growth strip down the middle so we could become our true selves. We slathered the strip with Butch Wax, and combed it straight up in spiky points, and were ready for a summer of great Indian Wars. We wanted facial tattoos like the Mohicans, but Mom drew lines of her own. Invisible to the eye, her lines were still as distinctive as the whorls and designs we sought for our bodies.

Within two weeks after school's end, we were as brown and bronzed as any tribal-born Sioux or Cheyenne. We decorated loincloths and ourselves with anything we could find to insure authenticity: Carole's pop beads, sequins from an old Halloween costume, tufts of my dog Patch's hair, saved after getting the burrs out, and various finger painted symbols as befitted great warriors.

We made tomahawks which was easy. We had lots of beach stones to select from for the business ends and we "borrowed" rawhide laces from my father's boots to hold the heads in place. We carved wooden knives and sewed sheathes out of scraps of material. We made headbands and ornamented them with sea-gull feathers found along the beach. We made teepees out of bed-sheets and clothes-line poles and hogans out of rushes and cattail fronds. We made pemmican and acorn bread and probably would have cooked up a stray dog if we thought we could have gotten away with it. We weren't too good at making bows, though, and had to redo our pitiful attempts frequently during each summer.

That was until Walt happened to drive by on the tractor as we were vainly trying to hit a homemade mockup of some hated enemy. After spending several moments laughing at the looping flight of the arrows and our general inability to launch them more than ten feet, he motioned us over.

Everybody knew our subdivision's caretaker, Walter. Walt was old, retired but not, whatever that meant. His family had been in the area since its settlement by the French in the 17th century. The black sheep son of a prosperous local farming family, Walter had somehow managed to have a good for life, minimal responsibility job at the Pointe aux Peaux Farms subdivision. His younger brother inherited the family farm when Walt's mother died and the brothers hadn't spoken since her death. Walt had been a soldier in the Great War and that's where he had picked up his family status of gone bad. We never knew for sure what had happened, but sometimes Walter did talk about some Heloise lady somewhere in France, usually after he had been paid. Walter really liked his beer.

Walt was skinny and bent by age, had false teeth that he seldom wore, had a purple bullet scar that he showed us often, owned just two pair of overalls, had huge hairy ears, and shaved only on the weekends. Walt moved slowly but he was steady. He cut grass on vacant lots with an old Ford tractor and alongside the roads, plowed snow during winter, patched potholes infrequently and acted as a guard at the subdivision's front gate during the weekends. Walt had a pistol, making him something special and slightly dangerous to us. He would wear it in a holster on Saturdays and Sundays during the summer when people migrated south for vacations from the city. Pointe aux Peaux was a private beach of sorts although it was pretty public during the week. Walt was important whenever he was at the gate, and he'd turn people away if they didn't have any business "driving around" in there.

The kids all liked toothless, old, Walt. He was always around and when we got into some scrape or another could usually be counted on to help out without telling parents. We brought him Sunday dinner leftovers, helped him rake grass and leaves, or just took time to listen to his tales. For Chip and me, this was the first example of a symbiotic relationship outside the family and that summer kept me particularly busy. I'd had to rely on Walt numerous times to help me out when something didn't go quite as I'd planned.

The subdivision provided Walter a small house for a home but it wasn't much. It was only about 50 or 60 feet square, but it contained all Walt needed: a hot plate, bed, and toilet. The little place was strewn with the leftovers of a long-lived life: clothing for different seasons, auto and tractor parts, although Walt didn't own a car, odd furniture parts, a wood stove for heat, his arrow head collection, other fossils, a stuffed fox, and other treasures that we glimpsed whenever we visited.

Walter had an interesting history and when he had a few beers in him, he'd recount pieces of his fall from family grace, or give us other character sketches of the subdivision's inhabitants. We found out all sorts of useful and startling information from Walt. The "beers" happened at least once a month alternating with occasions when he could accumulate additional money for a six-pack. Walt's only real friend, other than the kids of the neighborhood, was Mr. Miller, the local realtor. Other than requests for roadwork, complaints of overly long grass and icy roads, I never saw Walt in deep conversations with anyone other than Mr. Miller.

The day Walt saw us with our pitiful bows he called to Chip and me. Normally when summoned by an adult, we assumed that we'd caused some rift in society's fabric but not when Walt called. Thinking that we were just going to be laughed at (we knew how poor the bows were), we ambled over slowly to the idling tractor. Instead of the good-natured teasing we expected, Walter asked us if we wanted to learn how to make a "real" bow and arrow set.

Hah! Did the Indians want to scalp white people? Of course, we did! Walt warned us that it wasn't a quick task, but we paid little mind to that part. How hard could it be? Every Indian that we had ever seen had one. He told us to report to his shack first thing in the morning. He also told us not to tell our mother.

We were definitely excited. We were going to have a real bow with real arrows, and we envisioned ourselves with other Indian weapons. Real knives and war clubs would be next. We might even get rifles decorated with brass tacks.

The next morning we were careful to behave as though it were just another summer day of carefree raiding and horse thieving by the Mohawks of Goddard Drive. Never let the white man, in this case Mom, know what's going on in the red man's mind. Easy enough for us, we practiced blank looks any time our parents asked us what we were doing.

Walter was ready for us when we got there after breakfast. He still had a cup of coffee and sent us back home to change clothes. We were wearing our Indian regalia and couldn't understand why we had to change, but Walt insisted. He said we had to find a tree first. We had a bit of a problem when we went back home trying to convince Mom that we weren't going to play Indian today. Since it was early in the summer, I don't think she believed us when we said were tired of that game already. Suspicions aside, she sent us back out in patched knee jeans and our requisite "Salvation Army" shirts cautioning us to be back for lunch.

Walter had finished his coffee and was standing outside his shack when we got there. He handed us an old rusty hand saw and told us to follow him. We set off across the fields behind the subdivision. Because of a very wet spring, the farmer hadn't plowed and planted yet so we couldn't get in trouble for trampling his current crops. We had in the past and would in the future but not that day. We had Walt with us, too, and therefore felt a bit immune to any potential shouts. Despite not having any Indian accessories, we just knew we were on an Indian mission.

Coming to the edge of the swamp, we skirted the borders of cattail and bramble bushes that marked its marshy beginnings. The freshwater marshes of Lake Erie were a very special place to us, and Chip and I were familiar with every spot therein since we'd spent many days and nights listening to loons, mosquitoes, frogs, and squirrels, wandering trails, and wading in the waterways or catching tadpoles. We knew where not to walk because of sinkholes, where the crab apple trees were, and where to go when the carp were spawning.

It was our own private marsh and we loved it. We knew adventurous areas for unlimited play and different places designated as those suited to playing pirates, army, cowboys and Indians or storming the beaches of an imaginary Normandy.

Walter seemed to know where we were headed, but we hadn't a clue as yet, and his only comment was that it wasn't too much further. We eventually came to an area we knew well because we visited it in the late summer to stock up on hand-grenades.

All self respecting Army grunts and Marines had to have jacket pockets stuffed full of these Osage Orange globes. If you couldn't blow up that German pillbox, you'd never get to Paris. The plus side to this ammo was that you would reduce anybody that got hit with one to tears. The fruits were green and all over knobby, hard as a coconut and virtually indestructible. They just fit a boy's hand. I had thrown and been hit by about a million and hoped for more of the same.

Walt stood before the tree and studied it for a long time explaining to us that the branches he was looking for had to be straight, no knots or small branches and about two inches in diameter. He went on to tell us about the nature of the tree, how it was a preferred wood for bows, and that local Indians made treks to find it when they were in the bow-making business. Good enough for us. He boosted me up into the tree, handed me the saw back when I was situated next to a selected branch and told me to cut the first of four I was to saw off.

The branches were about 2 ½ inches in diameter, between 40 to 48 inches long, and covered with a rough, peeling bark. The shorter branches would be reserved for Chip's bow, the longer ones designated for mine. We had one extra of each in case we "royally screwed the first one up," as Walt put it.

We told Walt that these branches didn't look much like the graceful bows we had dreamed of, but he assured us that within each stick a bow was hiding. It would be up to us to release it from bark and bole, and only us. Thinking we were heading back, we started to scamper back the way we had come. Walt stopped us with a word and told us we had yet to get anything to shoot with the bows in the unlikely event we managed to make them. We set off to another section of the marsh toward a hickory grove on the south end of

Walter's family farm. It was another area that we harvested nuts for Mom's cookies and ammunition for our slingshots. We knew where we were going.

As we walked, Walter taught us more of the lesson and how he had acquired the skills that he was going to pass on to us. When he was a boy, his father often hired extra help in the summer and fall months to plant and harvest. Because their farm was more than two full sections, twelve hundred acres, the number of temporary help needed yearly was large, and his father employed ten to fifteen men for the work. At the turn of the century, most of the work of the farm was done by man and horse, wages were cheap, very little mechanized equipment was available, and there was plenty of food to feed the extra mouths. One of the men his father hired was a mixture of French and Indian heritage.

Walter knew him simply as "Chief," as stereotypical as it sounds, people weren't as conscious of real or imagined prejudices then. Chief had taken Walt under his wing and regaled him with tales of his own childhood. It seems that his people, the native inhabitants of the areas surrounding Lake Erie's western shore, had been farmers and hunters, warriors and philosophers. Walt remembered songs that the Chief had sung, descriptions of the areas before autos and trains, how they built their homes, how it was before the People were scattered. Walt didn't sing to us, but as we walked through the woods and fields he told those same tales

We soon reached the hickory grove and I shinnied up one not too tall example. Walt told me to cut branches about a yard long, as straight as possible and approximately ½ inch in diameter. I climbed up and down three or four trees before Walt was satisfied with the double handful of branches we had. Now we would head home. We were getting tired of the preparation part and wanted to get to the doing. What we really wanted was to get to was the shooting arrows part, but that would prove to be much farther away than we imagined.

Walter pulled a pocketknife and some twine from his pocket and sat down underneath one of the hickory trees to trim up the branches of both the Osage and hickory. He stripped the bark from the hickory but not from the Osage, explaining that he wanted the hickory to dry out a bit so it could be straightened for the arrows. The Osage had the bark left on to hold the moisture in longer so the wood could be cured properly over a slow fire, just as the original makers had done. Walt further explained that this would temper the bow, insuring a good pull and long life. Boy, oh boy, we were finding out stuff now; we could hardly wait! Walt bound the smaller and larger branches into two bundles and tied them crossways on my back. Chip carried the saw and Patch found her own stick. We finally set off for home, the trip shortened by tidbits and tales of both the Chief's and Walter's past years.

We got back just late enough that Mom gave us the devil for delaying lunch. It wasn't full blown pitchfork, hooves, and a tail, but it was one of his imps, and added to the first morning suspicions regarding the clothes-changing episode.

I have since figured out that parents, mothers especially, have this internal add and subtract meter. It automatically adds up clues, words and deeds, looks and appearances. When the meter approaches some predetermined level, alarms go off. Although kids don't hear a whisper, they are klaxon to mothers demanding action before overload is reached. Kids never know when they will go off, but mothers have this warning, similar I suppose to water approaching its boiling point. Mom's meter hadn't progressed much past the green portion yet but it was edging its way up. After all, we were still operating under a cloak of secrecy imposed by Walter.

After lunch, we headed back to Walt's only to find that he had work to do and couldn't be bothered with us for the rest of the day. We promised to be back early the next day knowing full well the ability of all adults to become disinclined to continue in any childish activities. We would learn this trait did not belong to Walt because he stuck with us throughout each and every step of the process. Before we turned to go, Walter told us that he had sent word to our local butcher shop and made arrangements for us to strip out some sinew when the butchering was being done.

How we were going to get there was another story. Walt didn't have a car and we hadn't included parents in the bow-making scheme, and the shop was several miles distant. Walt had said the butcher shop would get in touch with Jones's Market, our small local grocery store who in turn would tell Walt. He didn't have a phone but would get word to us, but beyond that was anyone's guess.

The next morning began with the lesson of how to construct a leg vise out of old leather harness that Walter had picked up somewhere. I suspected he had gone on a midnight raid to his family farm as that was the only barn still standing close to the subdivision. We learned how to sew a loop for our foot to take the strain of the branch while we applied a drawknife and spoke shave to shape and smooth the bow. We spent several days practicing on scrap wood before Walt was satisfied with our efforts and we learned how to maintain the hand tools as well. We spent more long hours sharpening the blades because Walt said he didn't have time to make them sharp and that it was our responsibility if we wanted a good bow.

We finally began the process of shaping the bow by scribing the outline of the bow through the bark. We were to shave slivers of wood off the branch with a pocket knife, stopping frequently to sharpen that, too. Walt told us that dull knives were more likely to cut us than were sharp ones. We didn't understand that until we figured out that it took more effort to push a dull knife through the wood. The Osage orange wood was tough. It seemed to dull the knife in a minute. This was proving to be a real task, but we were dedicated to the Indian way. We worked on the bows almost every day. Walter took time to track our progress, stopping his grass cutting long enough to offer suggestions or show us how to better use the spoke shave.

Eventually we got to the point that the branches began to look like something other than storm damage. We were making progress. We hadn't cut off any fingers; our arms and legs were gash free, and Mom's suspicion meter had returned to its normal middle of the green area. This bow-making business seriously cut into playtime. Every once in a while, we skipped working on them, just so we wouldn't forget how to be Indians but not very often.

The branches became graceful works of craft, thick in the middle for hands, tapering gracefully toward either end, flat and smooth beyond compare. Finally Walter was satisfied with our results and he told us to take time off from the work until Saturday when he would show us how to temper the bows with fire. He said it would take us all day and that we had to prepare by gathering dried wood and bringing it to his shack. We spent several hours picking up windfall wood, dragging it to Walt's and returning for more. We managed to pick up quite a bit along the shoreline because Lake Erie almost always put some on the beach every night.

The next day, Walt stopped by to tell us that he had arranged with the Monroe County Book Mobile to give us a ride to the butcher shop that very day. We would have to go now, without any real planning or be forced to wait for two more weeks when the book mobile would return on its summer schedule. The square van got to the beach about 10 am, stayed for two hours, and returned to the Monroe County Library branch near the butcher shop. How Walt had managed to engage the help of the driver, a county employee, into the sinew scheme I never found out, but that driver helped us out and dropped us off at the butcher shop without many questions.

We left the known world and safety blanket of the beach without permission, a serious breach of trust. Staying within established boundaries was one of the first of hundreds of "Commandments" we lived by and identical in stature to number one of the ten handed down to Moses. This unauthorized departure was definitely a sin. I'd even convinced my younger brother to participate in this transgression and probably another one. I told myself that we were going with another adult so it really wasn't bad, but I knew better. Several less obvious sins would surely be heaped upon us if we were found out, and we might expect to be shut up in the crawl space under the house for several years if discovered. We would be put there after having belts, brooms and hands applied to appropriate places. That was supposing we survived the verbal assault delivered when the sin was first revealed.

Walt had also worked it out with the butcher to take us back to Pointe aux Peaux as he was delivering cut meats to Jones's Market. This was going to work out great. We were shadow warriors sneaking in and out under parents' very noses. We went secure in the book-mobile hanging on to the built-in bookshelves.

Once at the butcher shop, we were given aprons which were stained and spotted with former cows and pigs. The butcher showed us to the back of the building where his helper was already busy with several sides of beef. Walter led us to a table and the man slapped down a quarter of beef. He showed us how to identify the sinew running from the meaty muscle to the joint. Walt did the cutting with the accuracy and detail of a surgeon and explained how we would separate the sinew from the flesh to utilize it as the bow string. He removed several lengths of the sinew, each carefully stretched out straight and wrapped in butcher's paper and tied the package up with string. We were set. We had to wait until the order for Jones's Market was ready before we could return to the safety of our home territory, but it was sure to be a short wait. It turned out much shorter than we expected.

My father worked at the local Ford plant polishing bumpers on the midnight shift. It was physical and exhausting work, but Dad worked overtime whenever he could. It wasn't easy keeping the Greene's four children clothed and fed and Dad took advantage of any opportunity for extra money that came his way. He'd worked over that day and because it was payday, decided to stop by the butcher's on his way home to spend some of that overtime pay. We were still in our bloody aprons when he walked through the front door. He came around the counter through the swinging doors and stood in front of the cutting table, and turned the same color as the slab of beef.

My father's temper was like a charge of gunpowder gone astray. Quick and smoky hot, it leveled most opposition and I tried to avoid it at all costs, but this time escape from his retribution seemed remote. I had a thought that my prospects were just about equal to the beef carcass lying before me; destined to be consumed.

I heard Dad asking, "Just whatinHell I was doing here, didmymotherknow,   howdidwegethere,   and somebodybetterstarttalking."

I wasn't about to answer any of those questions. I had forgotten the first part of the question and my father's mercurial progression took away the middle stuff. I was hopelessly lost by the time he finished. Silence wasn't golden at that point, but I hoped dumbness in any form might provoke some mercy.

Walt came to our rescue. Like some grizzled Knight Templar, he plunged into the fearsome breach blown open by my father. An unlikely hero at best, he still managed to defray and absorb some of Dad's fearsome temper. It took him several minutes to get Dad calmed down, but Walt was older and by rights was accorded some respect. Regardless his station in life, he was a very integral part of our community; he took care of and protected our home in his own way, so my father listened as he was told of the entire summer's efforts and goals. Despite a multitude of dark looks from my father, Dad put aside any more slashing questions and eventually motioned both Chip and me into the car. Walter came along, too, him in the front equal with Dad and us in the back, appropriate enough to our current standing.

There wasn't much talking for part of the way home, but my father pulled over to the side of the road before going through the flanking pillars into Pointe Aux Peaux. Turning in the front seat, he told us what we deserved, how much he wanted to administer those just deserts, and how disappointed he was, trust given and betrayed, etc., etc. We knew this stuff chapter and verse but paid attention while he went through various penances and punishments delivered on him as a boy. Dad got in trouble, too?

We'd just been given a reason for our behavior! Now we knew where we got it! We got it from him! I'd recall his revelations every time I was carpeted in the future but I never brought them up.

Then we got another surprise. I was so astonished I asked Dad to repeat it. It came out of his lips again! We weren't going to tell Mom! I was too shocked to even contemplate the reasons. Unbelievable! Unheard of! Withholding sins? Was that another one? We were virtually to go unscathed, a reprieve, a new life. We were going to pretend it didn't happen and keep a secret from our Mother. I was pretty sure it was another transgression. Chip got caught up in the guilt thing and it took several more minutes for Dad to convince him that this non-confession was the best course for us to take, but no way was I arguing against this.

While my father's temper was awesome to behold, it withered in comparison to the severity of Mom's iron bands for atonement. Mom didn't shout or rant and rave at us, but she was a firm believer in select sins never being expunged and keeping these mortal sins alive and well for future reference. This would be one that hung around a long time if discovered. We were always sure where her focus lay because she emphasized the word "mortal" and she selected which sins would remain un-forgiven.

Walter was pretty relieved at this idea, too. I'd seen him bear the brunt of Mom's wrath once when he ran over some of her tulips with the tractor. I'd bet he remembered it, too.

Dad let us off at the gate and Chip and I walked the rest of the way home. Either he was distancing us from the probable discovery of our adventure or he was developing a strategy to become Walt's houseguest if Mom did find out. We talked about the fact that the bow project was no longer a secret from one of our parents. We actually had tacit approval. This was something to fall back on if discovered by Mom.

The secret was intact when we got home, and we greeted Dad as if we hadn't seen him for years spreading it on a bit thick. He soon told us, "Enough!"

But we did have lots to be thankful for and my father was the giver of that joy. What a guy.

We knew he could take it away, too. When Chip and I talked later, safe in our bunk beds, I told him I thought Dad was just trying to insure the continuance of the Greene name, but he didn't understand what I was talking about.

The next Saturday completed the tempering process of the bows. We didn't forget Walt's intervention for us and after having pooled our allowances, purchased Walt a package of Redman chewing tobacco as an offering to our newly recognized deity. It took some talking to convince Mr. Jones at the corner store that I wasn't going to chew this stuff personally, but I did have to explain where it was going. I couldn't talk him into selling us a bottle of beer to go along with the tobacco. The specter of my mother overshadowed decisions in all sorts of places.

The tempering process was carefully explained to us and watched over by Walt.

Let the fire burn until it turns to coals, still blistering hot, but no flames. Slowly, but not too, draw the length through the coals keeping the bow moving along its length and rotating it at the same time. The wood can't get hot enough to char, but it has to turn a golden color.

This is particularly difficult as the bow tapers at each end and is thick at the handle, but the entire bow must reach the same degree of hardness and flexibility. Walt helped us wrap the thinner ends of the bows with cloth that we were instructed to keep wet during the bulk of the tempering. The bows had to get hot enough to make holding them uncomfortable and it wasn't long before our hands glowed with their heat.

Walt told us that this was how the Indian transferred something of himself into his bow. I recall the words: "Something of yourself." I liked that.

Every so often, Walt would tell us to pick up a handful of the feathery burnt ash at the edge of the fire and rub it down the length of the bow. We had to break for lunch because Mom's meter had been quietly creeping up since our overjoyed greeting of Dad on Thursday. At lunch, our blackened and reddened hands probably sent the meter up a few degrees more, but we were getting things done and didn't pay attention to her skeptical looks when we answered. We told Mom that we had helped Todd Belisle fix his flat bike tires and that was the reason for black hands. She didn't ask further questions but she did notice.

After lunch, we alternated the heating and rubbing processes until Walt was satisfied. The bows had taken on an ashy tan color and glowed with the sheen of a job well done. When Walt flicked them with a work-hardened fingernail, the bows quivered with a taught sound, solid, strong and well made. Walt declared them finished except for the leather grip coverings, but that we had much more to do before we'd use them. Those bows felt good, and we were both amazed at how slick and smooth they were. They belonged to us. No one had given them to us. They were the result of our hard work.

It had taken us about five weeks to reach this point, and the feeling of accomplishment was strong. I think Walt was pleased with the results as well. After all, he had been reliving his own long ago with Chief as his teacher and that had to be an enjoyable journey for him.

But, unknown to any of the humans, my mother had tracked her two poor liars. My ever faithful and vigilant Patch should have told me but she didn't.

The reddened hands must have had a huge effect on her internal meter. It was high up in the yellow area now. Mom was always good at this following stuff. She had often tracked us, showing up at the best and worst of times and in the most unlikely of places my entire life. I suspected she had Indian blood in her and lots of it.

Mom had been watching our endeavors from the shaded security of a lilac bush, either until she was satisfied of our honest labors or had enough evidence for a conviction. I personally think it was some combination of both, weighted toward the guilty of something part.

She startled us with a statement, "Clark Malcolm, you know better than to play with fire."

The specter of Mom standing with hands on hips pushed all other thoughts somewhere beyond my grasp. Having once again been reduced to speechlessness by the appearance of a vengeful parent, I stood there wishing simply to be somewhere else. China. Russia. I wasn't the only one.

Walter immediately decided that there was grass much too long somewhere, clambered up on the tractor and feigned not hearing Mom over the noise of the Ford's un-muffled engine. He put it in gear and drove away before he was sucked into the vortex of sin cleansing. Older was smarter.

We were in for another surprise when Mom later questioned our activities over the past summer weeks. While we talked, (mostly we answered in short yes/no sentences; it was much less incriminating) Mom picked up both bows and ran her hands over their smooth finishes. Her look of unhappiness changed to appreciation at the products her boys' labor had produced and sort of balanced her disapproval of the sneaking. However, "sort of" does not mean complete acceptance and forgiveness. As we related the work and care given to the task, I thought I felt her softening just a bit.

My mother knew how caught up with Indians and their lifestyles we were, and I suppose that she accepted our quest for complete realism, but she certainly didn't approve of the cloak and dagger methods. I saw her thinking about some appropriate comeuppance for us, but right then she was praising our labors. After several more admiring comments, which hinted at a chance of salvation, Mom turned to go.

She left us standing open-mouthed. "Those are really nice, boys, but we'll have some things to talk about after dinner, won't we? Don't be late."

This was a familiar and effective strategy of hers: leave them on a note of unending uncertainty. That way the next several hours would be spent in a re-living of the fall from grace. Contemplating punishments always adds to their severity. It sucked the fun out of the rest of the day.

Both Chip and I decided we should go home and cut the grass, or weed Mom's flowers, or give Patch a bath and a comb out, or clean our rooms.

Paint the house.

Join the Foreign Legion.

Pick out a funeral plot.

Dinner that evening was tense, at least along the boy's side of the table. Chip and I always sat alongside one another. Mom believed that I'd assume some positive role in his growth as a Greene family member although this probably didn't fall into that category. I believe our seating was just a more efficient way to confront us. Withering stares were more effective if Mom or Dad didn't have to keep swiveling their heads to include more than one guilty party.

Dad had obviously been brought up to speed on our latest transgressions, and I could tell by the short blessing before dinner that the word was still mum on his previous awareness. He didn't say anything about saving his sons from Hell or Mom, so the secret was still in effect. I think he was worried about his own complicity. Both Chip and I struggled through dinner. I knew how the condemned man felt as his thoughts turned to the final after dinner activities. I'd been the recipient of many "the dishes are washed and put away, Clark, come in here" sentences. There was always penance.

After dinner Carole cleared the table, but Chip and I stood before Judge and Jury, Mom. She was also the Sentence Giver.

My father was The Enforcer. Witness to the event and giggling to magnify our disgrace were sisters Carole and Phoebe, but the focus was entirely on us boys. A parent's shame in their offspring is a mighty sword and always a good starting place. It lets the child know that while you have failed the parent, the parent might share some of the blame…if the child exhibits enough sorrow for doing the foul deed. We were well practiced at this exhibiting part. "Sorrowful Sams" were we. Chip managed several good blubbers, a calculated action for him, and I said it was my fault alone. I thought about saying that I made Chip do it but reconsidered that as just a bit too farfetched. Mom and Dad, for completely different reasons, would know better than that. The pleading and confessions were over none too soon. Sentencing came next: grounded for two weeks. No going over to Walt's. No progress on the bows.

While the grounding was pretty bad, we still had lots of possibilities at home. We had rabbits, a flying squirrel, several cats, and my dog Patch to tend, and we had grass to mow, flower and vegetable gardens to weed, all under the ever vigilant eyes of my mother. Kids would come over to play, no restrictions there. Still any summer punishment was horrific to us because we were always on the go, doing something that if not constructive, was always entertaining.

There was another unwritten rule at our house: We could never say we were bored. "You're bored?"

These were openings all adults sprang into.

This was second only to "moping" around. You didn't want to be known as a Moper in the Greene house. "Quit moping or I'll give you something to mope about!"

Any lag in an immediate behavior change was countered with lists of absolutely pointless work for the child who could not think for themselves. I never said I had nothing to do and I seldom moped where anybody could see me.

Two weeks was a severe summer punishment, and we would have to stay occupied without "getting underfoot," "getting on my nerves," "pushing our luck," or "cruising for a bruising" (my father's favorite).

Mom actually came to the rescue. It never failed to amaze me how parents can do something that alters perceived punishments and changes them to enjoyable tasks. Mom had spoken with Walt after all. I pictured her chasing him down on the tractor. She probably didn't do that but she might have laid in wait behind the lilac bush. Worked once with us, why not again with him? Even Walt had to come home eventually.

Several mornings later, after breakfast, Mom sent us out to clean the garage. When we first moved in my father and Grandpa Clark had built the garage, but our car hadn't fit inside the garage since the day after it was completed three years ago.

Once my father drove away to work following his week's vacation, Mom began excavating treasures stored in attic and crawlspace, closet and cardboard box, under bed, behind the piano and in chests of drawers. Picture frames, stools, broken chairs, winter clothes, beach balls, baseball and bats, horse shoe and croquet and badminton sets, benches, boxes, pots and pans, old rugs, a baby carriage and crib, a cradle, leaves for the dining room table, coffee tins of nuts and bolts, kites hung on the wall, bicycles for all four children, rakes and shovels, Christmas ornaments and wrapping paper, Dad's Navy footlocker, an old tricycle, wagons, sled, wheelbarrow, bundled up newspapers stacked high, all were rushed to fill up this new vacant space. The result of this was that the garage was always reminiscent of images of post-tornado newsreels.

Whenever our parents thought we didn't have enough to do, we were sent out to clean up the garage, but that morning we were surprised to see Walt standing beside one of our wagons. In the wagon were neatly stacked the bows, arrow shafts, and tools, all of the items necessary to continue doing in public what we had been sneaking around to do in secret.

My mother was a shape changer. One minute she was a banshee or wraith, the next minute an angel in form and fashion. We kids didn't have a clue. I certainly didn't question the reasons she had talked Walt into bringing the operation to our house. Chip and I were happy enough just to have the bows. Our parents usually took things away from us when we managed some horrid deed but this time it was different.

Walt, Chip, and I had to listen to Mom's new rules regarding when we could work on them (after chores and animal care), how we would work on them (only under adult supervision), what we could do with them when they were done (never aim at animal or person, no birds, cats, or neighbors), where we would keep them (not in the house) and what would happen if we by gosh broke any of the rules (unsaid: scourging, drawn and quartered, the rack and iron maiden as well as spanking with a belt).

Fair enough.

Now that we were pretty much done with the bows, it was time to start on the arrows. Walt had stored the arrow branches under the eaves of his shack pressed tightly between two pieces of planking to keep them from warping. These thinner branches had to be scraped smooth and straight, and Walt had fashioned two special scrapers out of an old lawnmower blade for us to use.

He had cut across the length of the blade and ground two different sized semicircular grooves into the long dimension. The other edge had been fitted with a slotted piece of wood forced on the blade to protect the hands from cuts and blisters. It was a modified wood shave that would round the shaft of the arrow when drawn down its length. As the scraper was drawn down the branch, thin slivers would curl off as the shaft became true and smooth, a tedious and time consuming task. We averaged only one straight arrow shaft every two or three days. The pile of finished shafts grew very slowly.

Tempering the arrow shafts was much quicker to do but no less demanding. As the shafts were heated, we also had to straighten them further by prying with another device that Walt had made to do the job. It consisted of scrap wood with a large hole drilled in one end. This hole was used to push and pry the heated shaft until it was as straight as possible. As the wood was heated and cooled, pushed and pulled in this direction and that, the shafts would hold their trueness.

Eventually we were ready to fletch the arrows and had asked Mr. Yost, a deacon in our church and the owner of Yost's Turkey Farm, for some feathers. He came through wonderfully and one Sunday had given us a grocery bag full of cast off turkey feathers. We had domestic white feathers, not so authentic, and a few barred metallic colored ones from the wild turkey. Mr. Yost had several customers that insisted on having "real" turkey for Thanksgiving and Christmas, so he would always have a few wild stock birds. The feathers were split, shaving the quill until it was as thin as could be.

We placed the feather sections around the end of the arrow shaft and tied them in place with fishing line. Walter got some hide glue from someplace (another raid to the homestead barn) that had to be heated up in a pan of water, and we coated the fishing line and quill slivers to hold every thing in place. Once the glue cooled and hardened, the feather end was notched to accommodate the bowstring once we'd figured that part out. We walked around for weeks afterward with glue stiffened fingers because the old-time hide glue was indestructible when set, but we didn't care.

The business end of the arrow had a whole set of rules made up for it: no sharp points, nothing that wouldn't come out if it went in (ruling out anything barbed), no sharp edges, nothing made out of stone. I had visions of finding or borrowing enough flint arrowheads to affix all the arrows with authentic points but knew better than to ask for Walt's. His collection was one thing that he prized highly. I knew several kids who had access to father's and cousin's collections, but my father had been a city boy and didn't collect anything when he was a kid. Rules about the tips did put a pretty big damper on the arrows, but we were able to talk Dad into getting us some target points. They are metal, but dull and rounded to protect the arrow from impact damage.

Compromise was learned very early in our house, mostly through the practical application of old homilies. Don't cut your nose off to spite your face; looking a gift horse in the mouth; for want of a nail the battle was lost; flies with honey; hell in a hand-basket; flash in the pan; counting chickens too early; chapter and verse, chapter and verse (this last one had to be repeated) were just a few of the phrases we heard morning, noon and night. They accompanied every task given, every transgression discovered, and every statement made. We would "be content with such things as we have."

We finished the bows shrinking leather cut from someone's cast off boots around the handgrip portion. This was hard to do and we enlisted my mother's help to soak, stretch, and sew the wet, pliable leather grips with a heavy rug thread. Once the grip dried and had shrunk, it was in place forever and cushioned the hand.

We had a lot of trouble with the sinew, and after trying and trying and trying until we ran out of the raw material, we gave up. We tried chewing it for pliability, taking baths with it, giving it to Patch to chew for us (which was really dumb), leaving it lie in the sun, soaking it in dog urine after we had chewed, not before, because Walt thought he remembered the Indians doing it this way. It was hard getting Patch to pee in a bowl. We wasted most of one day following her around with the bowl ready. It didn't work.

Despite all of our efforts, we broke sinew after sinew after sinew. They just weren't strong enough to hold up to the strength of the bows, but Walt didn't remember how to make them better.

We were faced with the very real possibility of never being able to shoot the bows. We had attempted to use packaging string (bad), fishing line (not heavy enough), butcher's string (waxed and a bit better, but it still broke), baling twine (too thick, but strong), and had tried braided rug thread.

Nothing worked. We were crushed.

We were also the objects of lots of neighborhood derision.

"Where's the bow at, Clark?"

"Some Indian you are..."

"Na-na, na-na, Na-naaaaaa!"

The last was a favorite, though I didn't know why. After we'd boasted about our skills, hard work and potential as fearsome, unconquerable Indian warriors, it didn't take long for every one to hear of our problems. It soon seemed like every neighbor boy and even a few girls made fun of us from the road.

We were still grounded and couldn't give chase for any vengeance wreaking, but I made a mental list. I could stand a little teasing, but Larry Hemry and Bobby Marshall were surely going to get it. Even I couldn't stay grounded forever. I thought about telling Patch to "Sic'em" but I had gotten in trouble for that before.

After Dad finished his breakfast a few Saturdays later, we were summoned. Like commoners approaching the throne, we met Dad at the head of the breakfast table. We children ate early on the weekends and Dad could sleep in on Saturday if he chose. Sundays were for church and early rising, but Saturdays were a Dad-day when society's rules were relaxed. We had been "moping" according to Mom and he wanted to know what the story was.

No moping was allowed here.

We told him all about the bowstrings and our failure. I threw in a short bit about our neighborhood status being in jeopardy, and Dad did one of the few spontaneous things I ever remember him doing. He called the local sporting goods store, asked about bowstrings, and was told to bring the bows in so they could be measured properly. When he hung up, he told us to gather up the bows and arrows.

We were going to Monroe and Walt was going, too! We didn't go to town very often and we sure didn't do it on the spur of the moment unless one of us was dying or we ran out of Bag-Balm. The twenty minute drive to town took forever.

When we got to the store, we presented our bows to the clerk and followed him into the back of the store. As we walked, the clerk marveled at the bows and initially disbelieved who the makers were until Walt told him the whole tale (leaving out the butcher shop and lilac bush parts). He ran his hands appreciatively over their surfaces, admired the stitching on the leather grip and flexed the bows by hand to feel their strength. In a workshop with piles of guns with cracked stocks, deflated rubber rafts, torn tents, waders with rock cut gashes, and broken (gasp!) bows, the clerk measured our bows. He measured both Chip and me for arm length and told us to come back next week.

We were reluctant to leave the bows. We didn't know this guy. Maybe he was going to sell our bows or he might even say they were lost or stolen.

Dad convinced us.

"If you ever wanted to shoot the Danged things, we ArebyGod going to leave them here and if we don't want to, we could JustbyGod get in the car and GotheHeck home."

After this clear and scintillating explanation, we left the bows and headed back to the car and home.

The next week crept by. The school year was fast approaching; the hot summer waning, and we were running out of days to spend with the fruits of a whole vacation's labor. Right then we had absolutely nothing to hold on to. We had given the bows to a complete stranger and had endless private and worried discussions about the likelihood of ever getting them back. The disarray of the workshop was an additional contributor to our anxiety. It would have been easy to lose a speedboat in that place. There was a point that we even talked about a conspiracy between the sporting goods store and my mother. She had gone on a good while about someone getting an eye shot out and belabored this point enough to worry us both.

The next Saturday it took physical restraint by my mother to allow Dad his normal sleep-in. We listened with ears pressed to their bedroom door to catch a change in his breathing patterns. We "accidentally" dropped large objects for sound effects until Mom chased us outside with dire warnings. Once outside, we teased Patch into barking incessantly in hopes this would hurry things along fully knowing how cranky Dad could be. Then we cut the grass outside his bedroom window.

That worked.

We were in a hurry, had to always "push our luck" one of Dad's favorite sayings. When he got up, he promised us "what for" if we didn't quit.

We quit.

Eventually Dad's breakfast was finished and we were on the way to reclaim our possessions. If that rat of a store clerk hadn't sold them or lost them. We took our arrows in hopes he was an okay guy.

We went to pick up Walt first and fidgeted the whole time we waited for him.

When we got to Monroe Sporting Goods, Chip and I managed to leap the span from parking lot to door without our feet hitting gravel despite a thirty-foot distance and my father's command, "Wait for me." We were through that door in a skinny minute. The clerk stood behind the glass shelves as if he had known we were on the way and had set the bows out on the counter. The new strings were already affixed, but the bows weren't strung taught. They were marvelous, sticky with wax, heavy, multiple-strand, reinforced at both ends and middle, honest to goodness bow strings. The clerk showed us how to string the bow by stepping between bow and string to bend the bow enough to slide one end up and affix it in the notch.

The bows were strung. They looked powerful, taut, and more than a little deadly. They were all of that and more. They were ours.

He showed us how to draw back on the string using three fingers, where to place the arrow shaft and how to position the wrist away from the path of the released string.

With more words of caution about the results of string zinging forearm, he asked my father, "Is it okay if I take a picture of them holding the bows?"

"Sure," said our benevolent father.

Our pictures were taken several times as we posed with bows drawn, bows held in front and across shoulder. We were Indians in a white man's blue jeans and shirt, smiling at the white man but just until we could escape back into wilderness and war.

We were glowing so much the pictures were probably overexposed.

We gathered our arrows possessively and were surprised when the clerk handed us two quivers to hold the arrows. They were brown canvas with fake fringe and a belt loop. We knew that real quivers were worn over the shoulder and made of deer or elk skin, but we remembered "gift horse in the mouth" and gave him an honest thank you. He said he wanted to make sure the feathers didn't get scruffed up and keeping the arrows in a quiver would insure their good condition. He also said we had done a good job.

This guy was not a rat.

We were almost to the shooting part.

The trip home included a lecture about being responsible. The potential for disaster was explained to us again and again.

"Don't think those bows are yours. You're only the keepers of the bows."

"I'm the real owner of the bows."

"I can withdraw my permission any time I see fit."

"I will take them away if you mess up."

He went on to detail all the reasons we shouldn't have the bows. Our only defense was that we had made them. Colored by the fact we had started out very sneakily, it wasn't a wise statement and I chose to just be dutiful. I listened and so did Chip. I also knew that if anything happened, I would bear the entire blame.

We stopped by Mr. Sisung's farm on the way home and Dad bought three bales of straw. After we threw them in the car, we headed toward home, and Chip and I knew we were about to enter a moment of truth for two young boys. We were being entrusted with a weapon of considerable power just as the clerk had told my father. When he thought we were out of earshot, he said both bows were capable of killing any large animal, like a deer, a fact we already relished.

What would any self-respecting Indian make a bow for if not to shoot a deer, a buffalo, or a bear? Did he think we were going to shoot a cauliflower?

Dad set the straw bales up in the vacant lot across from the house situated across Goddard Drive, between the street and the Hicks' cinderblock house. He helped us mark out distances of twenty-five, fifty and seventy-five feet before we ran out of vacant lot. We put the straw bales on their sides and stacked one on top of the other to give the largest area for a target. Our first targets were just rude bull's-eyes drawn with black and red crayon on old butcher's paper that Mom had saved and stored in the broom closet. We had practiced in dreams and with our first poor homemade bows until we just knew we were experts.

We made the other neighborhood kids "GettheHeckouttathere!"

Toeing the twenty-five foot mark, I remember when I first drew the arrow on that loaded string, the bow audibly hummed. The arrow flew straight, flat and went clear through the straw bales, sticking in the dirt about fifteen feet on the other side. A good thing we made Steve Hicks move before we started.

I didn't see the arrow's flight or it stick in the ground. I couldn't see anything. My eyes were watering as if they'd been doused with lemon juice. The clerk talking about wrist and forearm position came forward with a rush just after letting the arrow fly. As the red welt rose on the inside of my left forearm, I remembered it chapter and verse but completely forgot the part of being a stoic Indian.

Dang, that hurt So Bad!

I continued to make this mistake until my wrists became strong enough to hold their proper position.

Walter and my dad watched us for a while, but as is the nature of parents and adults of every age and era, soon lost interest in the doings of children. Dad walked to the house to see about lunch and Walter ambled off to drink a beer or two with Mr. Miller. With final solemn words and cautions about eyes poked out, inevitable loss of said bows if something bad happened, and a farewell "Be careful," we found ourselves left to our own devices. We hollered thanks to their retreating figures and got back to shooting.

Our Mohawk haircuts had grown out considerably by then. At some point every summer, Mom usually stopped shaving the sides of our heads. She wanted both of us fairly presentable when school resumed. Mom was accustomed to her "little heathens," but she knew Jefferson Schools wouldn't be. It was enough she had to explain our wild and aberrant behavior to the church group, she didn't want to have to explain it to the whole school. Nonetheless, we still felt as if our veins coursed full of the blood of Sitting Bull, Tecumseh or Pontiac. We practiced until it was too dark to see the target and went into the house. We would be back tomorrow.

Although we still had two weeks until school started, summer vacation ended that Saturday. We still went swimming, still played Indians, still cut grass, and still explored the marsh, but everything else was a second ending, another kind of finish. We had passed not out of childhood but into something with added value. We'd gone from having playthings to the making and shaping of a tool and from having a dream to building a reality.

The summer had been full of unexpected work taught by an unexpected teacher, supported at unexpected moments by both parents, singly and in concert. Mom and Dad may have recognized that their two young boys might be ready for a different set of operating rules and allowed them to bear both the fruits and consequences of their actions. Now I suppose that's what good parenting is, but then I just knew that most of my parents' lessons were tough ones.

Walter Nadeau's teaching of two boys came to an end that day, maybe at the same moment I released the arrow. It wasn't anything that he or we really decided but instead appeared as a slow dawning that the lesson was learned and the task finished. We still waved and chased the tractor or stopped by for a chat and Mom baked cookies for him every once in a while, but we never again joined as closely as we did in that June, July and August of 1954. The next summer we were older and so was Walt. He either did not have enough energy or the inclination to give any more of himself to us. Maybe we were too busy and had moved on although we played with and enjoyed the bows for many, many years. Walter would stop and watch us practice every once in a while, but he never looked that closely again. For a while, Walter Nadeau played an indelible part in our lives, well apart from my parents. He taught Chip and me that doing any job the best way that we can is self-satisfying. We learned it's sometimes okay to bend rules if the goal is worthy enough, but we shouldn't tell that to everyone. He taught us that everybody has something to offer even if appearances don't make the offering evident.

Chapter 4
Fair Trades

I had nine new puppy tails in my pocket and I was looking to trade.

These were even more special than the first batch I'd had because they were really and truly Airedale tails. No mutts in this place!

We were always able to determine when Patch was falling under the breeding spell. She'd stop beating up trespassing males. In fact, she started treating all dogs nicely, male or female. Any other time she was quick to run off intruders but when she was in season, she sent signal advertisements for the opportunity.

We had been lucky during Patch's breeding seasons twice now since her first litter and had managed to keep her confined inside both times. We used a whole variety of different tactics for the duration and she didn't go outside at all unless accompanied by at least one of us kids. In addition to escort, she had to have two leads just in case she managed to break one, and if a male dog had been seen in the vicinity, two of us were liable to be called for guard duty. In the house, she wore a homemade diaper every second while she was fertile so if she did manage to escape, the protective cloth was supposed to thwart any male's unauthorized advances. It was a tussle every time and when she came in season late last January, Mom said we should breed her to another registered Airedale.

We took her all the way to Port Huron, Michigan, where the closest non-related male dog lived. We had to contact the AKC in Detroit to find him. There just weren't that many Airedales around anywhere.

He was a pretty male but not much larger than Patch, and the dog's owner was surprised at Patch's bulk. This male wasn't nearly as big as Patch's sire, but we were here, and we wanted purebred dogs. Besides, Patch wasn't choosy. My dad always said Patch was wanton when she was ready to mate and he was right. Patch would have been happy with a dachshund. She had liked this choice fine enough and that's why we had puppies.

We were so intrigued by the promise of Patch's pedigree pups, and she was kept confined when her term was coming to a finish. These offspring deserved a better maternity ward than the space under the house. My bedroom was now the birthing room, and we had a crowd for witness. Patch had been acting differently all day, and Mom said the little ones would be coming anytime.

Mom made sure all four of us were there as she explained each step in the process.

"Come here quick, children! Patch's water just broke and the puppies will start coming right away. Come on, you've got to see this."

We all tucked in around Patch to watch her heaving and straining in labor. No jockeying for position now; we're too enthralled with the prospect of babies.

"See, there's the snout of the first one, right there. Watch close. See the head starting there? It's okay, girl. It's okay," Mom soothed to comfort Patch who was already panting and whining with the strain of birth.

"Look now, children, the head is the biggest part and after that the little body will come out in a rush. These puppies are God's miracle of birth. See the little umbilical cord? That's how the baby got nourishment when it was in her belly. You all had a cord, too, right where your belly button is now. Only God can do this, children, only God."

Puppy birth and God lessons all rolled into one. Mom didn't miss one single opportunity.

As the puppy made its entrance, Patch curled her head around to start removing the birth sack. The baby gave a little yip as it sucked in a breath of air while Patch continued and Mom let Patch chew and sever the umbilical cord before taking the puppy in a towel. Patch pushed the puppies out with regularity, just having time between each one to clean them up before the next started its birth journey. Mom gave each more cleaning and handed them to us until we all had puppies in our laps.

"Watch how she cleans them up. She's such a good momma. See her licking each one to stimulate their breathing reflex. Here comes the afterbirth, see it? No, Chip, she'll use that herself. You just let it be. What a good girl she is. Now, let's get them at the teats. Nuzzle their noses right up there. They'll latch on all by themselves. We've got to get her off that blanket, it's soaked. Clark, go get a dry one for her and the little ones."

I went because this teat stuff was mostly for Chip and Peg anyway. Chip wasn't two and Peg wasn't around for the first litter Patch gave us. The birthing part was interesting but I was already an old pro at the nursing arrangement. We got the mass of puppies transferred and situated on one of Dad's old woolen Navy blankets with "USN" stenciled across both ends. Soon sounds of soft slurping and puppy happiness grunts came from the blanket. They were such hungry little babies, pushing and kneading on Patch while they each looked for the very best nipple.

Ten babies, five males, five females. We had puppies in the house again! In my room again! Puppy smells and puppy noises! All Right!

Two weeks after those ten curly haired puppies were born we took them to have their tails docked. A real veterinarian, not our family doctor, performed the operation this time because we were going to make big money with these dogs, thirty dollars for the males and twenty-five for the females. We sold one male dog before it was even born. When my father mentioned at work we'd had Patch bred to another registered dog, several of the guys were interested right away. One man wanted a dog for his kids and gave my father the money right then and there! When he came over to pick one pup out, he said not to cut its tail.

I remembered when we picked up Patch my father had said only idiots didn't have Airedale's tails docked. I wondered why my dad had agreed to sell one of these special pups to an idiot, but I didn't ask him.

Which is why I'd had only nine tails, but they're all the real McCoy. Puppies in my room and tails in my pocket and these Airedale puppy-dog stubs were worth a lot, too. I'd gotten advance offers from two kids and I headed over to see one of them right away. Jimmy Reaume wanted a tail so bad he said I could choose from a whole bunch of the stuff in his room. But it had to be secret because his mom doesn't like dogs. Jimmy was afraid she wouldn't like them all the way down to a tail.

We often spent much of our summer times paying homage to one relative or another.

One of our yearly traditions was a visit to Uncle Ernest and Aunt Etta's farm in Avoca, Michigan. The date was as vague as the first robin of spring or as early as a dandelion pushing its way through the last translucent snow but equally treasured and marked on Mom's kitchen calendar.

Uncle Ernest and Aunt Etta were my uncle and aunt but not really. They were my grand-uncle and grand-aunt, if such titles exist. Ernest was one of Grandpa Clark's older brothers, one of the five Greene sons, and he owned a huge dairy farm. Their farm was much more businesslike than my grandparents' place in Manchester. Whenever we visited, Uncle Ernest expected us to help out while we enjoyed a taste of true farm life. While we'd always helped in the gardens and orchards of Grandma Phoebe and Grandpa Teddy, at this one we worked right alongside the hired help and we were required to keep the pace.

Our trip to their small town north of Port Huron was a carefully planned expedition. It had to be for six people and a dog. Driving the seventy-five miles or so between Pointe aux Peaux and their farm was no small feat. This was before I-75 joined the ranks of interstate freeways that snaked their way through the U.S., when Ike was president. A journey of this magnitude must be well prepared for: lunch of course, and blankets (if the car broke down), old clothing for everyone (you wouldn't be wearing anything good on this farm), and a requisite pie, loaf of bread or cake (just to show our country kin Mom hadn't forgotten how).The preparation and drive took most of the day.

Ernest had been a logger in Michigan before he was a farmer and still carried the whipcord muscles he'd developed as a young man. Although in his sixties and seventies when we visited, he ruled over cows, farmhands, and land by sheer force of strength. He hired high school kids, itinerant workers, and press-ganged every cousin, nephew and niece, and cajoled his brothers for the numerous tasks the farm required. He operated on the principle that everyone better keep up with him, and he was always at the head of the pack.

If milking began at five in the morning, Ernest began at four (and so did everyone else). He came upstairs and kicked our feet until we woke and responded. Of course, Aunt Etta had been up before that preparing breakfast for all the hungry mouths, but that was an unspoken expectation and meal making included every woman and girl who came to visit. When noon-time rolled around, despite the ringing dinner bell, nobody better glance toward the house until Ernest took off his hat and wiped his brow, a signal for lunch. Dinnertime was the same. If there was light in the sky and work still waited, everybody kept right on working and the women kept the dinner hot until the work was done.

My father told me it was a lesson Ernest learned during the Depression when he'd almost lost the farm to foreclosure. Don't let work wait. First it piles up and then it doesn't get done.

Ernest never forgot.

Despite the inevitable work, our one and two week visits were always looked forward to with great excitement and anticipation. They were a renewable rite of passage, a chance to show cousins that we could stand the pace and to measure one another against the growing-up ruler Uncle Ernest kept in his head. Aunt Etta greeted us with unfeigned delight at each visit, but he waited for a time until he had watched us work and we'd proved our mettle. His appraisal was important to us and part of being family.

We could just make out the faded and numerous barns and outbuildings that surrounded their house when we turned onto their road. The country road on which their farm sat was one of surprising peril. Unpaved and only smoothed when Ernest found the time to do it (which wasn't often) with his old tractor drawn scraper, it was always touch and go whenever we made the final turn especially if there'd been rain. There was a good chance our car would get bogged down. When we did get stuck, my father would have to walk the rest of the way to the farm, take someone away from their regular work and bring the tractor or horses to pull us free. Theirs was the only farm for several miles, and it was lonely and overgrown with wide, deep ditches that had a chorus of frogs.

We viewed the road as a sort of weather vane for how the visit would go.

My father, no stranger to farm life, always cussed his way down the road when he had to get assistance and often managed to lose more than his shoes to the muck. He knew what was coming from his failure to negotiate his way around the ruts. Dad, always short of temper, would have to ask for help from Ernest who wasn't long on it, himself. If we got stuck, you could be sure Uncle Ernest would repeat the tale at least once during every meal we ate for the entire visit. Ernest laughed until his face turned scarlet at Dad's misfortune. My father's ears turned even redder.

It didn't help that once when we were mired to the floorboards, one of the big pulling horses kicked out the headlight, dented the grill and knocked off the chrome ring on the front of our car. Uncle Ernest told that story for years.

Yet, when we were there and had unloaded all the Greene trappings, we settled into the regimen of farm life almost immediately. It must have been due to some inherent work ethic as if the family knew the secrets of industry. Mostly we did the grunt work of the farm, but when the farm consists of seventy-five or so milking cows and another thirty odd steers and heifers for sale or eating, as well as chickens, horses and pigs, there are plenty of tasks available. In addition, Uncle Ernest raised all his own livestock feed: wheat, corn and oats, and vegetables and fruit enough for the entire family (and I suspected the county, too). The farm grew enough of everything for Aunt Etta to have a produce stand at the summer-weekend farmers' market in Avoca. The only thing that didn't grow at his farm was moss. Nothing stood still long enough.

His hired help spent the night in a separate cabin adjacent to the main barn. All the related kids, regardless of relationship, age, or gender, slept in the farmhouse attic. It was high peaked, full of cobwebs and night sounds that crept through the eaves, had a solitary naked light bulb, and was the storage space for people and farm oddities alike. Aunt Etta kept a dressmaker's form up there, odd cribs and chairs, several iron bed frames and trunks full of clothes that smelled of camphor.

There was little worry about mixing boy and girl sleeping arrangements. Beds were made on the floor and it didn't matter if Clark slept next to Cousin Helen. The farm work made sure everybody started dreaming as soon as their heads hit the feather tick pillows. A visit to their farm was the only time I didn't read myself to sleep each night.

Mealtimes were as carefully planned as the rest of the farm chores. My mother helped prepare the gargantuan platters of toast, eggs and biscuits, ham, bacon, potatoes and milk gravy that made up their usual breakfasts. No one went hungry at Aunt Etta's table, ever, as long as you were timely. Morning and lunch meals were generally a sumptuous but frantic affair, as if eating were an impediment to getting all the work done. We all sat at a common table fifteen feet long, family and hired help alike, and everyone was equal. Every meal I had there was a contest to make sure there was food enough on your plate to keep you going strong until the next feeding. The only rule at meals was "don't reach." For one thing it was impolite and for another, more importantly, Uncle Ernest would crack the offender's knuckles with the handle of his knife even if he had to get up and walk around the table to do it. He was quick, quicker than a snake.

In the early mornings after the hasty breakfast, milking began. Once Ernest pushed away from the table with his big hands, the only sound you heard was the scraping of every other chair. The rush had begun.

During each morning and afternoon milking, Patch was kept tethered. Uncle Ernest took every precaution during this time and Patch was liable to introduce some excitement to the normally sedate herd. When the morning chores were done, the first thing I did was unhook her. She was then allowed to run free, another farm dog expected to do her share.

She and Ernest's dog, a black and white, part something, part collie named Sue, could most often be found at the three or four acre stock pond inside the main pastures. Sue had been around the farm forever and had once been a pretty good herding dog. Now she'd reached the age where she usually wanted to herd the ground underneath her.

Ernest had several milking stations but not as many as he had cows. This meant that six or so cows could be milked, stripped, and sent out to pasture, then another six, and so on. Ernest milked Jersey cows. They are known for calmness, docility and their excellent high butterfat milk production. They led into and out of the milking stalls easily to get their udders washed and fed a ration of grain while they were being milked.

There is a song sung by milking machines: slurp, chutter-chutter, slurp...slurp, chutter-chutter, slurp...slurp, rhythmic and soft, cadenced as regularly as the beat of a heart. Accompanying the music is the rich and sweet warm smell of milk, mixed with the sharp tang of cow. Senses are filled unlike at any other time, and once you've listened to the tune and inhaled the perfume of milking, you never forget.

At any other instance, one could be lulled to sleep by the atmosphere but not at Ernest's. The mornings were scurry and scuttle. The milk had to be milked; the milk had to be stripped; the milk had to be separated; the milk had to be cooled. At eleven o'clock every morning (and there are NO off days), the dairy truck would be there to pick up the previous night's and the morning's production. Every jounce of labor was centered toward...The milk, the milk, the milk...

One of the children's jobs was to remove the already milked cows from their stanchions, strip and clean their udders, and turn them out into the big holding pasture until the rest were tended. Stripping is hand milking the last drops from the cow's udder. It entails progressively squeezing each teat starting next to the udder and pulling down gently at the same time. I'd learned how to milk with the goats we'd kept when we lived in Manchester and had the lesson reinforced by Ernest every time we visited. He'd follow along behind us at each cow insuring that they were properly emptied. The lash of his tongue when we didn't get it right was enough to guarantee we didn't do it badly a second time.

We stripped their udders into buckets or toward one of the farm's many cats. What the cats didn't get went to the house and was strained for the family's use.

The milk house where the foamy liquid was stored was a squat stone shed and cool regardless the outside weather. It was redolent with the smell of butter-fat as if the white painted stone had been smeared with heavy cream. There were two big stainless steel tanks and pipes that went hither and yon to a large spigot for the tank truck. It was scrubbed and soaked completely each afternoon under Ernest's stern gaze, and he was more than mad if it wasn't done to his satisfaction. There was a refrigeration system in an attached shed that Ernest had to kick and cuss every day, and his loud and repeated fussing provided us kids with huge and secret laughter.

It wasn't until I was a teenager that I ever saw the inside. No children and only a few hired help were ever allowed to go in the milk house and it had a huge padlock on the stout door. The milk house was sacred.

Once the cows were finished, we settled down into the countless supporting tasks necessary to keep a six hundred acre farm up and running: clean stalls, cows to day pasture, fodder and feed to distribute, something to plow, plant or harvest, this or that to repair, and that or this to haul. Uncle Ernest directed the whole affair as if he were a general ordering troops about. A score of important every day tasks and at least that many unexpected ones which simply MUST be done before the end of the day.

In addition to all the ladylike cows on the farm, there was Hector. All of the sedate niceties found in the cows were absent in Hector, the Jersey bull. He was tawny, huge and muscled, with a scrotum that almost clunked when he walked. His maw was continually bedecked with ropy drool and his breathing was a good imitation of a freight train leaving the station. Hector spent most of his day eating, slobbering and bellowing; he sounded like the MGM lion. He stayed in his own pasture close to the farmhouse so Ernest could keep an eye on him until those days when he was put to the pleasurable service for which he was intended. He charged the fence, pawed the ground throwing clots of earth into the air, and swung his head from side to side whenever anyone approached his pasture, even my uncle. Hector also had a habit of hooking his horns into the gate to the pasture and rattling it when anyone walked by.

Although the farm was owned by Ernest and Etta, everybody knew who the cows really belonged to.

Hector.

He had an extra special corral that the kids gave a wide berth to. Uncle Ernest had scrounged railroad ties from somewhere and used them for the posts around the enclosure. In between these heavy timbers, he'd strung stout wire and old water-pipe and had interlaced those with barbed wire. The whole of it appeared to be strong enough to enclose a penal institution for elephants. The only thing it lacked was armed guards.

Except Sunday morning church, there was little time that farm work wasn't all anyone ever thought about. Nonetheless, every so often, Ernest either forgot or ran out of things for the kids to tend. We were always thoroughly instructed in the do's and don'ts of the farm on the trip up and on any new ones that were thought up when we arrived. The only piece left out of the equations was a grownup's inability to remember all the things to tell cousins not to do. We were inventive when it came to occupying ourselves when no one was looking.

The farm's livestock pond was located between the two back pastures and was really two ponds in one. A small creek ran down the side of a hill and onto the property feeding the ponds. The upper pool was surrounded by exposed stone outcroppings and cottonwood trees and had been dammed years ago forming a small deep pond roughly seventy-five feet in diameter. On one of the overhanging tree limbs, someone had tied a stout rope swing that arced out over the surface. Although Uncle Ernest professed to know nothing about it, we suspected he did it in a moment of "letting the kids have some fun," weakness. At the spillway on the lower end of that pond, a continuation of the stream fed the stock pond. The lower one was good for watering the cows. The upper one was good for watering kids.

Children and a swimming hole are identical to holding the opposite ends of two magnets together, a strong attraction, especially on hot and sultry days. We also knew that if we ever did get the opportunity to sneak off, Ernest would not spare anyone's time to hunt us up. We might catch the devil at dinnertime, but that was in the future. What we were interested in was the now.

Boys in dungarees, girls in shorts and wetly transparent tops, cannonballs, dog-paddles, belly flops, rainbows of sunlight in splashes, streaming hair in faces, shouts of glee and everyone trying to be the one whose "kersploosh" went the farthest out. Faces were plastered with cottonwood seedpods, skinny dipping when gender allowed, but someone had to keep watch, crawling up the slick rocky outcroppings to take another turn, swinging up and out to the sky, and all the while knowing it would last forever.

One year in August, (I was twelve or thirteen) when we'd delayed our trip until the end of summer, our troop of cousins made a get away. These escapes were a regular part of summer. It had been so hot Uncle Ernest wondered aloud that the eggs didn't come out of the chickens already cooked. We snuck up the track away from the house to the pond, and splashed and sported the afternoon away until someone finally noticed the insistent clangor of Aunt Etta's distant dinner bell coming from the farm.

The charge we immediately made back to the house for dinner was one of necessity; if there were empty chairs, the food that was meant for twenty would be eaten by the dozen or so who showed up on time. More vittles for them and none for us if we were late.

Our normal foot-dragging pace back to the world of work was forgotten, and we raced and whooped and hollered our way down the lane screaming like oblivious hooligans and banshees. A gaggle of cousins aged between seven and fourteen can make enough noise to stop traffic. The shortest distance between the two points of pond and house led along the side of Hector territory. The cacophony was definitely loud enough to get Hector's attention, but I wasn't satisfied with just having him notice us.

I was caught up in the wildness of our run for lunch, but determined to spare a few seconds to show how brave I was. With the recklessness of youth, I made a show-off beeline to the gate and whooped and hollered.

"YAHHHH, HECTOR! YAAAHHH! YAAAHhhh…" The end of the scream died in my throat.

Hector bellowed loudly in reply, charged in my direction, and hooked the six by eight foot heavy gate with his horns, ripping it off the hinges! It took only a second to realize what I'd done.

I was almost frozen with fear but not quite. I took off like a shot, scattering the group of cousins like billiard balls. Our previous racket was nothing compared to that now blared from each of us.

The gate teetered back and forth on his horns. Hector bellowed again.

Hector was loose! Hector was loose!

We screamed, "Uncle Ernest! Aunt Etta!"

Hector swung his head violently, the gate still caught on his horns cutting back and forth, an ominous swath in the still air. There were lots of targets for his ground tearing rage, and he was trying to get a fix on one. Most of the group put on extra speed when they saw Hector tear the gate off. Several others froze at the sight of Hector on the loose; my sister Carole, my cousin Susan and her eight-year-old brother, Jimmy, didn't run anywhere. Jimmy was squealing and trying to get away, but Susan had a death grip on his hand. Being struck immobile by fear didn't mean quiet. Everyone was shrieking. In the distance, I heard the screen door screech and slam again and again as adults poured out of the house. They added their noise to the now explosive August day.

Hector stood outside the pasture, his shoulders bunched and thick. He was blowing hard, a hoarse coarse rumble, wet and hypnotizing, "MUHHUUH, MUHHUUH!"

He whirled his head to glare at the reinforcements coming from the house, pawing clods of dust and dirt into the air. Aunt Etta looked out the window and ran from the house fluttering and flashing her apron. One of the men ran toward the barn, grabbed two pitchforks, and dashed back to hand one to Uncle Ernest. The adults made a rough (and very large) semi-circle around Hector.

"You kids! You kids! Shut up! Stand still, but shut up!" Ernest commanded. He glared at his wife. "Etta, quit flapping that damned apron."

He might have saved his breath about the shushing. Sue and Jimmy were making so much noise they wouldn't have heard the last trumpet. The rest of us weren't doing too well either. Hector continued to look back and forth at the audience, each swinging whip of his head making a slicing noise in the dirty powdered air. None of the adults could figure out how to get close enough with that wicked gate cutting the air, and they stood there with pitchforks in their hand and questioning looks on their faces.

Two lightning bolts of fur, one black and white, one black and tan, shot into the farmyard arena. Ernest's dog raced to the front of the bull shrilly yapping and growling. Patch went at the other end, her deep hoarse bark smothering the still expanding screams of the group. The bull whirled, facing Patch, then again to face Sue, bellowing in rage with each breath, this way and that, again and again. The dust clouded up so heavily it tore at our already hoarse throats. Every time he'd face one, the other dog would dart in and worry the end which they'd claimed, back and forth, back and forth.

Sue ducked under the swinging gate and lunged at the bull. On the back-swing, the edge of the heavy gate caught her shoulder, and she yelped as she rolled with the blow. The gate clattered off the bull's horns. He glared at Sue for a second and charged. I jittered myself one foot to the other in excitement and saw Patch rush in and bite Hector's back hock. He whirled again, bellowing even louder and Patch flew around, still attached. Hector continued to spin in a lumbering circle, around and around and around. Patch still didn't let go. The air got dusty-dirty-smoky like a trash fire had been lit.

The whirling lasted only a few moments, but it seemed like an eternity. Finally Hector began to slow, his circles going from dervish to stagger to stop. Patch got her feet planted and acted like an anchor to the bull's gyrations. She only released her hold when Hector stood head down, tongue lolling, his breath ragged and rattled. Ernest and one of the farm hands moved in to herd him back toward his enclosure, but they didn't get there in time. As soon as Patch let go, Hector shook his head, whirled once more and shambled off down the lane, heading toward the back pastures. Both dogs hurried after him barking not sure if the game were at an end.

The bull led a procession toward the rear of the property, a distance of more than a half mile. The dogs kept worrying and nipping at him, but once he got a head of steam up, he paid them scant attention. It was as if he wanted some attention from his women. Once he got in sight of the herd, Hector picked up speed. By the time he got there, nothing as puny as plain farm wire could have slowed him down. The cows knew he was coming and were gathered at the perimeter to greet him. He burst through the wire strands as if they were thread.

Even a slowly trundling bull can outrun a group of people, and by the time he'd knocked down the fence, everybody was a hundred yards behind him. When we did get there and were standing at the ruined enclosure, Hector's arrival had excited the normally lady-like cows. His flanks were wet with sweat and his guttural breathing hadn't slowed. He curled his lips repeatedly as he wove through the milling cows sniffing and arousing them into a frantically whirling mass. The dogs weren't helping. They'd followed Hector into the pasture, found another contest in progress, and joined in with gusto. Their snapping and barking added fuel to Hector's fire. Once the herd gained momentum, they poured through the downed fence, bawling as they headed back down the lane toward the house.

Their escape was certainly no wild-west stampede, but when fifty or sixty eight hundred pound animals get moving, the very best action to take is to get out of their way. People hugged fence posts, clambered up and stood with their feet thrust through the wires, or clung to the top strands and scooched up close. The fencing on both sides of the lane must have looked like a strong wind had come along and blown people into it. In just a few moments, the only animal left in the grazing meadow was Hector. He bawled once more and went over to the edge of the pond and lay down.

The dogs ran yapping after the runaways. Uncle Ernest took several steps into the pasture. He looked back at the herd of escaping cows and turned around. It was the only time I ever saw him indecisive. The end of the lane by the farm house was open into the barnyard. Beyond the house nothing stood between the cows and the road. He hastily resurrected one of the fence posts and draped the sagged and snapped wire over the top. It wouldn't do much but maybe it would fool Hector.

He whirled shouting, "C'mon, the damn bull can do whatever he wants. We've got to get those cows!"

The crowd started jogging after the cows.

By the time we got back to the barns, the cows had disappeared from the farm. One of the farm hands ran to the road and yelled, "They're headed toward town!"

The group clambered on Ernest's old flat bed truck, his and Etta's family car and Grandpa Clark's big, shiny Lincoln. One by one we sped out of the driveway and turned to follow the Jerseys. We quickly caught up, but all we could do was follow them. Passing was out of the question on the narrow and muddy road.

Tagging along behind a herd of running milk cows is unique. Although their front ends go wherever they happen to be pointed, their back ends take a different approach. Their huge and swollen udders have such mass and weight that it causes their hind legs to sway at right angles to their forward progress. The result is an elliptical gait, right rear leg steps forward, udder swings to right, left leg swings forward, udder pendulums in that direction and moves the rear end of the cow back and forth. Leaning over the sides of the farm truck to watch the procession, we kids thought it looked hilarious.

Uncle Ernest's commentary during the slow drive made it seem even more so. We caught snatches of his furious voice over the wind.

"Goddamn bull, I'll castrate that..."

"Those damn cows..."

"...too excited to let their milk down."

"...we'll be milking till midnight."

We followed the cows down the dirt road for about three miles. There was no way to get ahead of them and stop their trek, and Ernest quickly figured out that honking his horn only kept them up to speed.

Only when the cows reached Avoca were we able to start slowing them down and stopping the few who'd run out of breath. The town was a small community and despite the hilarity that the now-walking herd caused the people in town, some quickly started to help us out waving their arms and hollering. A few of the cows took side streets; some doubled back down alleys; others stood stock still in the middle of the road; some looked in store windows. The owner of the hardware store ran out with a length of rope and we fashioned halters for the runaways. Just when we'd get one or two under control, another would bolt anew and head off in a new direction. It took the farm hands, kids, adults and townspeople until almost midnight just to gather them all up. It took several more hours to lead them back to the farm and many more to get them milked.

Uncle Ernest was right about milking an excited cow. The cows were reluctant, recalcitrant, and downright rude when they were finally led into the milking stanchions. They kicked and fidgeted and stamped their feet without exception when the milking tubes were hooked up. Stripping them was worse yet. It took forever and everyone was stumbling with sleepiness by the time we were through. Most of the cows remained squirmy, and milking was a long and drawn-out affair for several more days.

At the dinner table the next evening, my father took exceptional delight in recounting the entire tale front to back. None of the kids mentioned my role in starting the whole thing, and I sure wasn't going to tell anyone. Now that the ordeal was over, most everyone laughed at Dad's descriptions of the udder-jouncing cows. We chuckled and chortled our way through the story, our exhaustion of the previous night forgotten, but Ernest didn't forget.

There are all sorts of traits that can be passed between generations. Ernest's ears turned red, too.

I seldom had to cast about for something to keep me occupied.

I recall only three times, each time that Patch had a litter of puppies. Although the squirming masses of pups were entertaining, I sometimes became bored watching them vie with one another for nuzzle and nurse. I could bear the part of attendant for a while, and Patch was very good at sharing her litters, but my mother would chase us away when she thought we'd spent too much time handling the puppies.

"You boys leave those poor puppies alone and go outside and play. You're going to wear the fur off them."

Second to playing with Patch, reading was a favorite pastime, and although no one would ever have said my parents were indulgent, two items were ever-present in our house; books and flashlight batteries, an odd combination to some. For me the two went hand in hand, like horse and cart or peas and pod. Despite the words "go to sleep," it was no *great* sin to read under the covers after the bedroom light was turned off. I'd been reading everything I could lay my hands on ever since I could remember, and I was encouraged on all sides to continue. There were few nights when my tented blankets didn't leak some bit of weak illumination into the darkened room.

By the age of eight, I'd been on voyages with Sinbad and Ulysses and helped Tarzan or Tom Swift save the day. I'd been on the deck of the Hispaniola and the Mary Deere and defended the walls of the Alamo. I'd ridden the banner stallion in the charge of the Light Brigade, traveled the red plains of Mars, and journeyed to the bottom of the sea with Captain Nemo. My "expeditions" weren't limited to words on a page. Chip and I often tried to scale the heights or dive the depths my eyes had wandered.

I'd recently finished or re-read Jules Verne's, *20,000 Leagues Under the Sea* and shared all the scary parts with Chip. He'd been mortified when the giant squid had attacked the Nautilus and almost wet his pants when Nemo, Ned, and the professor were attacked by sharks as they hunted in the undersea forest. We had a lake at our doorstep, and all we needed was a means to get under it longer than our expanded lungs allowed. We had the means but didn't know how to get to use them.

Although we were encouraged to explore and adventure just about everyplace we could imagine, there were a few places that were forbidden: the boggy septic tank area behind our garage, my parents' bedroom on Sunday afternoon, Carole's bedroom all the time, and the underside of our house. Our Goddard Drive home was a converted summer cottage and was built over a dirt crawl space. Except for the times when our pipes froze in the winter and the occasion when Patch had her first litter under the house, we were denied access to this dusty and dark area. My mother and father also used this crawlspace to store items for which they had no earthly use.

Being denied admission was one way to insure that we wanted to know everything about the place. Chip and I lifted the hinged squeaking doors many times and had always been caught when the rusty pins announced our trespass. In the few moments before my mother's voice or hand fell on us, we'd discovered a treasure trove of things *we* couldn't live without: an old tattered canvas fold-up bathtub, which when inverted, could have made a great army tank, wooden skis that we'd have been delighted to try being dragged behind Dad's car on, ancient tumbrels and devices which we'd have turned into something, if only we'd had the chance. Other things once belonging to my Grandpa Clark rested in the way-way-back among the nail spiked boards, spider-webs, and left over tile pipes.

My grandfather was one of seven sons, born and bred to farm life in Michigan. Similar to so many children brought up on the hard toil, hard scrabble, hard existence of 1880's agriculture, as soon as he was able, he got off the farm. Grandpa did this by joining the Navy at age fifteen, a choice that insured far away, far off and far from the farm. He'd been a salvage/repair diver in the Navy when the century was just turning from nineteen to twenty. After his stint in the Navy and well before he was a politician and a sometime gangster, well before he became respectable, he'd tried many different avocations: real estate in burgeoning Detroit, timber cutting in Michigan's jack-pine forests, and mining in Michigan's copper country.

Diving was a chancy job in the service when he had to do it. He'd tried to find something along the lines of his service-taught profession, but undersea diving in the early 1900s wasn't considered to contribute toward long life. I don't think Grandpa tried very hard.

Of the flotsam and jetsam underneath our house was Grandpa's old cast iron Navy diving bell. How he'd managed to keep possession of it I never knew, but it lay there just inviting someone to give it another try. I'd had brief glimpses of it for several years. It was covered with flaking rust; the clear face plate had been broken long ago, and the air inlet brass was banged and bunged, but to me it looked like my mind's picture of one worn by the captain of the Nautilus.

Chip and I had previously tried many strategies in order to stay submerged when we swam in Lake Erie. We'd held muscle quivering rocks from the shore pressed tight to our bellies as we plunged off the three pillars or from the concrete jetty we called the pier. The large rocks worked well enough, but the jagged edges scraped and reddened our stomachs, and they lasted for only one breath. We'd hauled a bag of hardened cement left over from the construction of our garage with much the same result; abrasions and bruises, and that almost got a foot when it was dropped after my breath ran out. We'd even hauled the garage-stored snow tires to our car down to the lake in hopes that they would prove the solution, but they weren't worth the effort.

I eventually hitched up enough courage to ask about the diving bell. It took a great deal of convincing for my mother to allow my brother and me to belly scoot under the house and drag it into the daylight. I suspect the only reason she did was because she thought and said it was too heavy to be of more than a passing intrigue. Mom was correct about the heavy part. It took us most of a full day to drag it clear of the deadly jackstraw pile of nail-spiked boards and battens that barricaded its freedom.

Once out, we didn't quite know what to do with it. It was sand-paper like with rust; it weighed a ton; even I could tell that the missing face plate was a problem. It was cast with lipped slots to accommodate shoulders and had a handle on the very top of the dome. It had smaller slots cut in front and back for straps to hold it in place, but they'd rotted away long ago. The faceplate frame was attached with brass screws, and it had a large threaded brass fitting in the top for the air hose connection.

Laying it down face up and lying on my back, I scooted into the bell. The bell had been made to fit a man, broad shoulders and all. I was anything but. When I tried it on, it was just big enough to fit my head and one shoulder in comfortably. Of course, that meant that it canted to one side alarmingly, but I figured that could be corrected with padding. The immediate issue was the missing faceplate, and I knew better than to ask my parents for help. One of many unspoken rules in our house was that we could do anything we wanted as long as we kept pleas for help to a bare minimum.

The 1950s were a time before plastic and aluminum had overcome glass and steel for containers. Perishables were not packaged in throw away bottles and cans. The milkman still picked up empties while any tin-cans were saved to give to a man who drove through the neighborhood every so often. Our garage was stuffed with bundles of old newspapers, bags of flattened soup cans, vegetable cans, and scavenged pop bottles that were worth two cents when we turned them in. The garage which was so full that there wasn't room for the car also contained every bit of debris that a family of six could accumulate. Chip and I scoured the teetering piles and lumps for hours before temporarily giving up on the face plate.

We put that aside for a while and concentrated on the clean-up and restoration of the bell. It needed scrubbing and a fresh coat of paint, new straps, some padding, and an air supply and hose. The hose wouldn't be a problem, our garage had many old, leaking hoses, hanging like starved Christmas wreathes on nails pounded into the joists. The shoulder padding was easy. Chip and I violated the bags of clothing meant for the Twin Wells Indian Mission in Arizona. We stripped the arms off a winter coat and glued them into place with Elmer's All Purpose.

The paint was easier still. Along the back of the garage squatted cans of drippy-edged, skinned over varnishes, house paints and stains that had once had real purpose. They were all just waiting for some renewed function and we had one in mind. The result was that the diving bell looked similar to Joseph's coat of many colors, but

Chip and I thought it would blend in better with the undersea vegetation.

I sent Chip in to snitch the fireplace bellows for our air supply but had him take them back when we couldn't figure out how to connect the bellows to the hose to the brass fitting. We had several hand pumps for blowing up our often patched bicycle tires, inner tubes for lake floating and assorted basketballs, footballs and multicolored beach balls. The hand pump produced only intermittent, minimal jets of air, but when Chip pushed the handle I could feel a small breeze on my cheek. I thought it would be enough if he pumped hard and I breathed slowly.

We still needed face plate material. I'd eyed the seed guards in our canary's cage. They were scuffed and scratched, but clear enough to sort of see through. I took the two plastic rectangles closest to the wall so my mother wouldn't notice immediately, and they fit the opening with some modification. We used roofing tar to seal them to the bell.

We next had to figure out how to get the thing in place on my shoulders. It weighed more than Chip did and half as much as me. Standing up with it over my head was out of the question and I owned the bruises to prove it. I could get it waist high with effort, but couldn't coordinate the necessary clean and jerk move to set it over my head. I'd even tried doing a sit-up with Chip pushing to keep it in place and shoving me upright at the same time. It slid off into my lap but didn't do permanent damage.

We ended up dragging it under the Catalpa tree in our side yard and threw a rope across a limb to hoist it up. Chip and I together managed to get it high enough, but Chip couldn't hold it when I let go to get under. It fell heavily, the front and back lips pronging deep into the dirt. We needed help. The help had to be beefy and it had to be quick since Chip was getting short on enthusiasm. He hadn't cared for his job as air supplier and I couldn't get it through his head that if I was having trouble with the weight, he would be even less likely to be able to bear it.

Chip almost got his wish to try the bell on. After listening to his five-year-old whining, I was convinced that anything was better than that. I found I could just hold it in place with the rope after he'd helped me raise it. We tugged it high, and I stood with my legs braced while he cautiously let go his strain. I thought I'd lower it down

CLARK MALCOLM GREENE

gently when he was in place not letting the full weight of it go. He'd
see just how heavy it really was and realize that he couldn't do it.
He'd just taken his position under the swinging bell, and raised his
arms to guide it down.

My mother's scream put an end to that trial.

Mom had just happened to stick her head out the back door to
make sure her boys were up to *some* good. Perhaps it was the infallible
boy-trouble-radar she possessed, perhaps it was just luck. Whatever
it was, the vision of her beloved younger son about to be hammered
into the ground by her (at that moment) not so cherished older son
was more than anyone could bear. My mother was normally calm
under fire; she'd had to have been with me in the house. Not that
time.

It was the only time I ever heard her scream.

We began another trial immediately. Mine.

The shrill cry startled me so much I let go of the rope. My hands
burned as the rope slid through raising welts. Beyond all reason, her
shriek also jolted Chip enough to cause him to leap out from under
the heavy diving bell. The bell hit the ground with a leaden thunk
narrowly missing him. It took my mother all of three seconds to cross
the yard, yet it seemed even quicker. She first checked Chip for
missing or damaged parts, then turned and tried to extricate me from
my clothes. I thought my ears might pull free from my head. I hoped
they would. I'm sure my head was canted more than the diving bell
was when I'd tried it on. Inasmuch as my mother was right handed,
I'm much surer my left foot did not contact the ground on the way
back to the house.

We put the diving bell away for a long time.

It went back under the forbidden recesses of the house. I was
surprised she didn't make my father get rid of it because out of sight
didn't mean out of mind.

The bell became a goal, a Mt. Olympus to reach, something I had
to do. Unfortunately, my mother believed it was something I should
do later, when I was much, much older. I whined and wheedled; I
begged and pleaded, but the answer was continually in the negative.

"Absolutely not, young man."

"You might have killed your brother."

"Whatever could you have been thinking?"

"It's really not something you should be doing."

"Why don't you practice with your snorkel?"

"I don't know if…"

"Wait until you're bigger."

Eventually I thought she might be weakening, but it was years before I dared another attempt.

My mother was extraordinarily skilled at judging her children's abilities. I always thought she'd started making up punch-lists every time she first laid eyes on her newest born.

Girls were pretty easy: hair fit for sausage curls, check; eye-lashes for fluttering, check; sweet smile, check; dresses appropriate for showing off at church, check.

Boys belonging to my mother required much closer inspections: accumulations found in nose and ears, check; squirmy, forbidden or foreign objects in pockets, check; age, odor and attendant color of underwear, check; severity of cuts, bruises and abrasions, check; specific reminders regarding body noises, check; possessions potentially falling into the weapons category, check; location of and what is he up to now, check.

Chip and I were observed, searched, monitored, investigated, rummaged around with, explored, surveyed, questioned or dealt with at every opportunity. Additionally, Mom often sneaked in while we were asleep just to make sure she hadn't missed something.

My mother had spent the passing time after Chip's near miss making up rules just in case I ever did ask again. The list was as heavy as the diving bell, but I'd managed to grow some during my diving bell-less years. If it hadn't been for the boy muscle I'd gained, I'd never have borne both. As it was, I had to prove to her that I could handle the apparatus to her satisfaction.

When finally she agreed to let us drag it back out, my mother stood with arms folded over her bosom in order not to appear welcoming to the idea of her boys' make-believe, and watched me closely.

I went through handling, manipulation, donning, removing, walking (actually staggering), turning, twisting, bending, and standing upright from a crouch. Mom helped me attach the air hose (for realism) and tighten the straps.

Mom made it perfectly clear that Chip's role would be one of attendant. Her litany dulled my brain, but I managed to get the gist of it. Any deviation would result in immediate sentencing. I was glad when she finally finished.

"Chip, you're to stay at that end of the hose and it better be stretched straight out," Mom said as she pointed. "You boys stay in the yard and play with that thing. Chip, you're not to get too close to Clark in case he falls over."

My mother left us to our own devices satisfied that her boys understood all the complex rules that accompanied the use of the diving bell.

I must not have heard the middle part.

Our side yard was partially hidden from view of the house by the garage my father and grandfather had built. My mother relied on her other senses to approximate the need for watchfulness. Screams of anguish required immediate attention while screams of play were only a reminder that she did have boys after all. Barking dogs, yells of triumph, and screeches of Indians attacking a fort were tolerated and even encouraged.

My mother checked on us once when she didn't hear the normal ninety decibels of our play, but I thought even she knew that you can't make much noise underwater.

Chip and I played at underwater exploration for quite a while. We swam in and out of deep-sea lilac bushes and explored the under-sea wreck of Patch's dog house. We found sunken treasure in the submerged forests of our catalpa and pear trees and found drift-wood cannons from a ravaged pirate ship. We looked for sharks and giant squid but couldn't find any.

It really didn't take long for us to wander far from the approved path. The diving bell was heavy and uncomfortable even with the padding for my shoulders. We got fed up with the really fake feeling we had in the side yard. After all, we did have a lake close by.

We loaded up the wagon.

On the way to the lake, Chip and I discussed the best points of water entry, jumping and easing. Chip favored the leap into water style of Sea Hunt with Lloyd Bridges, but I was convinced that the best method was to walk into the water. As I was the one who was to do the task, my reasoning won out.

The lake side at Pointe aux Peaux was rocky, stony and perilous to bare feet. Why we never wore old tennis shoes I never figured out.

Maybe it was because the only tennis shoes we had were old ones, or maybe it was because walking tenderly over the rocks proved something. At any rate there were only two spots along the shore where it was possible to get wet without risking serious injury, the pier and the ramp along side the three old pillars that jutted out of the water. The pier was only good for jumping and it was dangerous enough by itself. It was old and crumbling and had jagged holes in the main body where the winter's ravage had torn the concrete out.

The three pillar's ramp sloped gently into the water, but was prone to have a slick growth of aquatic weeds where it was underwater.

We got set up just fine. I lifted the heavy apparatus in place, strapped it on properly, wiped my breath's fog from the face plate and hooked up the hose. I made sure Chip was convinced of his importance in the scheme with a final grab of his arm and started down the ramp. It was a treacherous few steps to the water and walking tilted backwards slightly to offset the top-heavy weight was no stroll in the park either. When I reached the water's edge, I turned back to watch Chip. He looked just like a combination of the hand-car men in my Lionel train set and the jumping wooden monkey on a stick that my grandfather had. Up and down, up and down, up and down, I felt the tiny blasts of air each time he pushed on the air pump's handle. I spread my arms to maintain balance and turned again to the beckoning water.

I came up from the depths very slowly, but I wasn't swimming. As I got closer to the surface, I remembered the sickening feeling I'd had when I attempted the first ever double-back flip with a diving bell. I had an odd feeling on the back of my head and my feet were wet, but that was all. I heard the whispering swoosh, swoosh, swoosh of the air and the sound of the waves as they continued their easy assault on the shore. I was looking up at the sky and I wondered why I couldn't remember any of my underwater adventure.

It was the turning part that hadn't been good.

I was still dazed when I undid the straps that held me in the diving bell and it seemed to take forever to scoot out of it. The sky moved alarmingly when I sat up and I vaguely heard Chip talking. He seemed far, far away.

"You got blood all over the back of your head. Mom's gonna be so mad."

Chip paused for a long minute, but then took off running toward our house. I knew my diving bell time was growing shorter by the minute, but that was alright.

After all, my Grandpa Clark didn't do it anymore either.

Chapter 5
Judgment Day

Molly usually drank mixed martinis but she slugged straight gin when she was in a hurry.

Men looked at Molly when she walked by and so did other women but for different reasons. Molly liked the men's looks when she sashayed by and didn't give a damn about the others.

She was flashy, smoked cigarettes stuck in an ebony holder, painted her lips real red, and rouged her cheeks. She dyed her hair midnight black and didn't have real eyebrows. Molly painted hers on with a brush. Molly wore extra tight black Capri pants and leopard print blouses tied in a knot to show off her belly button. She was unlike any other woman I knew as a child. I liked her, maybe even loved her.

She also scared the hell out of me.

Molly lived and breathed kitty-corner from our house. This seemed appropriate due to the leopard print blouses and the fact that she was slinky like a cat. She ever seemed to be in the thick of things. She was loud and brash, and I never knew what exciting incident would come alive because of her. Everybody knew a great deal of the neighborhood turmoil began in her house and lots of it came from inside to outside where God and everybody could see it. Her yard would sometimes be littered with broken dishes and vases, and on more than one occasion, the screen door was torn off the front of her house. Molly saved my skin several times from a parental paddling and could be counted on to smother me in a hug. She gave me more punishment for misdeeds than anyone besides Mom, Dad, and my grandmothers.

Molly had been married several times; she had outlived one or more husband, thrown out another, and had settled in with number four or five or six. No one was sure which number was right and Molly never told. The multiplicity of her marital partners was just one of the traits that endeared her to me. Her many husbands weren't bad; they just put her in a category different from the rest of the women (although two of my grandmothers had had more than one husband) and mothers that we grew up with. She would regale us with the inadequacies of each in progressive comparison during her frequent bouts with the bottle. She couldn't win the fight she had with alcohol, but we came away more enlightened from the stories she told.

Her several trips to the altar are little wonder. I can remember my father referring to her as a hellion. He was right. She handed out hell to anyone she decided was in the need, adults, children and strangers. Her sentences were punctuated with vocabulary I never learned in school. I would get lots of favors and affection from Molly because she liked me, but I also got the best, longest, and most pointed cussing that I ever got. One of her former husbands must have been a sailor.

I worked odd jobs for Molly, cutting the lawn, washing windows, or raking leaves in the fall. As a middle class child in the 1950s, when middle class meant having very little pocket money, I was always looking for ways to put change in my pockets. While there was mostly enough money for food and clothes, there never seemed to be enough to put us kids into the category of "change jinglers," and this was the reason for cutting other people's grass. I'd worked several springs at Kress Park cleaning the beach, picking up bottles in the ditches along the road, and begging people's old papers to bundle up and sell to the paper mill in town at three cents per hundred pounds.

I was continually looking for some way to put a quarter in my pocket, and Molly paid well. After doing the work, payday arrived and Molly would dig through closets, find purses, opening and discarding many, but eventually would find sufficient coins for my waiting hand. Her search for money was always accompanied by scintillating commentary on the rest of the neighborhood's occupants. I'd find out which person had come in late last night, which spouse had been fighting with what spouse, and who had been caught in places where they shouldn't have ventured, all to my heart's content. Many times the spouse fighting stories were about her spouse, although spouse was not the word she called him.

To be privy to adult complaint, speculation, and gossip was something that simply didn't happen in the Greene household, and I was careful to store these tidbits for later embellishment and passing on. Molly regaled me with commentary on her past husbands, current affairs in the literal sense, and generally kept me up to date on all things great and small.

I was cleaning out her eaves one day when I got first hand experience with the HonesttoGod hellion part.

My father was right about Molly.

She'd asked me if I wanted to earn some money by cleaning her gutters and I'd lugged Dad's ladder over to her house, got my wagon stationed just right at the foot of the ladder so I could toss the leaves into it without climbing down and was busily at work slopping out the wet gunk. The mushy work went quickly at first for my mind was on the fifty cents she'd promised and I was already thinking of what I would do with the money. Nobody's birthday was looming on the calendar; I didn't have to buy the Thanksgiving turkey, and Christmas was a long way off. The riches would be all mine.

I found out a truth that day. I'd read a Rudyard Kipling poem with a line, "The female of the species is more deadly than the male." I had wondered how he found out.

Where work was concerned, I could be distracted if the fruit was tasty enough. This "apple" was baseball, something we boys took seriously because we all dreamed of being the next Stan Musial or Mickey Mantle. Several boys came by Molly's house with a bat and a ball which tempted me terribly.

I saw the boys, heard their enticing words and climbed right down the ladder. I obeyed base desire. I played ball.

Despite everything, all that I knew about work first, play second, I took time out to play catch with them. I ignored another law, too. Ball playing was strictly forbidden around houses. I had been told hundreds of times with a finger pointed for emphasis.

"There's a ball-field right over there!"

At first we just fooled around, but catch turned into three flies, six grounders, I'm up. One of us, it doesn't matter who, committed the unpardonable. I watched in dismay as Molly's huge picture window was shattered by an errantly hit ball. The other four or five wannabe Mantles disappeared like smoke, but I knew that flight was futile. I began imagining just what I could tell Molly when she returned, but I really wanted to run away, too. I finished up the gutters, hoping the completed task would blunt her fury, then sat on her porch picturing the devil that I would catch when she saw what had happened. I didn't have to wait long.

I got the Satan all the way down to the tail.

Her driveway was alongside the house and so she couldn't see the window as she turned into her side yard, but somehow she knew from the dejected boy on her porch that something was not right. Maybe the big brother gossip network had already given her the news. I remember her closing the car door and walking around the house to stand in front of what was once a big pane of glass but which was then just letting bugs in.

The next part I remember was being hoisted to my feet by both ears. I can still feel it happening, slowly and painfully, but I know she was as quick as a snake. I thought that the sound of the slamming car door coincided with her hands on my ears even though she was looking at the broken window for a little while. Having your ears grabbed by your grandma or mom is one thing a boy (or at least I) was programmed to expect. Humans are given few appendages that when grabbed will stop you in your tracks. If you're a boy, one of them is covered by your jeans, but the other two are hanging out there at adult arm level just for that purpose.

It was as if I had two pair of pliers on my ears. Molly had long red painted nails and they dug in real good. She walked me backwards in a circle around her front yard several times. Then she went around the other way pulling me by the ears. I matched her step for step. It was like trying to hold a large sack by the corners and move backward and forward. She had to straddle-walk me to do it but that didn't slow her a bit.

My father would seldom cuss. Every once in a while "Dammit"

would sneak out but not very often. My Grandpas Clark and Teddy were both much better at it, but despite the vast knowledge that would be lost between generations, we children were NOT encouraged to emulate them. Big kids at school and on the bus could do better yet, but they would whisper to avoid teacher detection or a bus driver's trip to their seats.

But, oh, could Molly go!

Every expletive was accented with a shake of my head while she completely explained the error of my ways. Explain might not be the right term, but I have never had anything made so perfectly clear to me before or since. I heard words that made me shudder and wince and probably caused at least one bird to fall out of the sky. I heard words to describe body parts I didn't know existed and I was ten. I heard my description given loudly and with enough questions that I would have to ask my mother if she found me on a doorstep. I knew immediately the gravity of my sin and that I wasn't likely to get redemption anytime in the near future. There were new rules for me to obey. There was a new law on the books. From this day forward, I would go out of my way to keep this particular commandment. It might even move ahead of Mom's many rules.

It was number eleven: "Thou shall not piss off Molly."

As painful as the ear pulling was and as much as my pride was smarting for the chewing out I was getting, I knew it wasn't the worst. Her demonstration shocked and flabbergasted me and made me mute with uncertainty, but it wouldn't be the end. First, there would be Mom with lots of hand wringing, where did I go wrong looks, and maybe the broom for emphasis. The real finale would wait until my dad got home.

After her ear pulling frenzy, Molly calmed down enough to take me into her house. She wanted me to survey the damage from another perspective. She wanted me to clean up the mess. She wanted a drink. I think she also wanted to make sure that my ears would return to normal before she sent me home.

Molly's house was normally in perfect order as if there was a sign that said, "No Kids Here!" Like the interior of a high-class hotel, she kept her place every bit as spotless and neat as if the maid had just been in. Now the inside was shattered in all ways; much worse than

I imagined and I had a vivid mind. The broken window had damaged the sofa when it smashed inward and jagged shards of glass had cut big gashes in the slipcovers.

Great sharp pieces had sliced the back and cushion covers, too, and she wrapped my hands in towels before she told me, "Pull them out and clean up the rest of that mess."

She walked over to her liquor cabinet, filled a glass with clear something, and sank down into a puffy chair to watch.

I carefully wrapped each piece in old newspaper and took it out to the garbage can. There was a terrible lot of glass, but Molly wasn't through with me yet. I knew there was going to be other punishment. She just needed a breather. I recall paying particular attention to door locations every time I walked past her on the way out the back door in case she wanted to start that ears stuff again. I wasn't about to let her get between me and escape.

I got the broom, swept up what could be gotten from the floor, took her Hoover with attachments from the closet, and carefully vacuumed the couch and surrounding areas as well as I could. I know she could have done it faster and better, but that wasn't part of life's lessons in the fifties. Adults must have had more patience then. I believe she would have made me do the cleanup even if I had to spend several birthdays' worth of time to accomplish the goal. I struggled with the broom and vacuum for a long time. She would point to little glitters of glass on carpets and windowsills and I would tend to the problem again and again. I wouldn't endanger my chances of survival by shoddy work at this point.

Meanwhile, Molly had several more drinks.

Her inspections of my work grew less specific in proportion to the number of straight gins she had, and in about an hour, she began dismissing the incident as trivial. Instead of pointing to places I had missed, she would airily wave toward the front of her house with a slurred word or two. I don't think she was quite happy about the broken window, but she might have been enjoying the breeze by then. Perhaps Molly reached a point where she wasn't sure that I was the one who even broke it or whether it mattered as much as she first thought. She started telling me about one of her former husbands. He was a bum and had the gall to die before she could turn him into something she wanted. With this revelation regarding something other than the window, I thought I might be on the road to salvation.

Molly got up from the chair, but the rising looked snakey and sinuous. She managed to get to the phone and call Marshall's Hardware on Dixie Highway and blurrily told Mr. Marshall to please come and replace her picture window. Part of the conversation was, "One of the neighborhood boys had an accident."

Man, I was in the clear! Molly hadn't even mentioned my name! Mr. Marshall was a good friend of my dad's and that avenue of information was, for the moment at least, closed. My hope that I might escape with nothing more than deformed ears and hurt pride grew.

Molly became fluid when she drank. The more she drank the more slick and pour-able she became. Three martinis and her blouse would slide off one shoulder. Four straight gins and the knot holding the blouse front together would slip loose. Six drinks and her hair sort of slid to one side and she couldn't keep her shoes on. Anything past that and there wasn't a chair in the world that could keep her captive. I'd watched in wonder several times at the progress from upright to wall leaning to chair to floor. She would have been a great addition to any circus.

"See The Lady With No, that's right, folks, I said, No Bones In Her Entire Body!"

I could have been the midway barker.

I'd finished the cleaning and began thinking of escape, but Molly said I couldn't go yet. Mr. Marshall showed up about an hour later, but by then Molly was way down her slope, almost to the bottom. Aside from an occasional mumble, she didn't talk much when he knocked at the door. Mr. Marshall did a classic double-take at the window and a second one at Molly when he came through the door. He didn't ask any questions. It was a small community and everybody knew everything about everybody. It was no secret that Molly Miller could put 'em away.

He took out his ruler and I helped him take the measurements on the window frame, but he had a hard time remembering and writing the dimensions. Molly was a good-looking woman and she was really slippery by the time he got there. Her disheveled figure was wedged into the overstuffed chair in the living room. She didn't get up to greet Mr. Marshall, and even her hair was lopsided by then.

He had to go back to his hardware store to cut the glass, but he first motioned to me to help him with Molly. She was a handful especially for someone hampered by a ten-year-old boy. He would get her hoisted up all right, but she'd just slide out of his grasp before he'd gone very far. I hoped he was being careful about where he put his hands because I sure was. Her bedroom was on the backside of the house, and by the time we got her to the door, Molly had managed to slide clear of pretty much everything except Capri pants and bra. I was real glad her husband wasn't there to see. We got her tucked in and covered up.

Mr. Marshall knew I had seen him peeking at Molly and I think he was embarrassed about some youngster being witness. How could he not peek for Pete's sake? I had been. At any rate, I'm sure he suspected me of the problem's beginning, although he didn't question me. I think he wanted to put some distance between himself and the eyes that watched his eyes. He told me to wait until he got back. When an adult spoke then, children listened. It didn't make any difference if it was family, friend, stranger or bum in the alley; we kids paid attention. I waited.

I called Mom to tell her where I was, and to tell her the story. She said she'd be right there despite my telling her there was no reason. I told you we lived close. I turned around from the kitchen phone, and as I was about to pick up a magazine, Mom charged through the door. She didn't knock or anything.

When the conversation started with, "Oh, Clark, how could you…" continued in the middle with, "I know that you know better than…" and finished with, "What is your father going to…"

I knew I was definitely not finished with this episode.

There were lots of other questions.

"How did it really happen?"

"Who was playing with you?"

"Who's going to pay for this?"

"Where's Mrs. Miller?"

"Where did you say Molly was?"

Mom looked in the bedroom and answered the last question herself.

The phone rang. When I answered it, Mr. Marshall said that he didn't have a piece of glass big enough for the window and that he had to have it sent from Detroit, which seemed practically cross-country. He was going to come back right now and tape a piece of plastic over the window. I told my mother the news after I hung up.

Mom said pointedly, "Molly won't notice."

The situation was definitely worsening, anger transference at the very best.

Mom was mad at me because I was involved with the shattered window. Mom was mad at Molly because she was passed out drunk. Mom was more than mad at me for seeing Molly passed out drunk. Finally, Mom was mad at Molly for letting me see her drunk. The whole situation was much too complex. I just stuck with the mad about the window part.

Mom started running the vacuum again even though I had done a pretty good job. Mom ended up spending a lot of time vacuuming by Molly's bedroom door, but the glass hadn't gone near that far. It looked like I wasn't the only one who would pay for sins that day.

It's a good thing there's a book somewhere that says, "Judge not."

I helped Mr. Marshall tape the plastic over the window frame while Mom stood by telling us both how to do it properly. After Mr. Marshall had come and gone, Mom left Molly a note telling her about the glass and that she would see that I (Clark, the bad one) would be over tomorrow to work out some penance.

We had Judgment Day every day at my house. My mother was really big into this immediate payback reinforcement; mean words and cuss words, Fels-Naptha in the mouth; hit brother or sister, (Chip, of course, and Carole, but never Peg) spank the offender; doesn't clean up his stuff, take stuff away (severity of squalor equals amount of stuff); doesn't do chores after only one request, no dinner, go to room. There was always a final trumpet ready to blow in our house and we knew whose lips were puckered to do it. I would report for duty at Molly's house.

Part of the Mom's note said, "Be hard on him," but she hid the rest with her hand.

Dad went flat out wild when he got home. Several of those "Dammits" slipped out and they all had a big loud God in front. Mom was gonna have some more anger transference here. I knew she was mad at me because I broke the window, mad that Molly was drunk because I broke the window, mad that I saw Molly drunk because I was there after I broke the window, and mad that Dad cussed big time because I broke the window, and mad that I heard Dad cuss because I was the object of the cuss and I was there in the first place. Yup, I understood and accepted all the punishment that came from my day's misadventures.

Of course, Dad paid for the window. It was expensive, probably $150 or $200 dollars, a huge sum in those days, equivalent to a few thousand today. He worked it out with Mr. Marshall and paid it in weekly installments. We just did not have that kind of cash. I was supposed to pay Dad back. I'm sure I never did. It was just one of the prices he paid for my experience. I paid, too, but in a different way. I got one heckofa whipping. Mom bought material and sewed new slipcovers for Molly's couch, good as new and probably better.

I never paid Mom back for the slipcovers either.

Molly was relentless with me even though she didn't have to pay for the window or the slipcover. Child-rearing was everyone's responsibility, just like in those villages in Africa. Molly was definite about it being her duty. I spent a good deal of time in her flowerbeds, very red geraniums as I recall, weeding and dividing and transplanting. There was never any question about grass cutting fees the rest of the year. I cut it many times before the cold ended the need. None of the others involved were ever accountable, but they shouldn't have been. I had been at fault and I got my own redemption.

Molly and I continued for years to have a special relationship. I really liked her. Despite me growing up and me having a deliberate disdain for my folks, Molly and I continued to get along very well. Her last husband passed away suddenly in 1962, and Molly took it very hard. She was slippery drunk at the funeral and had to be supported by friends and neighbors. Her bright and brassy appearance turned dull and cheap as if life had tarnished her. She still gave me the devil when I needed it, but she did it sadly without her normal vigor.

She went away to a hospital to get "better" and when she returned, she was. The going away happened twice more, but the better didn't last very long. Then she didn't go away any more in spite of encouragement. She became less and less coherent when I stopped by to see how she was doing or did some odd job for her. Sometimes she just left the money in an envelope stuck in the door. Other times she wouldn't answer the door. I carried the trash out to the road for her every week, bags and buckets of bottles, all empty. Sadness and drink finally killed her. Molly died during the fall of 1963 when I was a senior in high school.

I always wished I could have done something more.

I was going to stay over at Jimmy's house after school.

Jimmy was my buddy and we liked lots of the same things: books, dinosaurs, and art among them. His mother had called my mother and they agreed a Friday night at his house would be okay. I'd ride the bus home with him, and Mom would pick me up from Jimmy's Saturday evening so I would be back for church with my family. Jimmy's mother said I could go to their church if I stayed two nights.

Mom said one was enough.

The Nadeau family was Catholic and although there was small chance I would bring home a statue of the Virgin, my mother didn't believe in a gamble. It looked like I could stay in an idol worshipping house just the one night. Mom even seemed to forget her oft-pronounced problem of Catholics drinking.

"All Catholics drink, even the priests, how Holy can they be." (It wasn't a question.)

She apparently approved of the Jimmy friendship, though. I think this was due in large part to the mural he and I created for the celebration of George Washington's and Abe Lincoln's birthday observation in February. Jimmy and I had done life-sized figures, each surrounded with pictorial accounts of their notable accomplishments. We worked on the mural for several weeks, even foregoing recesses while it was in progress. The mural must have been done fairly well because our grade-school teacher hung it in the school building right inside the entrance. Finally, a picture of it and us accompanied a story in the local paper. When the story was followed by an invitation to display the artwork at the county library, we earned some small celebrity, but even more important, Jimmy was awarded acceptance from my mother.

It was evident to Mom that anybody who could draw and paint that well must be of the caliber of people she wanted her son to associate with.

My mother reviewed my playmates through a pretty powerful magnifying glass before I was allowed to enter into a relationship. I was always just a bit astonished by the interrogation I was forced to endure whenever I mentioned a new name from school. I was expected to learn and convey their lineage as well as religion before any kid was allowed to be my friend. Woe be unto any family that wasn't a Born-Again-something. This staying overnight would mark new territory for Mom and for me. I took a giant step away from her influence when I got on Jimmy's bus.

There was a list of "do and don't" for me to follow. The don't part was longer than the do section.

All the "do" parts were a given, but Mom went over them anyway; the do's left unsaid. "(Do) help set the table. (Do) say grace before meals even if they don't. (Do) use your napkin. (Do) clean your plate. (Do) help with dishes. (Do) brush your teeth even if I'm not there to remind you. (Do) say your prayers before sleep. (Do) behave. (Do) say thank you to Mrs. Nadeau. (Do) remember God's watching you."

All the don't parts started with an emphasized "Don't."

"Don't look at the Catholic statues. Don't play with the rosary beads. Don't chew with your mouth open. Don't burp. Don't pass gas. Don't play with your food. Don't get dirty. Don't look at the Catholic statues. Don't play with the rosary beads. Don't be a brat. Don't track mud in their house. Don't be a smart aleck. Don't go barefoot (early spring and Mom knew my tendency). Don't play on the road (Jimmy's house was on a busy street). Don't ride bikes on the road. Don't do anything you wouldn't do at home. Don't make me wish I hadn't let you go. Oh yes, Clark, one more thing. Don't look at or touch the Catholic statues or the rosary beads."

I rode Jimmy's bus home and found out they said grace at dinner. I couldn't wait to tell Mom.

Jimmy's older brother Paul was almost as old as my sister Carole. Paul was thirteen. He wore his hair slicked back, wore a black leather jacket with zippers, cussed well and often, and smoked cigarettes. He didn't do the last two in front of his parents, but he sure did whenever they weren't there. As was the trend in the late 1950s, Paul styled himself after James Dean and Marlon Brando. Jimmy and I would have done the same thing but weren't old enough; we were still kids and knew our place.

After breakfast on Saturday, Jimmy's mother asked us if we wanted to go to town with her, maybe see a movie or feed nickels into the arcade games on First Street while she went shopping. I had never been in the arcade, but other kids in school had told me of the games there. There were pictures of Egyptian and Gypsy women in silky veils, who whirled and shed their gauzes while the cards flipped past and could be viewed for a penny. Other forbidden activities might be there, too, but I had a keen interest in those foreign dancers. I thought it was a great idea, but Jimmy said we would stay here and hang around with his older brother.

"Okay, I guess." I hid my disappointment at staying there.

The opportunity to cross the arcade's taboo doorways wouldn't happen very often. The same magnifying glass Mom used on me was used for shady and suspect places as well.

Oh, well, I thought. I only had two nickels anyway.

Just as soon as their mother pulled out of the driveway, Paul said, "Follow me."

Hanging around with an older kid was a new experience for me. I had kids my own age in the neighborhood to play with. My sister's friends, all the older girls and boys, put up with me not at all. By the time I was ten, I supposed that all teenagers left patience behind when they passed into the realm of pretty dresses, saddle shoes, rolled up jeans or motorcycle boots. They probably rolled that and tolerance up in a ball and put it away with their old dolls and cap guns, forgotten now that they considered themselves grown-up. Experience with Carole taught me it was far wiser to just stay away.

But now, there was a big kid who wanted us to follow him around. I was astounded. We could have been headed toward the gates of Hell and I'd have stuck like a shadow.

We walked a short distance down the road to a huge culvert that carried a small stream of water under the road. The round concrete tube was about twenty feet across and sixty or more feet long. A gravel path led down the steep bank to a walkway on one side of the culvert's interior, probably used by county road crews to clear wood and debris when necessary. It was a great place, a dark hideaway, and we could hear the cars thump as they whizzed over the road. Nobody could see us.

Paul fished into one of the pockets of his leather coat and took out a pack of Winston cigarettes. He had a pack of matches, and when he lit it, he did kind of look like James Dean.

"Here, ya want one?"

Like a good Christian boy well schooled in the avoidance of vices just such as this I shook my head.

"Whaddya…chicken?"

I shook my head again, but I sure wanted to be accepted.

The second temptation was worse yet. When the devil looked this cool and the devil's little brother took a puff, how could I win? I refused a second time and earned a real look of scorn from Paul. Jimmy chided me, too.

"One puff won't hurt ya. C'mon, take a drag."

I took a first mouthful of smoke when he offered me the "weed" for the third time. I knew Mom was probably sneaking up on me, but I did it anyway. I pinched the cigarette like I was picking up a dead mouse.

"No, hold it like this, between two fingers."

Okay, now I was cool, just like they were.

I hadn't in actual fact disobeyed, not really. I would have done this at home if I thought I could get away with it. I watched with envy as my father smoked, but I knew Mom disproved of his doing it. I was pretty sure she kept count of the cigarettes he puffed so she could tell how bad a sinner my father was. I couldn't remember ever having heard quotes in the Bible against smoking but listened to Mom get after Dad again and again about his cigarettes. I didn't see a link with the Commandments but I was convinced there was an anti-smoking verse in there somewhere.

After getting me to succumb to the temptation, Jimmy's brother decided he didn't want to be bothered with us any more and said he was going over to a buddy's house. He'd perfectly fit the mold of tempter. Once broken, the continuing sin is always easier, and Paul didn't have to concentrate on me or Jimmy any longer. I was bound for Hell already.

"No, you can't come. I'm not hangin' around with you punks all day."

Now he was talking the big kid's language I understood. Jimmy asked Paul if I could ride his old bike, the one leaning up against the garage wall.

"Yeah...but it's got a flat tire, you'll have to pump it up." He told us.

We ended up having to fix the tire with a patch before we could go bike riding, but this was something every self-respecting kid knew how to do. I had learned to repair bike tires several years before when my father got tired of doing it for me. I'd heard "You want to ride a bike, learn how to keep the tires fixed" every time I had a flat. I still heard it whenever my tires needed repair, but now only in my head. I fixed my own.

When we finished and aired up the tire, Jimmy thought it was funny that I pushed the bike all the way to the side street.

"My mom told me not to ride on this street," I told him.

He hooted with laughter, "I'll bet she said don't smoke, too!"

No, she hadn't, not directly, not specifically. I'm sure she would have if she would have thought of it, but her thoughts didn't drift to cigarettes when she was listing all my don'ts. Anyway, I was making up for it right now, pushing this bike while Jimmy laughed and rode circles around me. I thought if you did one good thing you might get to take one bad thing away. I knew this was contrary to the "not of good works" saying, but I was convinced God wouldn't overlook my good deed.

Jimmy's house was by the Monroe Country Club, just one street away from manicured fairways dotted with sand pits called traps. There were also "greens," something I didn't know anything about. There wasn't much that was green right now anyway. Every thing was still wearing Michigan's winter gray and there were plenty of places the snow hadn't yet melted. This early in March there could still be more snow for our area but not that day. We were going to ride all over the place; there were little hills we could coast down and broad open places where we could reach top speeds. It would be wonderful fun. We knew spring was headed our way and like the horses my grandpa kept stabled in the winter, we wanted to get out and cavort with the first warm days. Spring couldn't come too soon for me, hence the warning about shedding shoes and socks from my mother.

The country club was the ideal place and had some really short grass areas that we could skid and spin wheels on. The long open places were obviously built to race on and we spent several hours seeing who could go the fastest or who could get up enough speed to clear the sand traps. Many of the sandy areas had sloping ramps to launch us high into the air. The short-grassed areas were the best. We dare-deviled our bikes over them time and again.

Someone far off hollered.

"Hey! Yougoddamnkids! GetOffTheGreens!"

Jimmy said, "Let'sgetouttahere!"

We did just that.

I followed Jimmy pedaling furiously. I didn't know what we'd done, but whenever an adult hollered like that, I knew something was wrong. There was a chance to get away because he was still far off, but he was coming fast. We left.

Yougoddamnkids! Yougoddamnkids! Yougoddamnkids! Yougoddamnkids!

The large voice chased us for a long time, but we lost sight of the man somewhere through a small stand of trees. We were both breathless from the scare and the pedaling when we stopped to look back and were relieved when we couldn't see anybody. No more big yells spooked us either. Jimmy couldn't tell me why the guy was so mad. He just shrugged. With adults, who knew? He did say to not mention the incident to his mother as he rode and I walked the bike back to their house. No sense in the telling because we got away. Any mention of an adult's displeasure wasn't wise and even the yells of a stranger told to a parent would certainly come to no good.

We went in to lunch and read Jimmy's comic books. I didn't get comic books at home. The closest I got was the Sunday funnies. The depictions of super heroes weren't for son Clark, no-sirree-Bob. Mom frequently said there were heroes aplenty in the Bible if I needed some. I had to look at Mom-approved reading material unless I was at Grandma Phoebe's house. That was okay with me. I loved Tarzan, Jim Hawkins, Tom Swift, Sherlock Holmes, Robin Hood, Gulliver, and King Arthur. I also liked Long John Silver, Mr. Hyde, Fagan, and the Black Knight but didn't advertise my affection for the bad guys. All of them did better stuff than Superman could do. If those characters weren't enough, there was always Joshua, Daniel, David,

Moses and Jesus to read about. The Bible had the true to life, real heroes Mom said. But it was still fun to look at comics, another forbidden fruit for that Saturday. I forgot the biking episode and it was soon time for Mom to come and get me.

On the way home I told Mom all about the stuff we did. I left out the parts about cigarettes, bike riding and comic books, but my telling must have suited Mom. She didn't pat me down looking for statues of the Virgin Mary or Jesus.

It took the Sheriff about three days to track us both down. Two days for Jimmy, three for me.

We were all at the dinner table when there was a knock at the door. I got up and when I saw the Sheriff's car pulled up in the driveway, I somehow knew he had come for me but still didn't know what I had done. I'd known that man had been hollering for good reason, and half of the reason was me. I wanted to bolt like a rabbit, but I was trapped between him and the eyes of my family.

"Your name Clark?" he wanted to know when I opened the door.

I said it was.

"Were you and another boy riding bikes last Saturday?"

"Yes," I barely whispered.

"Out at the country club?"

I nodded. I heard my father's chair scrape on the dining room floor and his footsteps down along the porch. Then Dad was beside me, arm on my shoulder; Protective.

Dad wanted to know what this was about, but first he had something to say to the deputy.

"You don't come in my house and start asking my boy questions without first asking my permission and By God! getting it before you start and you ought to know better than that around here and you will know better than that in my house, so who are you and what do you want anyhow?"

Dad could get more words out in one breath than any man I ever saw when he felt invaded.

"Sorry, Mr. Greene, you're right."

The deputy told my father that two boys on bicycles had torn up the putting greens at the country club last Saturday. My father looked at me. Looked askance, looked very sideways at me.

"That right, son?"

I gulped my yes wishing I were somewhere else.

"Just whatinHell were you thinking?" my father asked.

When I told Dad and the deputy we had just been riding around, the deputy said we should have been pedaling our brains. The sarcasm of his comment was the second thing he did wrong.

My father was always good at punishments. He was especially good at lecturing an errant son. He made penalties something to remember. Penance would do when that worked, but he never backed away when more severity was deemed proper for the crime. What he did not need was help. What he didn't want was somebody else talking wise-ass to his son. Not only did he not want it, he did not allow a stranger the right to ever speak to his children that way. The uniform didn't matter.

My father was also really good at losing his temper, if "good" is the right expression. The word "instantaneous" is better suited.

My father gently pulled me back from the deputy sheriff, scooted me behind his back, and stepped close to the deputy. Like really close. If the deputy could have moved, he would have, but Dad had him right up against the closed door. Dad definitely counterattacked. This was Dad's turf. It was now the deputy's turn to be invaded.

"You can go now," my father said. "In fact, you'd better go now."

"I'm not done yet, Mr. Greene."

Arguing with my dad...That was his third mistake, and my father was committed to the three strikes rule.

"Buddy, you don't know how done you are. First you come in here and start to question my son without my permission, and then you want to smart talk him, too. You don't talk to my son like that. If that's not enough, then you're disrespectful to me. If you don't leave on your own, I'll help you go."

"They want someone to pay for..."

"Get out of my house!"

"They..."

My father reached around the deputy and opened the door.

"I'll take him over to the country club on Saturday and work it out with them. I'm telling you for the last time, mister, Get Out Of My House!"

The deputy turned without another word and walked back to his car. He sat there a long time writing and talking on his radio. I know it was a long time because my father and I stayed on the front porch until he drove away. Only then did Dad turn to me and ask what Jimmy and I had done. I explained as best I could, but he said I should have known better than to go somewhere like that even if Jimmy had not. For sure I would know better in the near future.

What I knew for sure was that I was going to get a spanking out of this. I wasn't wrong either, because he wheeled me right into the living room, sat on the couch, and pulled me down over his knees.

Whack!

"You know better!"

Whack!

"You know better!"

Whack!

"You know better!"

Well, I did for sure after the whacks. At least I didn't cry. I always felt humiliated when I got a whipping, but I knew I didn't get spanked without good reason. I had figured out that spankings came with irresponsible actions I could have controlled but made a choice not to or didn't have enough sense to restrain. I also recognized that my howls wouldn't shorten the punishment, not by one whack. Even so, they hurt like fire.

The "Respecting Other People's Property" lecture went on well past everyone's dinner. Dad's dinner was cold by the time he was through with me, but my dinner was ended when the first knock at the door came. Mom and Carole were clearing the table, and Dad was still going strong. I had to know that other people felt about their possessions the same way I did about mine, the same way anybody felt when people hurt or damaged things that didn't belong to them. My parents' sermons were worse than the whippings mostly because I knew they were right.

"You can go to your room and think about this. No more dinner."

I needed to think about knowing better. I would think about knowing better. I would think better to know better. I wondered if my parents ever thought that we might need to have better nourishment for our brains while we thought about being better. Probably not, the lesson was in the taking away.

The next Saturday my father and I went to the country club to survey the destruction Jimmy and I had done. We were accompanied by one of the officers from the club, who started telling me how bad I was to have done this much damage. I didn't say anything but my father said he'd been all through that with me. He also told the man to stop. I didn't need to hear any more from a stranger.

One putting green had a big skid mark torn through it, the flap of grass lying like a torn skin in the middle of it. One more had tire marks but the grass wasn't torn up too bad, but I was surprised at the amount of grass we had hurt. So was my father. The man said someone would have to pay for all the work required to fix it back up. Dad said I could start work right now if that's what the man wanted.

"No, we want someone to pay for this," the man said. "Besides, he looks pretty little."

My father said I could do something; something a ten-year-old could accomplish to pay for the time and money spent to repair the putting greens.

"I want him to work for this," Dad finished.

Mr. Germain, his name as I found out later, nodded in understanding and said there was probably something for me to do at the club. He told my father to bring me back next Saturday and he'd have jobs lined up for me to do: cleaning the member's golf clubs, scrubbing the floors in the kitchen, washing windows in the dining room. I would have to work several Saturdays but Mr. Germain was okay with that if Dad was.

"What about it, Clark?"

Nod. Nod. I thought, *Sure, anything to get past this.*

I worked at the country club for three Saturdays. I ended up doing all the jobs Mr. Germain had mentioned plus lots of other ones the members thought up. Polishing golf shoes, cleaning the locker and shower area, carrying them a drink from the bar, all sorts of jobs, but I knew how to work. I'd been learning that ever since I could carry a full garbage bag to the burning barrel.

I was introduced as "the boy who tore up #15 and #16 greens," but by the second Saturday, everyone called me Clark.

When my father picked me up the last day, Mr. Germain told him I had worked out pretty well. I had learned my lesson and was polite too. I told him I was sorry to have caused the trouble, but I didn't even know I was doing anything wrong when we were riding on the golf course. I was sorry. I just didn't realize at the time we'd hurt anything.

"Ignorance happens with us all sometimes, but you made up for the mistake. Just think about things before you do them the next time."

I was really surprised when he handed me a five-dollar bill.

Jimmy didn't get a spanking, but he did get a lecture and he was grounded to boot. His father paid the country club thirty dollars for Jimmy's part of the damage. He said his father never spanked him, no matter what he'd done.

Sometimes that happens, too.

We always told our folks where we were going.

At least, we always told our parents where we intended to go. Our continued freedom was built on the foundation that Mom and Dad would always know where to look for us. Straying was allowed but only within limits. If we could be seen from the spot we said we would be, we considered ourselves still there. If we got out of parents' searching eyesight, "within the sound of my voice" might be used infrequently. We were expected to be where we had been given approval to go.

When we said we were going to "The Lake," the words meant the lakefront in Pointe aux Peaux. The beach in our subdivision was entirely made up of rocks. Despite Mom's instructions to bring them all home for her flower garden or the driveway and sidewalk, there wasn't anything but stones. There was a picnic area consisting of a wide strip of grass between the shore and the road, but the beach was formidable to feet. Our entire family swam these rocky waters and we had to be tough to get wet.

For our band of brothers and sisters, it became a race of callus development every year, and there was competition to see who could brave the stony beach without wincing. By the middle of each summer, we had been barefoot enough so the soles of our feet had grown leather thick. We might get wet without tenderly dancing across the rocks, but for visitors this beach was as painful as a mystic's fire walk.

The only exception to the sharp treachery of the rocks was the smooth concrete next to the first pillar that sloped down into the water. This slick-with-algae surface was just another form of potential pain because it was impossible to navigate without falling. Anyone who attempted the slide was fortunate if their brains didn't get rattled when they fell. Ending up "ass over teakettle," my father said.

If we said "The Sandy Beach," it meant we were going to another area altogether. A sandy stretch along Lakeshore Drive into the peninsula was quite wide and spotted with seaweed along the shore. The beach extended all the way to the tip of the peninsula, but we limited our water play to the space adjacent to Kress Park and parallel to the road. Beyond the first house and concrete break-wall was considered private and we didn't go that far after Grandpa Clark and Grandma Grace sold their house and moved back to Detroit.

This was a much-preferred beach, but its ownership was frequently contested with kids from Stoney Pointe. The disputes never happened when parents were there, but when the swimming was "kids only," the "seaweed wars" were likely to break out. "Us against them" consisted of who could take the wet slaps in the face the longest, sand in your eyes, and the taste of dead fish in your mouth. These conflicts lasted from year to year and regardless the number or ferocity of contests, the issue was never resolved.

Just like everything else in our lives, we had rules to follow when we were swimming. Identical in nature to house, church, and animal rules, with the exception of a few, the majority began with "don't."

Splashing was allowed especially if the water was cold and we were brave enough to be the first one in. This wasn't a rule as such but was instead an empowerment of being foremost and most cold hardy. Carole especially hated this.

The first rule was time based. "Don't go swimming after you eat until twenty minutes have gone by." This third of an hour is the longest period of time that exists; just ask any kid waiting to reenter the water. We had been warned about the surety of the dreaded "cramps" if we went in the water sooner than twenty minutes after the meal. Our inner clocks were accurate to the second when parents were around. With Mom watching, we obeyed this rule in mortal fear of sinking like a stone if one were foolish enough to disregard this dire warning. When she was absent, we pushed these clocks ahead but breathed more easily after the time was actually up.

There was an even more sinister side of spasms. The condition could strike without warning at any time and would immobilize anyone. Our church upbringing in the surety of God's vengeance intimated the onset just might have to do with the clarity of our souls. This condition was the bane of all "unsaved" swimmers, but we believed cramps could paralyze even the best of us. In our hearts, we knew it was only a matter of time until the contractions got one of us but we kept on; we just swam in the face of impending disaster. Parents constantly reminded us of a boy in Stoney Point who had been "out too far" and drowned ten years ago when the cramps got him.

The rules may have started with the twenty-minute wait but rule number two said "Don't go out too far."

This distance was different depending on the area we swam. At the pier it was limited to a forty foot radius of the abutment. While at the three pillars, the area we were allowed to swim extended in a straight line directly out from the rocky beach to the second concrete piling. The water at the base of the pillars was jumbled with broken off concrete chunks and large stones used to stabilize the bases. The sunken concrete bristled with rusty reinforcing rods that could scrape skin off in a blink, and we swam with just a little fear at the three pillars. Kids could dive safely off a limited number of sides because of the debris hidden in the water. Even though there were hazards, we knew we'd be safe if we swam only to the middle pillar. Mom and Dad said so.

Carole, Chip, Peg, and I all knew the real reason that boy had drowned was that he went swimming out too far only five minutes after he ate. He broke two out of the three rules at the same time. No wonder.

The third rule broke with beach tradition and started with "No." As in "No Throwing Sand."

We were led to believe that this was "common" behavior and to be avoided at all costs. The children who did throw hands-full of wet sand were low class while we, on the other hand, were not. Automatic lower status was awarded to those kids who did, a classification my mother never forgot. She once told a friend of mine she remembered him "throwing sand" when he was seven or eight. At the time of this revelation, he and I were seniors in high school.

If we were caught in this despicable activity, we could be sure of a spanking right then and there. Not only did the spanking hurt more because of the thin bathing suits, everybody else got to watch. The humiliation always hurt more and lasted longer. Piled on top of the immediate punishment was a sure swimming ban for the rest of the day. In addition to all of this, personal experience with eyes full of sand taught us how uncomfortable that was. We didn't throw sand when Mom was around, neither did we do it much when she wasn't. This rule was only in effect at the Sandy Beach swimming area. The pier and pillars didn't have enough sand to make a good handful.

The Sandy Beach had different "out too far" limits yet. There were usually two distinct sandbars, one fairly close to shore that everyone except babies could get to. The shifting sandbars were separated by sixty feet of deeper water. If we could traverse the greater depth all the while keeping feet on the bottom or by swimming, we could go out to the second shallow area. The Greene children had to make this journey without assistance. Needing help through the deep water meant that you were either too short or lacked both courage and swimming skills.

A right of passage for the Greene children took place at "The Lake." We all earned our wings only one way. First we had to learn to swim "with our face in the water." Despite our Tarzan's (Johnny Weismuller) style in order for us to be considered real swimmers, we had to submerge our faces and turn our heads to the side to take a breath. Each child, also, in succession had to swim the distance between the pier and the third pillar, climb to the top of the old concrete structure, dive from the top and swim the return leg. The swim required was no less important to us than swimming the English Channel. Equally as far and twice as difficult in our minds, we practiced our techniques but dreaded the necessity of our attempt. The distance was about two hundred yards between the two structures, and twenty feet from the pier, the bottom of the lake fell away to deep water.

This was a swim contrary to our conditioned wisdom of "out too far," but we all had to do it. We could have a partner while we splashed our way, but he or she couldn't help and this included Patch. If we needed help, we had to start over. I didn't attempt the swim until I was nine. I hadn't gained sufficient courage until a year after my Camp Birkett experience in 1956. Even after that success, I still had fears, perhaps left over from Grandpa's sinking sailboat, and insisted that Dad swim alongside me.

Just like everyone else I waited for calm water the first time I successfully swam the trial.

Chapter 6
More Than I Knew

On the first day back to school in 1957, I thought I knew everything and I was pretty sure I was right about that.

My introduction to the sixth grade proved me to be lacking in many areas although I denied the evidence. I was leaving the "Garage Building" of grades 4 and 5. I was going to the "Big Building," someplace I had only been when I attended PTA meetings with my mother or I "needed a conference" to straighten out something I'd done wrong. My mom went to these summit meetings too. I had been to the junior high building enough to know my way to the principal's office.

I had convinced Mom to give me one last Mohawk trim late in the summer and was determined to have the broad strip prominently on top of my head when school started. A declaration of sorts that I had arrived and everybody should ooh and ah in appreciation of the entrance. Why she gave me that last side shave, I don't know. I already had several checkmarks next to my name under the column "Paddling" in my records. Last year I got into a wrestling match with someone who was making fun of my mostly grown out Indian haircut. When I showed him how Indians really act, he started crying and my folks had to come to school for a conference.

The bigger kids noticed my haircut right away on the bus, but I put up with the jeers and teasing from them. I knew the penalties associated with causing disturbances on the bus. One kid, Wayne, began to play to the audience more and more, pulling my hair, and making fun of the difference, calling me "Dirty Injun" and shoving. I put up with the names. I knocked his hand away from my hair several times while he taunted. I had heard "sticks and stones can break my bones, but names will never hurt me" plenty of times but didn't believe it. Names always hurt.

When he pushed me again just a little, I shoved him back hard enough to make him lose his balance and holler when he fell in the aisle. The bus driver said she'd report us if we didn't stop messing around, and we had to go sit in the front of the bus. Front seats were reserved; only bad kids sat there. Bus drivers were #3 in overall authority behind only parents and teachers. When they spoke, we listened. Her "report" could mean being thrown off the bus and definitely something to be avoided. Most families didn't have two cars in the 1950s, so transportation to and from school would be difficult. If you got thrown off the bus even for a day, you were going to get a whipping. You would have a sore butt as you walked to school because you were definitely going to walk. You'd keep walking until you could talk the driver into giving you another chance. On the school bus the drivers were the ultimate authority and had decision-making power for crime, punishment, and duration.

Wayne's fall caused the laughing to find a new target; him instead of me. He said he'd "get" me at recess.

"I'll get you good!" he sneered at me softly so the bus driver couldn't hear.

Wayne was in the seventh grade and bigger. I told him he'd be lucky to even "get" close while I really hoped I could keep away from him. Secretly I was worried. Littler kids never knew what to expect from bigger kids. Big kids were liable to run faster, have bigger friends, hit harder, and be tougher all around. Little kids were always getting "got" from one another. Then it was really no big deal. Our "gets" could be knuckle rubs or tickling or just chasing until one or the other was exhausted. Maybe "get" meant something else in junior high school. None of my classmates knew for sure, though two kids had brothers who got into fights, but they were in high school.

By recess, I had forgotten all about the altercation and was just goofing around on the monkey bars, playing tag or swinging by bended knees; I didn't even see Wayne come up behind me. He shoved me hard face first into the monkey bars. At first I just thought someone had bumped into me by accident, but before I could turn around, I got slammed into the bars again. This time my mouth made first contact and my upper lip split, immediately filling my mouth with blood.

I spun around, my right hand swinging with the turn and luckily hit Wayne flush on the jaw hard enough to knock him on the ground. When I saw it was Wayne who had shoved me, the whole episode of the morning came back quickly. I had always been possessed by a terrible temper. Usually I was able to keep it in check. My restraint was gained by learning that my father's loss of happy thoughts was much more meaningful than mine. During the boxing lessons Dad insisted on giving me when I was four, I also found that a temper under your control is an asset when you are in a fight.

Another thing I'd learned was to press any advantage. It was one of those lessons that I became skilled at the first time, from my very first attempt. As soon as I saw Wayne fall, I jumped on him and started slapping his face back and forth with hard stinging slaps. SLAP! WHAP! SLAP! I was dripping blood all over him from my burst lip; it was really bleeding and it tasted terrible. SLAP! WHAP! SLAP! It was dripping on his shirt and his face. SLAP! WHAP! SLAP! The fight drew kids like a magic flute, and all of them were screaming.

His friends were hollering to him, "Get up and kick his ass!"

My friends were screaming, "PUNCH HIM! PUNCH HIM!"

The fury must have overwhelmed him, because he started to howl. I just kept flailing away, really getting into the slapping. His wails made all the blood worthwhile.

But for the second time that day, someone snuck up on me. I should have known it, too, because the hollering quieted down a lot. Our school superintendent, Mr. Sodt, yanked me off Wayne like I was Raggedy Andy and he started hollering, too. The schoolyard screamers must have rubbed off on him. I knew it was an adult just as soon as he pulled me off and just stood me there, though I still had my blood up.

Mr. Sodt was squeezing my shoulder really hard, but he was looking at Wayne. The bigger boy's face and shirt were covered with blood. It was all my blood, but our school's leader didn't know that. Wayne was really blubbering and crying, his breath going in and out in little hitches. Mr. Sodt shook me really hard thinking I had done Wayne some serious damage. He shook me hard enough to rattle my teeth, and he got some blood on his suit and shirt from my bobbing head. I started to cry, too, not as bad as that sissy still lying on the ground, but here was this big guy "getting" me and he scared me to boot.

"WHAT HAVE YOU DONE? NO FIGHTING IN my SCHOOL! YOU'RE OUT! YOU'RE OUT OF SCHOOL!"

I looked at my principal and tried to talk but my lip had puffed up like a sausage and I sounded idiotic.

"Mffph...mhee...marded...mi!"

Even I didn't know what I had just said.

Mr. Sodt wouldn't have been receiving even if my diction were perfect. I tried to tell him I was just defending myself, but I was already the guilty one in his eyes. The other poor boy was still lying in the dirt crying, for Pete's sake. Wayne on the ground and the image of this Mohawk-haired savage looking boy, who couldn't even talk for God's sake, sealed my fate that day. I just pointed to my lip and reached up to take his hand away. He didn't let go at first, but I kept holding his wrist until he did.

Another thing I had absorbed from both parents was, "Don't hang your head when you know you're right."

But it sure was hard not to study my feet.

I knew I was in deep doo-doo, in real trouble. I expected to get whacks at school from Mr. Sodt and a whipping or two at home, one from Mom and another from Dad. I had been warned about school behavior, not being sassy to teachers, not talking in class, not chewing gum. NOT FIGHTING. I didn't care, that sissy baby Wayne would take a long time living down his public bawling. And everybody on the playground knew I didn't start it. But I did finish it.

"Mess with the bull, you get the horn," Grandpa Teddy always said.

I would deal with whatever punishment I got. I had been whacked before.

Mr. Sodt told one of the other teachers who had come running to call my parents to come and get me adding that he would not have

119

boys who started fights in his school. I would later learn that Mrs. Teigs, our school nurse, called Mom with the news. She was a friend of my mother's and told her what she had seen. While I was sitting in the office waiting for my mom, Mrs. Teigs gave me a washcloth with an ice cube wrapped in it for my lip. Mr. Sodt told me I had a paddling coming but he was going to wait until he decided if I could even come back to school. If I was allowed to return, there was a paddle with holes drilled in it hanging in his office. If he didn't let me back in school, my folks would murder me. He wanted me to "sweat" a little. I was doing just fine. Wayne didn't even come to the office.

It didn't take Mom but a few minutes to cover the several miles to the school, and she looked girded when she came through the big school building doors.

I still had a speech impediment from the swollen lip, but I was ready, too. While I was waiting, I asked for several sheets of paper and a pencil from Mrs. Avendt, one of the secretaries in the office. She gave me both though she looked reluctant. I smeared blood from my hands on the pages as I wrote. The schoolyard had a communication network that rivaled the one in our neighborhood. The story of a terrible Clark, half heathen and the half savage, had gone out across the school gossip airwaves. I took the time while waiting to write the whole story out including the bus episode that morning leaving nothing out. I added that I could have been better on the bus and should have held my temper but could not manage it. About the playground, I stated that nobody was allowed to hit from behind and that had caused me to lose my temper again.

Mom stormed the office in a fury that was originally meant for me, I'm sure, but she looked at my swollen lip and paused long enough to read my account. It helped that I'd dripped some blood on one page for emphasis. At least my mother wiped the smear with her thumb.

"Is this true, Clark?" she asked.

I nodded yes.

"Every word true, son, no exaggerations?"

I nodded and shook my head, hoping the order was correct.

"Come on then, let's go see Mr. Sodt."

We walked to the counter at the front of the office.

"Hold your head up, son. If what you say is true, you won't be sitting in this office long."

"Hi, Mary (the secretary's first name), is Harold in?" she asked the secretary.

"Oh, yes, he's in," she replied. "I think he's expecting you."

We were ushered in to Mr. Sodt's office. He began to tell my mother what an out of control and terrible boy she had raised. Mr. Sodt didn't get very far before Mom raised her hand in front of his face.

"You need to read this, Harold."

It wasn't a request.

Mr. Sodt took the time to read my side of the story. He didn't dismiss the pages out of hand. Mom waited until he looked up from the papers but he didn't speak.

"So, Harold Sodt, Mr. Superintendent, perhaps you let appearances judge before you found out what really happened?"

Mom sounded just like she did when I was catching it.

I wondered silently, *Was Mr. Sodt catching the devil?*

It sure sounded like it, but I had never heard of a grownup doing the catching before.

"Did you see Clark start the fight?"

Mr. Sodt shook his head.

"I'm going to have to investigate this, Mrs. Greene," he said. "The other boy has already been taken home. I'll have to see if this is true."

"It's true. My son knows he's in enough trouble without adding lies to his problems. If you like, I'll stop by Wayne's house on the way home and talk to his mother. Clark's got every right to defend himself. I didn't raise a boy to run away from trouble."

"You remember that, Harold," she went on. "Now, why hasn't someone done something about his lip?"

Mom could press an advantage when she had one. Mr. Sodt told her that my school suspension would stand until he found out what had really happened. Mom was to call at the end of the school day tomorrow and they would talk.

"No, Harold, we'll be here tomorrow at the end of the day," Mom said. "I'll see you then. Clark better not be marked absent for tomorrow."

I had a bunch of explaining to do when I could finally talk again. My darling brother and sisters had great fun with my lip although Chip had heard of the fight while he was still at school. I had to tell him all about it, and how I slapped Wayne because he fought dirty sneaking up from behind. Chip was proud of me for whipping Wayne, who was constantly picking on little kids, himself included.

"But how come you didn't really punch him?" Chip wanted to know.

"Indians slapped when they fought," I told him knowingly. "They thought a rolled up fist was cowardly."

I had to repeat the story several more times to Mom and Dad. Like any good police officers, my folks wanted to see if my tale changed in the retelling, a sure indication of fabrication. My father seemed pleased even though he didn't like all the trouble I had caused. He hadn't been involved in any of the negotiations yet. Mom had done all of that, but he wasn't crazy about trouble this early in the school year.

Mom told him not to worry. She'd get it straightened out. She was going to go to the bus stop in the morning to talk to the driver. Then she was going to talk to Wayne's mother. By the time she went to school tomorrow, Mr. Sodt had better have all the same answers she had.

Mom set off on her fact-finding quest but wouldn't tell me the results when she came back.

She just said, "I've got the whole story."

It was unlike her not to give information.

What if she believed Wayne's story? What if his mother convinced my mother? What if Mr. Sodt believed Wayne's mother? What if I didn't get to go back to school?

I did entertain the possibility of not going to school anymore but I knew that would never happen. I was sweating the afternoon meeting.

I shouldn't have. Mr. Sodt talked to everyone, the bus driver, kids on the playground, Wayne's mother, and those boys who were Wayne's friends. He found out what really happened.

His answers were the same as those Mom had gotten.

"Praise the Lord!"

When I went back to school the next day, Mr. Sodt lectured me about fighting but not for very long. This was due largely to the statement by my mother regarding "his" school and "his" students having to defend themselves from cowards who attacked them when they weren't looking. I was judged innocent of starting anything. Wayne was suspended from school for three days. Ha!

The word of my acquittal took much longer to get around the school than the word of the fight. I wasn't the savage of two days ago, some people thought. Others waited for further evidence.

Others, Harold Sodt included, harbored other thoughts. Clark would bear watching. After my return to school, it didn't matter that I was only defending myself, and it didn't matter what I did from then on, people were going to watch Clark closely.

Mr. Eaton, my 6th grade homeroom and geometry teacher, heard and obeyed. He would watch Clark. Bill Eaton was also very good at dealing with boys who got out of line. Mr. Eaton used rulers to measure how far off kilter we were. I didn't even realize there was a line.

Jimmy and I were really enjoying art class. The first six weeks had been spent learning cartoon techniques, training our hands to do repetitions of the same figure in order that animation could be created with multiple pages flipping past. We were both getting better and became recognized caricature illustrators of kids in class, teachers, and our coach. In particular, we enjoyed creating portrayals of Coach Fletcher.

Coach Fletcher was new to Jefferson Schools. When he swung in for the first day of gym class that fall, he was on crutches. He had been in a terrible car accident while he was moving to the area to take this job. As a result of the accident, he'd broken his leg. What luck. He was a perfect target of our artistic attempts; why, the possibilities were endless. We made him into a Joe Blitzfig, Al Capp's character in Lil' Abner. We put our character on crutches with the requisite black cloud over his head. We devised scenarios in which he was fitted with multiple casts, always outsized or of grotesque shapes. A particularly effective one showed him with huge plaster casts on each finger and toe being wheeled through gym class exercises. We thought we were hilarious.

Everybody else did too. But the coach stopped enjoying these cartoons after a while. Mr. Eaton didn't like them from the very start.

He and the coach were teacher lounge buddies. Apparently Coach Fletcher commented to him about the cartoons. Perhaps he said he was getting tired of them, enough of a good laugh is one thing while too much of anything becomes nauseating. Perhaps they both felt the drawings didn't show enough respect. Jimmy and I weren't clever enough to read the subtle signs. We weren't smart at all unless you finished the phrase with ass. All the kids laughed each time we unveiled a new portrait or a new tableau of imagined situations. Blinded and dumb by schoolmate's adulation and enjoyment, we kept right on, each of us trying to produce the most outlandish pictures.

We didn't know enough to quit while the cartoons were still funny to the adults.

Coach tried to get through to us in gym class. Extra laps, pushups, additional towel duties, and calisthenics made no impression. Most of the boys, at eleven, were clumsy and uncoordinated enough to earn demerits at an equal pace with us or so it seemed. We didn't notice we were being singled out. There were kids doing added physical activities so often it seemed a whim of the coach. Then "Bertha" joined the group. She was a beauty.

Another teacher, Mr. Kinner, taught woodshop class and he was a good teacher. He taught us to work carefully with our hands and the tools required to do woodworking. We made cutting boards for the mothers and footstools for the dads. My cutting board turned out well enough that the pig shaped board became a family heirloom, but the stool broke quickly when Chip and I were rough-housing.

While we were busy with our first project, Mr. Kinner had created Bertha for coach. He did a good job.

The paddle was about 2 ½ feet long with a nice place for both hands improving applied force, a lesson in physics yet to be learned. On one side of the broad business end, Mr. Kinner had used a wood-burning tool to write in large script the paddle's soon to be infamous name. Through the wider end, he had also drilled about eighteen holes, one half inch in diameter, which would eventually teach several of us about aerodynamics and wind resistance. Highly polished with a varnish coating, it also had a heavy leather thong through another hole in the handle end. We all thought Coach Fletcher was kidding when he showed it to us even though he swung it so hard it whistled. He was laughing and smiling.

I need to explain something about the culture of paddling in the 1950s. It was an accepted practice at every level of school. Before

Madeline O'Hare condemned the use of prayer in schools, teachers and school administrators believed in "spare the rod and spoil the child." They quoted it fearlessly, because parents also believed also in the sanctity of teacher decisions. Most likely a paddling in school brought to the attention of the kid's parents earned the child an extra helping at home. If you were fortunate enough to not have to take a note home for a signature that documented your Revelation, you were always smart enough to keep your mouth shut about it. Children knew if their behavior warranted the use of force in school, they were sure to have trouble sitting down for the remainder of the day. Teachers were not reluctant then; they were relentless. Cause and effect was in high form at school the whole time I attended, kindergarten through twelfth grade.

Right after I had unveiled my latest masterpiece by taping it to his door, I found out the coach meant the paddle for more than just show.

When I failed to do some activity in the proscribed manner or without the expected effort, the coach told me to go to his office. I really don't remember what the infraction was or even if there actually was one. He told me to lean over the desk and I did, but I thought he was carrying the joke or charade or whatever it was just a bit too far. I heard the little whistle Bertha made. SWAT! He hit me hard enough to buckle my knees. Only once. It was enough.

"You keep fooling around, Greene, and there'll be more. Got it?"

Yes, I did. I surely got it.

Coach Fletcher left his door open during my swat, and the whole gym class gathered to watch the first to be punished. I couldn't help the tears, never mind the hoots from several of the watchers. I was sure I wouldn't be the last and wanted to see some of those laughing now when they got their first kiss from Bertha. I hoped I would remember who was laughing, but my eyes were blurred making identification difficult. My butt stung like fire, like it was glowing. The gym shorts and cotton underwear I was wearing offered no padding, no protection from the force of the paddle. Damn, that hurt!

I am embarrassed to say it, but I ended up getting another paddling of one whack and then Jimmy got two more swats on different occasions before we determined that Coach Fletcher was paying us just a little too much attention. Okay, you are not my friendly neighborhood coach. The only reason I was doing the cartoons in the first place was because I had liked him and thought he was pretty neat. So had Jimmy. We didn't think so now. The cartoons of coach stopped. We didn't want to draw comic likenesses of Coach Fletcher anymore, exactly what he had planned. The swats, for us specifically, ceased but continued as punishment in gym class.

We turned our attention to Mr. Eaton. He supplied plenty of material right there in our homeroom class. Mr. Eaton had a twitch. Not a nervous twitch or facial tic, he just had a habit of quickly shrugging his shoulders and giving his pants a tug upward. He did it repeatedly and several of us would mimic his gestures in the hall, or if his back was turned, in his class. He even joked about it with us saying it was something he picked up as a kid somewhere and he now did it unconsciously. We must have thought that public acknowledgment meant public domain.

Mr. Eaton also had another unique aspect. He believed in stopping trouble quickly; when someone was disruptive or deliberate in refusing to participate, that someone paid a price. Bill Eaton would smack their outstretched hands with a ruler. He whacked the hands of boys and girls alike. He hit hands with equal opportunity in 1957. He made sure the result was effective by gripping the fingers of the offending hand and bending them backwards enough to insure maximum effect. He also used three or four rulers tied together with rubber bands to provide mass.

Whacks on the hand numbered 5, 10 or 20, always in those increments, never a variation. Five smacks were the limit for girls and mostly quelled the disturbances made by boys. Ten clouts denoted more severe displeasure encompassing such acts as farting, shooting rubber band missiles, or smart aleck behavior. Twenty strokes meant fighting or cheating or down right belligerence toward Mr. Eaton. The fives and tens were terrible enough and you remembered them the rest of the day. Twenty thwacks meant your hand was swollen for several days and your parents would most likely notice.

Jimmy and I could create great cartoons. Mr. Eaton laughed at every single one. He roared at a chalkboard mural we did one day. It was a whole tableau of him in a ruler store, buying thousands of rulers in different sizes and colors all stacked neatly in a grocery cart. The word balloon above his head asked the checkout clerk, "Where do you keep the rubber bands?" It took him twenty minutes to calm the class down. Ten minutes because of the cartoon. Ten minutes more while Jimmy and I got our twenty strokes after finger pointing laid the blame.

But we didn't stop. He just provided too much good material. Jimmy and I spent lunch times in creative fervor each cartoon more gaudy and spectacular than the last. We kept getting whacks, too, but had made an unspoken pact to continue. This had to be what our social studies teacher meant when he talked about freedom of the press. I brought colored pencils from home and we hooked paints from art class. We made cartoon series and stapled them together to pass them around school. At the end we might have had ten or twelve flipping animations of Mr. Eaton being laughed at in school. He gave up.

He kept us after the first hour bell rang and told us that we had to stop because he found himself getting mad when we got whacks.

"It's not that I don't like the cartoons," he said, "but you've allowed them to get out of hand and that's what I don't like. You've done too much, and this makes me mad. How about a truce?"

This was different. Here was a teacher who actually talked to us. Of course, it only took about 500 whacks for him to try a new approach but we eventually reached an understanding. We were so used to him grabbing our hands for whacks that we all laughed when Jimmy and I both hesitated when he stuck out his hand to shake.

He was one of my favorite teachers.

Chip and I were seldom daunted by failure.

We could have been because we didn't reach the mark nearly as often as we would have liked. Mostly, we fell somewhere between abysmal failures and almost, but either a short attention span or an attempt to erase our shortcomings through other activities, we didn't stay dejected for long.

Usually three minutes was enough.

I had set spring snares for small animals for several years and while seldom successful, I was still convinced this was the perfect way to claim kinship with my Indian brothers. At any given time I might have had eight or ten separate snares set across trails, around crabapple trees, or at the gently sloping areas where I'd seen animal tracks. I'd taught Chip and he was good with them, as well. The snares required continual monitoring because if sprung and not relieved of their captured prey, the escape wriggles of the animal would eventually ruin the snare. Worse still, the thought of wasting something that had managed to become ensnared would be shameful. We'd heard "waste not, want not" our entire lives. While our snares were limited to small game, when we had traps set, Chip and/or I looked at them daily. We got just as excited when we found the snare tripped and empty as we did when a rabbit dangled from the noose, but we were getting tired of bunny rabbits.

We had carefully thought out and prepared for our next trap. We snitched some stout clothesline left over from the last stringing in our back yard, made several sharpened and notched stakes to drive in the ground, and had a spool of our old stand-by, rug thread, for the trip line.

It was time to try for big game.

Spring snares can come in all shapes and sizes and are simple to make. A cord tied in a noose, a small branch plunged into the ground for the springing mechanism and a trigger wire or line to trip the whole contraption. They sometimes weren't reliable, but that didn't matter. We only cared about having the snares.

From the edge of the woods, a well-worn path led from the oak trees to veer off toward several watering spots. Another trail frequented by deer wound down the center of one peninsula jutting into the water of the marsh. We'd seen deer and their tracks enough to recognize this as a favorite route.

Perfect.

The trail was lined with maple and locust saplings some growing right next to the well trod dirt of the narrow lane.

Perfect.

As Chip and I inspected the jutting finger of land for a suitable spot, we found the trail abruptly turned at a right angle for three or four feet before winding again to resume its original course. Whatever animal came this way would be forced to alter foot position from its normal stride.

Perfect.

Nearby were several suitable young trees, three inches in diameter at the ground gracefully tapering twenty feet high and far enough away from the bare earth path to provide the snare a powerful pull.

I boosted Chip up one slender trunk as far as I could and watched him shinny up another several feet until the tree began to sway from his weight. Wrapping his legs around the trunk, he hoisted my Scout axe with the rope he'd tied to his wrist and lopped off the branches within reach. He tied the rope's end to the thinned and denuded whip as high as he could reach before he started back down. As he scooted down, the axe chunked the remaining small limbs until the length from the ground upward for fourteen feet was smooth and springy. Chip, who had just turned eight, was getting better at this Indian stuff.

I pulled on the rope bending it in the shape of a wide mouth "U," and tested the strength of the tree. It whipped back and forth to vertical each time I released the tension. This was going to work.

Perfect.

Once Chip was down, we cleared brush and weeds away from an area on opposite sides of the trail and drove one stake deep into the ground on either side. Stringing the rug thread double between the stakes for the trigger, we were ready to tie and hook the noose rope.

It took us both to pull the tree down and we had to struggle to do it. Once it was far enough so I could whip a loop to tie it off on a nearby tree limb, I estimated the required length while I fashioned the slip knot noose. Almost ready, Chip and I both held the rope while we pulled the loop from the restraining branch and knelt to hook the rope under the closest stake's notch.

My attention was on reaching the stake, and I accidentally allowed the rope to slip through my hands. With a terrible screech, Chip was sling-shotted into the air, unerringly launched upward at the tree trunk. Chip hadn't let go. In fact, he couldn't turn loose because he'd looped the rope around his wrist several times in order to pull better, and when our combined weights were reduced as a result of my involuntary release, kinetic energy took over.

"CLAAAAARK! YEEOORRROOOW! HELPHELPHELP!"

In an instant he was clinging monkey-like to the wildly whipping tree, and he looked like an upside down clock pendulum. Every swing produced another wild yell.

"HELPHELP! HEY! HELPHELP!"

Once I got over my astonishment at his flight, I asked Chip if he was okay, but all I got was more hollering for an answer. Chip looked pretty funny up there even as the tree slowed its violent back and forth motion. Even when the tree only swayed slightly, he refused to slide down the trunk. Gesturing wildly with one hand, he began instead to tell me how much trouble I'd be in when Mom found out.

I couldn't help laughing.

My hysterics didn't help Chip get down the tree either. It took several more moments of convincing before Chip slid down, and even when he did touch earth, I spent many more trying to persuade him it was accidental. The laughter that continued to bubble up each time I reviewed the picture of him stuck to the swaying trunk didn't help my argument. I couldn't talk him into trying to set the snare again. Chip looked incredulous when I asked, as if he wondered if I was so stupid as to imagine he would. He absolutely refused to retrieve the clothesline still tied and I had to climb the slender trunk. Chip got in a few laughs of his own as I struggled to pull myself up.

Despite my attempts to convince him otherwise, Chip still had suspicions of the actual cause of his sling shot ride, but he didn't tell anyone and I didn't either.

Perfect.

The sky turned yellow black a week later when we had one of those extraordinary summer storms that bluster and blunder and thrash and tear up trees, flowers, and crops.

These storms pour rain so hard you can't take a breath if you are caught out, and the winds cause shingles ripped off rooftops to fly away. Thunder booms and lightning shatters tree trunks and punctures the earth. This storm was no exception and had whipped up the surface of the lake to froth before building the water to huge waves. Driftwood logs that had lain in place for years were pushed to new vantage points. The Navy-surplus raft at Kress Park tore from its moorings and was shredded against the concrete of the breakwater. Trashcans, tree-limbs, and even entire trees found themselves in new yards, disconnected from original places, away from owners.

Power was out, out, out. Candles and oil lamps were the only light in the houses for miles around on that night. The entire subdivision looked like a giant had come through the subdivision gates with his big scythe swinging back and forth in terrible arcs.

Following the storm, there was work for everyone and everyone worked. Walter Nadeau gathered tools and troops to attack the damage. We spent days dragging and sawing and chopping scattered limbs and downed trees. The old tractor worked overtime and paths were dragged free of grass as limb after limb was dragged along the same path to the beach. People pulled tarps over holes in their roofs or boarded up broken windows until they could fix them properly. Detroit Edison trucks converged in the beach to determine damage and heal the wounds caused by the storm. The whole subdivision worked; debris from trees was pulled down to the beach area and piled high, about fifteen feet by forty feet wide. That pile would lie there until next year when it was dry enough to burn.

As we worked, we talked about the marshmallow and wiener roast we'd have. We'd get moms to make potato salad and get corn for roasting, and hamburgers would be made. Kool-Aid and lemon-aide, and some dads would bring beer. Mine would not, wasn't allowed by Mom. The plans were big already and we were still piling up brush, and would be for another week before the fields and yards were normal.

The pile attracted Johnny's younger brother Tommy, like a magnet. Tommy was a special child, and while we didn't think of him as a problem we did know he was different. He didn't have to go to school. He didn't have to do chores. He loved to wave branches and he had an unlimited supply after the storm. He just could not stay away and as long as he was waving a branch, he was pretty docile. He had a private reason, a dance or waltz with the branches to a music that only he could hear. The only person who could make him give up a branch was his mother.

Johnny and I had been part of all Walt's work details and took some amount of pride in our contributions to the pile of tree limbs and trunks. One could not fail to notice the huge pile and Patch was no exception. She burrowed into a gap in the branches woofing and barking at some imaginary game. We encouraged her to find the grizzly bear until she was completely under the pile and then had a heck of a time trying to get her back out. It was great fun now and more fun would come next year at the bonfire. The pile smelled of tree sap, sharp and biting and sweet, good boy-type smells. We had worked hard.

At the end of each day, we went swimming after we had finished with the cleanup. We were at the lake already and we usually wore our bathing suits under our jeans. If we went swimming, we wouldn't have to take a bath. Mom encouraged us to swim in the summer. To her, Lake Erie and warm weather equaled clean kids. We would normally just strip off the outer layer and "ooh" and "aah" our way over the sharp, rocky beach, and carefully wade through the shallows to plunge into deeper water. We were always dry from the hot sun by the time we walked home and so we didn't use up towels either, another plus for Mom.

Tommy had followed us about all day, helping in his own way, though always reluctant to put "his" branch on the pile. Only with the assurance of another would he surrender the one he had, and we couldn't talk Tommy into laying his last branch down to join us in the swim. Johnny and I paddled and splashed about thoroughly enjoying the water after a day of work. Patch joined the swim and buried her head under the water to retrieve rocks we would "plunk-plonk," splash for her.

I was still playing with Patch when Johnny climbed out to get Tommy washed off before we headed to our respective homes for dinners. It was getting to be that time and it didn't do to be late for dinner. I didn't know about Johnny, but we were apt to have extra kids to feed and sometimes the food didn't go quite far enough. He started a tug of war with Tommy for the branch.

Johnny won. Tommy howled.

Johnny took the current special branch and tossed it on the nearby pile. Despite Tommy's gyrations and his continued attempts to regain the branch Johnny got his jeans and t-shirt off and got him into the water. Then he turned Tommy loose.

Before Johnny knew what had happened, Tommy had reached under the water, picked up a rock about the size of a football, and had crashed it down on Johnny's head. I didn't see what had happened, but Patch began barking furiously. I turned at her sound and hollered. Tommy had lost his grip on the heavy stone and was groping about for another.

"Onny ook my eeee, Onny ook my eeee! Onny ish!" Tommy screeched.

I swam/waded to them both and told Tommy, "Go get it, go get it. It's right over there. Johnny won't care."

Tommy splashed out of the water, intent on regaining his branch. Johnny had gone down in about eighteen inches of water, but he was face down. By the time I got to him, only a few seconds, the water around his curly hair was laced with a thick tendril of viscous red blood.

He was out cold, more than just stunned, and I rolled him over on his back to get his face out of the water. I held his head out of the water and got him pointed toward the shore. His eyelids fluttered and he took a couple of shuddering breaths as I towed him toward shore, all the while keeping an eye on Tommy. Frequently Tommy's rage would cast about for others to tend but luckily not this time. As it turned out, I didn't have to worry because he was already heading back to the pile of brush. That quick spurt of violence was gone forever from his mind. I got Johnny half in and half out of the water. That would do for now.

Close inspection revealed that Johnny had a nasty three inch gash at his hairline and the blood was streaming around his nose into his closed eyes.

"Man, you're bleeding!" I hollered to no one.

He was starting to come around, but he sure looked like the dickens. The entire front of his face was sticky crimson. It scared the Hell out of me.

"Please, please," I breathed to myself. I ran back to the beach for something to wipe him off so I could get a better look. He'd passed out again by the time I got back.

I wet his t-shirt in the lake and wiped his face off. The wiping must have helped, because he weakly struggled to sit up.

"What happened?" Johnny asked.

I had to explain the whole thing to him several times before he understood, but he was coming back around the whole time so it was a well-spent effort. It gave the bleeding a chance to slow down too. After getting the blood washed off as best we could, I helped him up, and we headed toward Johnny's house.

I supported him the whole way home because he still didn't have his legs under him well enough for a solo. It turned out to be a good thing we washed off as much blood as we did because Mrs. Weiman went wild enough as it was. Johnny was still pretty woozy, so while his mother patched him up, I had to tell her the whole story. I played down my role of getting Johnny out of the water. That was between just him and me. Johnny didn't go to the hospital and didn't even get stitches.

"Head wounds bleed," his mother said. I think Mrs. Weiman put Bag-Balm on his head. She told Johnny that he knew better than to take Tommy's things. He was the only one to blame.

She sounded just like my mother when Chip and I went at it. She sounded just like Mom when I got hurt. And, she used Bag-Balm just like my mom did.

Johnny was in good hands.

Everything was gonna be okay.

I'd see him tomorrow.

Summertime meant gardens full of good food, but we had to work to bring in the produce.

Grandpa Teddy's gardens required tending and everyone worked. Hoes and rakes and cultivators were passed out like weapons to fight the war of the weeds. No child was ever too young for garden work unless still babes in arms and then the infant still went. Bassinets were as common as cornstalks in the garden, and I remember each of my younger siblings and cousins cooing between the rows. As soon as we walked, we went to farm school and had endless details to learn. First came "mind your feet," marching precisely down rows so trampling and squashing didn't happen. Little eyes were taught to know the unwanted from the wanted, and small hands were told to pull the one without uprooting the other.

I learned good bugs by finding praying mantises, counting ladybugs, and watching wasps lay eggs on caterpillars. Bad ones were learned when Grandpa put a bug that bit me in my hand. Grandchildren were paid a penny apiece for striped potato bugs and earned a nickel bounty for every big green tomato worm or black grasshopper we turned in. I wasn't supposed to learn that all girls hate June bugs but I did. We trailed behind Grandpa when he dusted his garden with poisonous powders, but we had to "get back now" when he did. Grandma planted marigolds twixt the vegetable rows to help with the pests. Both grandparents thought Patch was another pest in the garden. I had to teach her to keep out, too.

All young ones had another garden goal to tend. No child was considered "big" until he or she could push the big-wheeled cultivator in a straight line. We had to practice in bare ground before Grandpa let us in the real garden, and no one did well without hours of exercise. If we were believed to be "too" little for mechanized work, we were still expected to labor. Methods of hoeing and raking and loosening the ground were taught and our work was inspected. We discovered how to scare some birds away but how to invite others with open arms.

Tomatoes, fruit trees, plants and canes got particular care. Tomato plants got pinching back and heavy mulching. Strawberries and rhubarb got tucked with mulch while blackberries and raspberries were tenderly weeded. Apple, peach, cherry and pear trees were stripped of suckers that had to be removed correctly. "Don't tear the bark."

My grandpa had a saying about fruit trees: "You have to treat them like a bad woman," but he never said it to anyone but us kids. To keep Grandpa's obsession with bark bound trees at bay, we wore ourselves out by hitting the woody rough trunks every year with a plastic bat. We'd better get it right if we wanted Gram's jellies, juices and jams, and we'd better keep our mouths shut about his reasoning.

Sometimes we ate new red-button potatoes if Grandpa got the patch planted early.

Grandma's flower plots were for touring and sightseeing, and while visits weren't quite mandatory, you'd be sorry if you didn't go. Her father had been a horticulturist and she was determined the knowledge given to her as a child was passed to the following generations. We learned Latin names for the poppy, aster, lily, snapdragon, rose and philodendron even though this last common name was tough enough for me. I learned to plant and divide and graft and root and take a cutting for propagation. So did every other child who came on the premises. Everyone was expected to know how to make all plants grow. The premise behind my grandparents' instruction was that we could grow our own food if necessary, but we'd have flowers because we wanted the beauty.

At Grandma and Grandpa's farm, summer also meant a month preordained for all at the same time parties, homemade ice cream, and mystery cakes baked with coins inside. We celebrated the birthdays of Chip, Greg, Henry and Uncle Don one weekend every July when uncles, aunts and cousins gathered in Manchester. Picnic tables were set up, cucumbers chilled and sliced, and chicken fried for everyone. The birthday picnics were huge and if we had been particularly productive, Gram would make sloppy-joes baked in wax paper. When it was time for ice cream Grandpa had to buy ice in a fifty pound block from a man who kept it in a sawdust-packed trailer. No store or service station had ice machines in those days and Grandpa had to drive out in the country to get it. Everyone took turns cranking the handle on big ice cream tub and it took a long, long time for the magic to happen. Many years Grandpa managed to persuade some of his strawberry plants into long-term berries and we mixed the sun-sweetened fruit in our ice cream. The children tried x-ray vision to determine where the nickels and dimes were hidden in the birthday cakes, but somehow it seemed the other person always got the right piece.

Summer was even more special because grandchildren often stayed longer than a family weekend. Favored children were scheduled on some mysterious Grandma calendar. We suspected it all came down to behavior, but we never knew for sure how the bonus worked. Sometimes the worst one (the Greene children thought) got to stay and the rest were flabbergasted. We considered ourselves lucky if we got to stay even though Grandma was tough on us. Her firmness was mixed with exactly equal and careful portions of pampering. We always got to "order" breakfast, and along with waffles and pancakes, I learned to love fresh tomatoes with vinegar and sugar. Grandpa also taught me to eat my toast burnt black and smothered in butter.

I loved every minute when I was chosen to be the golden child.

Chapter 7
Delivery

Summertime was also always adventurous.

Small adventures and big adventures were met with wide-eyed sparkle when I first discovered that a new quest was unfolding.

I grew up in a time when exposed breasts were found in the National Geographic, or not at all. You had to discount the women breastfeeding their babies which sometimes took place at baseball games in the back of our church, or at the Monroe County Fair. For young boys, these overexposures equaled "Mother," not a real girl and, consequently, not a real breast.

When I was seven or eight, the Sunday Detroit News magazine had an article on the Mayan Indians of South America. In the magazine was a sketch of a Mayan maiden with an arm outstretched, one breast partially exposed. I was enchanted by the wonderful curve of her breast but didn't know why. When everyone had finished reading the paper, I quietly tore out the page when I took the trash out.

I stashed that sketch, privately, shoved secretly under my mattress folded up, and pushed way in so Mom couldn't find it. I admired the breast for two years, satisfying my attraction until Mom discovered the picture. I got my first sex education class only when I had entered the 9th grade and that only after a tremendous battle of parents vs. school. It was a big deal to kiss a girl and you had better really like her if you did because before you got over the flush, everybody else would know.

Advertisements then did not feature tight jeans and brassieres, but instead showed clothing and underwear limply lying alone on shelves and tables and never bulged with buttocks and breasts. The Sears' and the Penney's catalogs were read primarily by moms and daughters. Bunnies were something Hugh had seen only in sporting magazines; Victoria hadn't thought of a secret worth keeping, and Dr. Ruth was considering veterinary science as a profession. We didn't have any videos rated anything and adult films were something you had to get from France or Italy and the actors all talked funny. Condoms were sometimes found on the beach looking lost or in the drugstore hidden away.

The sexiest movies were *Some Like it Hot* and *On the Beach*, with Bert Lancaster and Deborah Kerr, which were "steamy." Was it better in those times? It was different.

My hormones, while beginning to move around a bit, were still far from raging or even racing. They weren't mad at all and hadn't even started walking fast yet. They had not clambered up to the door of my brain and demanded that the current inhabitants immediately vacate the premises. There was an awakening of sorts, and on several mornings, I hurriedly cleaned up the evidence of midnight fantasies or my body's practice, but for the most part I did not associate these startling feelings with girls. When Mom eventually discovered remnants of the evidence I had not totally obliterated, she told my father.

My father's answer to his first son's puberty and sex education was to give me several U.S. Navy manuals that were required reading for servicemen heading overseas. He got them in 1941, when he shipped out for the South Pacific during World War II.

"Read these," he said in his best sensitive and fatherly tone.

One had "GONORRHEA" and "SYPHILIS" printed in big black letters across the olive drab front. Inside were pictures of men's genitalia disfigured and ravaged by these diseases, "the clap" and "syph." It listed all the symptoms and results if left untreated and who to see if you got it. There were several pictures of big syringes accompanied by details of the treatment. The pamphlet ended with a whole chapter entitled "How to Avoid the Foreign Prostitute."

Wow, how and where did a person catch this stuff again? What was the middle part? After reading it through, I asked my father if he was sending me overseas. He said I'd missed the point.

I probably had but it didn't stop the wondering part.

Other friends were wondering, too.

One of the neighborhood girls, Kaye, had the rightfully bestowed reputation of being a tomboy. She could play baseball better than most boys her age except that she couldn't hit very well. Catching and throwing were her specialties and she delighted in fielding a line drive or throwing someone out after grabbing a "hot" one on the first bounce. She played ball with us during pickup games but never when we played against our rivals from Stoney Pointe. She was the second fastest runner in Pointe aux Peaux and nobody could catch her or could even come close. If Kaye could have only learned to swing a bat, we would have made an exception and let her be on the team.

I was twelve going on thirteen that summer and did have a pretty good curiosity. I was growing up, the silky blond hair on my legs turning dark, overnight it seemed. A few boys, but not me, had noticed the beginnings of chin whiskers or mustaches. I had a few new hairs struggling to make themselves evident on my chest and groin but it wasn't enough to brag about.

At age ten, I had determined it was time for me to be bathing without the watchful eyes of my mother's inspections. I had a difficult time with bath privacy because Mom was accustomed to giving her boys a bath. I supposed she viewed my sudden modesty as a milestone she wasn't happy about passing.

Chip and I still had to take baths together to conserve the hot water, but I got Mom out of the bathroom. I had to promise that I would make sure Chip scrubbed all the important parts if I didn't want Mom in there. I promised religiously and enforced the promise with a fervor built of worry that she would renege if she found Chip below standard. I was not about to let his ears' and fingers' and knees' cleanliness ratings fall once I had gotten her out of the habit of watching me bathe. Chip had been clean enough for almost three years now because Mom no longer made attempts to storm the bathroom while I was in there. We had an inside lock on the bathroom door but weren't allowed to use it. It was much too suspicious for kids to want to lock anything, especially for boys.

Being in a family that included two sisters, I was not ignorant of the differences between boys and girls. I knew for instance that we never took baths together and I knew about the toilet seat thing. They liked talcum powder and toilet water, and I liked the smells of the marsh and my dog. My older sister Carole had three seconds worth of patience allocated for me daily and I always ran over that limit while I could wait for a turtle to surface in the swamp for hours at a time. I figured Carole's problem was girl related.

Mom was a girl but that didn't count. I couldn't relate any mother stuff with some developments that were appearing on many girls in school and in the neighborhood. I would have had to be blind not to notice some parts getting slimmer, other parts getting bigger, the different ways they walked, talked and smelled. I was covert in my observations and determined to avoid discovery while I studied these differences. I inwardly congratulated myself on remaining undetected.

Kaye was about six months older than I and had already turned thirteen. In addition to playing baseball and running, she could wrestle and for years she enjoyed "pinning" most of us. She was wiry and twisty and agile and strong, and she could tussle right along with the best of us. Her father used to get a big kick out of our humiliations, because he enjoyed watching us get whipped. He wanted a son, but instead he got a daughter that could play ball, run, and wrestle as well as anyone. He encouraged his daughter in all sports, including wrestling, but was surprisingly blind that his little girl was growing up. Just last week he cheered when she put my shoulders to the ground two out of three. I might have let her, maybe not. She was growing and up wasn't the only direction.

She was also cute. Her athletic abilities endowed her with tight muscles and long legs, only adding to her attractiveness.

"She's pert," her mother used to say, "a pert girl."

I agreed.

I collected for The Monroe Evening News on Thursdays. I also collected on Fridays, Saturdays, and Mondays through the next Thursday if I couldn't "catch" someone at home or if they didn't have the money. While collecting, it wasn't unusual for me to be invited inside houses while my customers searched purses and pockets for the forty cents. There were some customers who would not answer the door and some who said come back later. In truth, I collected virtually every day of the week, and it always seemed a struggle to keep people current with the weekly cost of the news.

I carried a black leather latch purse every day, a bag that once used to carry money for the Newport Community Bank. One of the deacons of our church was the president of the bank and had given it to me when he found out that I had commerce to carry out. I had plenty of commerce to carry out, the only problem was that the amount I had to carry was difficult to get. The problems I encountered collecting such a paltry sum today seems impossible, but those four dimes were sometimes hard for people to scratch together in the 1950s.

One day as I collected, I was invited into Kaye's house and waited for her mother to get the newspaper money. I stood by the front door and Kaye walked out of the bathroom with a towel wrapped around her waist and one around her head. I gaped. Between the two towels, new country was visible, all curvy smooth and hilly creamy. She didn't scream with embarrassment like my older sister would have done. She let me have a long look, and she turned at the waist, this way and that, before she smiled and walked through her bedroom door.

Wow! Young breasts! Not a picture, though I would see them as plainly as if I carried a photograph in my pocket from that day forward. Breasts put a whole new meaning to the word budding, far better than trees and flowers. Budding, yeah, I liked it! Pert, too. If someone said she was pert, I could definitely agree. New meanings for two words today!

Mom would have been so proud about the new words growing in my vocabulary…but not about Kaye.

I got my newspaper money and her mother asked, "Did you see Kaye?"

"No, is she here?" I responded quickly.

I just knew her mother would see the scarlet of my face and my lie. I expected immediate suspicion, trial, conviction and sentence. She didn't see "LIAR" painted scarlet across my forehead, but I knew it was there if she looked. I had seen Kaye all right. More than I expected. Her mom hadn't seen my heightened color, a reprieve.

Kaye's mother had turned and called to her daughter, "Kaye, honey, Clark's here collecting. Do you want to see him?"

The question allowed just enough time for the red heat of my face to pale to normal. The word must have disappeared from my forehead, too, because Kaye's mother didn't scream anything at me.

When Kaye's voice floated out from her room, I just nodded an okay.

"No, I'll see him later."

Her mother gave me a tip for having to wait, but I already had one. I said a thank-you meant for both, but only got "you're welcome" from her mother.

I finished up my paper route with questions at every step. "What was that about?" Step. "Was she surprised and just froze like some opossum in the headlights?" Step. "What did that turning and showing thing mean?" Step. "What was that smile about?" Step. "Did she like me looking at her?" Step. "Or did she like me just looking stupid?" Step.

I was pretty sure "yes" was the answer to the last question. Kaye had become a whole new person in the space of a few heartbeats, mine and hers.

Papers delivered, I turned back on Goddard toward home when behind me her voice asked.

"Well, what did you think?"

Before I could answer, she ran away and I knew I couldn't catch her. She was quicker than I was in lots of ways, though I hadn't formed the thought. I had plenty of questions that needed some answers, and some questions I couldn't even think of then. I was sure they would come to me. I was overly good at asking questions. The questions all would have to wait, because Kaye was already small in my sight, still running, just turning into her yard.

She carried on this question and flight tactic for several days sneaking up behind or alongside me and dashing away.

Her question was always the same, "What did you think?"

I was quickly fed up with the game, if that's what it was. "What were the rules? Who made the rules? Chase? Grab? Lay in wait?" I obviously didn't know. I hadn't recognized the game for sure. I was accustomed to talking with Kaye even if it was just a "hi." I had done so every day for so long I couldn't remember when we hadn't. We had been neighbors and friends forever; now this girl had suddenly become a stranger, certainly coming from a different place.

During summer, we normally wore bathing suits every day under jeans or shorts. That way when an opportunity presented itself we didn't have to say, "I can't; I don't have my suit on" or "I've got to go home and change first." It was easier to just cool off, enjoy Lake Erie with a quick swim. My mother, other moms, and most all the kids spent part of every summer day at the lake. We had had picnic lunches in between splashing furiously, but waiting the twenty minutes after each meal, so we didn't get the cramps, something dreaded and avoided, only to finally submerge back in the water, timed to the second.

Several more days passed. I certainly hadn't forgotten the vision, but I'd become accustomed to the run away questioning from Kaye. Our family had spent an entire day at the beach when Mom reminded me.

"Papers need to be delivered, son. It's three o'clock; you'd better get home and change," she instructed. "Take Patch with you. We're going to stay a while longer. See you at dinner."

Patch and I headed back to the house where I tied Patch up in the back yard. She barked her disapproval at the enforced lock-up, but experience had taught me she was capable of leading me astray from paper route duties, and there might be time for more swimming stuff before dinner if I hurried. If I pedaled hard, threw papers to porches along the way, maybe another splash or two were still waiting. Though I usually took my time and enjoyed the walk or ride and really liked my route, I could hurry if I needed to.

As I headed back to the front door so I could change, I saw Kaye standing by the lilac bush at the edge of our yard.

She called, "Clark, come here a minute, take a look at *this*."

I thought she had found something, a snake or a kitten, maybe a baby bird. Instead, she took my hand and we walked secretively to her house and around the back behind some lilac bushes.

"Come on."

She ducked her head and scooted under their home's back porch through a small, hinged-on-the-top door. It was dark and cool, smelled of dirt and sort-of-musty. I could see a blanket spread smooth on the dirt. The sunlight made sharp lines in the dust as it crept through cracks in the porch surrounding. This had to be more of the game we were playing, like extra innings or second quarter play. Count me in.

"Did you like them? Want to look some more?" Kaye pulled her bathing suit down off her shoulders, pulled and stretched until it was at her waist. "Want to touch them?"

Yeah. Yes, okay, sure. Of course. You bet! Yessireebob, I do! all came to mind, but I had left my voice somewhere else.

Kaye had found a baby bird all right, but now it was somehow trapped in my chest, fluttering, trying to fly somewhere, a first flight. Kaye took my hand, my own left hand, and placed it on her breast, her own right breast, and I could feel her heart beating. Not nearly as fast as mine was, but pitter-patter sweet and I reached out with my other hand to hold this delight a little better, a little closer. They felt far better than they looked, even though two minutes ago I would have said that was impossible. At the identical time my first molecule touched her first molecule, and all the other molecules in my body were finding new life, changing the shape of my bathing suit dramatically. I had had erections before but this one was insistent, demanding and shouting in languages I had never heard.

At the same instant, we both thought that kissing would be a good idea. It was good. Really! Good! We did this for some time, melting slowly, lying down side by side instead of that uncomfortable kneeling face-to-face stuff we started with. Boy, did she feel good; boy, did I feel good; we both felt good together, and she was making these little noises in her throat. I felt like shouting.

This was something, this was, "Oh, my God!!!!" as she put her hand down the front of my suit. Like middle of the night, wake me up feelings, but much, much better. We kissed and kissed and kissed and kissed. I liked every part of this and the kissing was right up there at the top. Kaye kept her hand where it was feeling another change taking place.

Wow, this was so…sweet. That's the right word, sweet.

"Ejaculation," whispered Kaye. "You ejaculated, what you just did," giggling sweetly. "I read about it."

I knew the word, too, but asked what book she had been reading. I don't remember which one she told me. We both laughed as I told of the ones my father had given me.

We lay together for a long time, just touching, arms across each other, little kisses on lips and faces. Not talking much after the laughs, just looking in eyes, seeing each other.

She sat up and said, "Let me see if anybody's around."

She pulled her top back in place, put her arms through the loops and turned. Man, she looked good from any angle, in the front, from the side and now going away, too. She pushed open the little door and sunlight stole through the crack.

"Its okay, nobody's around, we better go," Kaye said and waited for me by the side of the porch, letting the door swing closed again, making the light go out.

I scooted over to the door and she gave me a good kiss. Sweet. A flash of sunlight through the door and she was gone.

I stuck my head out and looked but didn't see Kaye, didn't see anyone. It was time I got the papers delivered, past time really. I walked back to my house, still searching for Kaye, still looking. I got my clothes changed but now there wouldn't be time for swimming before dinner. I didn't mind, this had been lots better than any swimming I'd ever done. Before I went down to pick up my papers, I went back and untied Patch. I needed to talk to someone and my dog was perfect for that sort of conversation.

Three days later Kaye beckoned to me from her bedroom window as I delivered papers.

"Meet me."

I held up the paper bag, nodding.

"After you're through with the papers; my mother went to town. She won't be back for hours."

I am sure that I established a paper route delivery record that day but Guinness never contacted me. Maybe I was supposed to call them, although I could not provide details of the record. I only hope the right people got their papers that day.

Kaye was already under the porch when I finished the route. I peered in the dimness and saw she was lying on the blanket, half covered by an additional sheet that she had brought. She looked what...? Beautiful, pretty, sweet, young, perfect, wondering, all the words fit, all seemed to describe her.

She stretched out her hand and said, "You better get under here before somebody sees you."

I got.

I crawled under the porch and sat by her, not touching yet, wondering if there were new rules to follow, maybe a new game to play.

I tugged my news-bag from my shoulders and Kaye said, "Take your clothes off and get under the blanket with me."

This was a new game, no clothes, under blankets. I had heard of this game. It was called "going all the way," but I didn't say so out-loud because my voice had flown away again. She picked up the corner of the sheet when I had struggled out of my clothes, a hard thing to do under the porch. I hadn't undressed in front of my mother for more than two years and I was a bit embarrassed. Looking at her as she held up the sheet, everything else went away, all thought, all sound. I could hear her breathing, I could feel my heart beating, but of everything else there was no sense. There wasn't another soul on this planet.

She was soft and smooth and dark between her legs, all the something I was not. I was rough, scabbed on the knees, and scruffy. I had an instant erection and had difficulty knowing what to do with it when we kissed. We kissed. We talked. We kissed some more. Talked some more, too. She felt indescribably good, like satin and kittens and silk, and how a baby's belly feels. This could not possibly be anything other than heaven. Kaye rolled over and pulled me on top. Suddenly there was a place for my erection.

Oh, my goodness, miraculous, a lightning-bolt good. I thought I would pass out. It dawned on me…this was what the difference was for! This was the why of boys and girls. Everybody should find out about this!

It was over pretty quickly, but Kaye whispered, "Let's kiss some more; you're not heavy. Stay right where you are."

I was planning on staying under this porch a long time. I'd stay until I was old, really, really old. I remember thinking how unlikely her choice of me had been.

As if reading my mind she said, "I've liked you a lot for a long time. I wanted us to do this."

We kissed again, little peppery kisses that stung sweetly, like heat prickles but nice and we made love this time. Getting the hang of this, getting sweaty, becoming more than two experimenters, we formed a small union, floated over a new country discovered for the first time by us. Kaye shuddered. So did I. We held each other a long, long, long time afterwards.

"Orgasm," she whispered.

I didn't know this word and she told me it was just like my ejaculation but for women.

"I am a woman now, you know," Kaye whispered. "I read about that, too."

I wanted to read her book. Maybe she'd swap for mine.

We lay facing one another, half covered, looking, touching hands, hills, valleys, chests, legs, knees, feet, toes, exploring and talking.

We talked about lots of things, if it was okay to do what we'd already done, what our parents would say if they found out.

"R.I.P. Clark, if mine do," I laughed.

"Go live with Grandma in Omaha for me," Kaye giggled.

We spoke of marriage and pregnancy and having babies, where we were going to run away to, all things that needed saying. Kids' talk, meaningless to anyone other than us, but we cemented our lovemaking with words of kindness and care. Being nice, being sweet. Neither of us knew it then, but we would never find this time or this place again, never.

We said a longing "Hi" when we saw one another over the next few days. We waved passionately with big smiles from streets and windows. I am surprised nobody asked me what was wrong with me. I hoped I didn't look as different as I felt and I expected to be accused of something at every turn. Kaye and I met and talked, walked hip to hip, held hands, and touched shoulders with shoulders or faces with fingertips. We were both surprised when walking by the lake a week later.

Kaye started to say, "I really want to do that again, but…"

Just as I was saying, "I don't know if we…"

We laughed together, arms around waists, foreheads together, touching, pleased with ourselves, but sad with spoken decisions. It would be too costly, too chancy to continue, and we couldn't continue. We would always be friends. Forever, we said.

I told Kaye I'd love her forever.

She laughed, "I know."

Another of my paper-route customers in Pointe aux Peaux was a young wife whose husband was in the Air Force and away in a foreign country.

Carolyn Champion had rented a neighborhood house the previous fall when her husband went overseas. To a place called Viet Nam, I later learned from her. I had never heard of the nation, and few others had at the time, but she told me he was there as a military advisor. I didn't know what that meant, either, and she didn't say.

When I saw this nice-looking young woman carting boxes into the house, I asked if she needed help carrying in boxes from the garage and unpacking them. This was sure to be one of those no pay jobs, but she said it was just a few boxes of stuff. Mrs. Champion was a pretty woman, an attribute I was noticing more and more lately.

The house she rented came with a garage, and when I opened the big door, the "few" boxes looked like "many" to me. There was an aisle down one side of the garage but the rest was cardboard from the dirt floor to the rafters. Stack upon stack marked "bedroom" or "dining room" or "dishes" or "clothes" waited for me to cart them into the house. This wasn't going to be a one-day task, but I told her I'd come back after my papers were delivered and we'd take care of them until everything was inside.

I carried and carted, lifted and lugged, and hefted and hauled for three weeks. In between the carrying, there was unwrapping and stacking and putting away and hanging. I opened boxes full of newspaper-swaddled dishes that had to be unwrapped and put away in her kitchen. I hung wall sconces, pictures, and lamps in the small living room. I unrolled rugs and put them down. I unpacked and placed doilies in the strategic places she designated. We put all their clothing away, his and hers, but she took care of her underwear and sent me elsewhere until it was done. We unpacked photo albums and took a break. We looked at her history and I saw her family's faces and childhood pets, found out where she grew up, where she had been, and whom she married.

In the very back of the garage covered by a ragged green tarp was a go-cart. I admit that I sneaked a quick look early on, just as soon as I saw it in fact. I didn't mention I had peeked, didn't like to admit I was pawing through her stuff without asking, but I began to hatch a plan. It was a machine of beauty. It had slick racing tires front and back with two engines on the rear and a racing type steering wheel. It had a roll bar and a headrest on the back of the seat and a seatbelt, something most cars didn't have yet. The engines were wrapped in plastic, but I could see the torpedo shaped mufflers poking out of the coverings. There was a small metal plaque that had the number "9" painted in red. What a piece of work. Wow.

If I could just...No this was something too special. If I would ask...But she wouldn't let me. She might...Yeah, right. Even supposing the unlikely chance my folks approved, there was small hope. I had progressed to using her first name during the unpacking.

"Call me Carolyn," she said. "Mrs. Champion makes me sound old and it takes too long. Call me Carolyn, please."

When Carolyn offered me ten dollars for my help, I did ask. I said I'd exchange the work for a chance to fool around with the cart. What did she think?

"Oh, I don't know, my husband used to race that cart. He built it with his father when he was in high school. He and his father went all over the country, as far as Nevada once to race that cart. Jim (her husband) said it was really fast. I don't even know if it still runs. He hasn't driven it since we got married. Besides, it's not mine, it's his."

"Oh, man...okay. Darn." It was great to dream, to imagine just a little. I bet it would have gone twenty miles an hour. I took the ten dollars, but I sure wanted to drive that cart.

Although I didn't forget about it, I put away most thoughts of ever trying it out.

"Might as well wish in one hand and shit in the other," Walter had whispered to us kids on many occasions. "See which one fills up first."

I enjoyed Walter's sayings lots more than Mom's. His were more evocative. Who'd be dumb enough to poop in their hand? I couldn't stop the wanting, but knew beyond my imagining there was small chance of the doing. I just couldn't quit hankering for a try.

Not a day passed that I didn't lust just a little after the go-cart. It was just sitting there, first calling me softy, but then really hollering. I was surprised nobody else heard it. Everybody else must have been deaf.

The neighborhood communication network in our subdivision was astounding. Adult messaging was infallible and separate, and we kids didn't get to listen. I was unaware of the conversations between my parents and the pretty young housewife, my customer. I heard, from my parents, after school was out that she had written to her husband to ask if I could take his go-cart from the garage and try to get it running. When he wrote back saying yes, Carolyn asked my folks if it was okay before she let me in on the approval. No sense getting my hopes up if my parents didn't want it to happen.

When I was eleven, my parents and I, particularly my father, began a period of barely veiled contempt for one another. I struggled in school and was continually harangued about the poor showing. I was indifferent to church and usually had to be threatened when it came time to attend. My folks were strict regarding my selection of friends, especially after my problems with Jimmy. Most of my friend choices brought frowns to their faces.

Therefore, when Carolyn first asked Mom and Dad, they obviously said no. I'm sure they thought I didn't need any other influences to hasten my ongoing descent. I'm amazed they were still claiming me during the time. My small triumph by school's end may have influenced them to offer a plum or maybe they thought they'd chance other responsibilities.

When I stopped by to collect one week soon into summer vacation, Carolyn invited me in. She had some news if I was still interested. What I heard fascinated me.

Carolyn handed me several sheets of paper and part of a letter. Her husband not only wrote his approval, he included information about the cart and engines.

The go-cart was equipped with:
Twin 10 horsepower McCullough chain saw engines from two-man professional saws
Tillotson carburetors
Engines and carbs modified for racing
Roll bar
Four wheel brakes
Centrifugal clutches

He wrote details about the best probable way for me to get the go-cart running:

1) Take the carburetors apart and clean them.

2) He thought there were gasket kits in his toolbox.

3) I could use his tools but had to replace any I lost.

4) Change the engine oil.

5) Take the top and bottom covers off the engines to clean them well.

He had never met me, but he wrote like he had. Chapter and verse, chapter and verse, he wrote of the rules in order for me to use (and keep using) the go-cart. His wife was to maintain custody and my parents were to hold its use over my head. He added that this go-cart was NOT a toy. He had been timed at more than 80 miles per hour when he and his father were racing. He closed the letter to me by saying again, "It is not a toy! Take care of it."

Of course, I would.

Carolyn talked to me a long time about the cart. Her husband had been older than I was by several years when he drove the cart. She read the pages written to me and was concerned about the speeds it could attain. There were her rules to follow, too, chapter and verse. I would have to be careful.

Of course, I would.

I wanted to push the go-cart over to my house but was told that it would stay at her house. Not only now, but it would sleep there every night, she laughed. If I got it running, I had to promise to bring it back each night.

Of course, I would.

In the garage I spread out the tarp that was used to cover the cart and found all the gaskets her husband wrote about. I took the carburetors apart again and again until I finally got them to stop pouring gas out every time I opened the valve at the tanks, but I eventually succeeded. I worked on the cart every day except of course on Sunday. I had to get special oil from Shorty's gas station for the engines and that took two weeks because Shorty had to order it. I hadn't been far thinking enough to order it before I needed it.

The day finally came when I was ready to start the engines. It took me aHeckofalong time to get both running. I could get one running or the other, but before I could get the second engine started, the first one would stall. That went on forever, at least aHeckofalong time and probably longer. I tried for days to get that cart drivable.

I eventually got both the engines running and they stayed that way, idling a bit rough, but I was sure they would smooth out.

"Even a blind pig can find an acorn," Walter said when we boasted of something.

I thought the carburetors probably had to get worn in or something, fix themselves maybe. I drove about twenty feet down the road before it quit, and it was a job to get it pushed back to the garage. No matter what I tried on the road, I just could not get the engines started again, and I tried aHeckofalot for aHeckofalong time. Carolyn came out and watched me the whole while applauding and jumping up and down when I finally got them both started and laughing just about the whole time after they quit, too.

I gave up. For good.

At least, just until the next morning.

"Out of gas. I don't believe it. What a dolt." I had RunOutofDinkingGas and I said it out loud. I ended up taking the blinking carburetors apart all over again because they were full of dirt and sediment from the bottom of the gas tank.

It was the middle of August already, and I had managed only one very short ride. I didn't even consider it a ride, as short as it had been.

After cleaning the gas tank and getting everything back together, the engines started right up, relatively speaking. I was ready for another trial run. This time I drove off and turned to wave before I rounded the slight bend in the road. And I almost ran over Bobby Girard who had heard the go-cart's engines. He dodged, I swerved, and I missed. Everything was okay now.

I kept having trouble with one of the engines. Every time the engine's speed would fall below a certain point, I had to reach behind me with one hand and close the choke on the carburetor a little to pull more gas into it. As long as the engine speed stayed high, it ran like a striped-ass zebra (one of Walter's better phrases). That was fine with me; I wanted to go fast anyhow. It was a problem to turn corners with the engines racing fast, but I thought that was just a learning-to-drive issue. I made several circuits of the neighborhood that day, and by the second lap I had drawn several onlookers. I had to keep the cart going between twenty-five to thirty miles an hour to keep it from stuttering badly, but I was getting better at the driving part. I "leaned" into corners and curves and left black marks on the paved sharp turns when the back tires skidded.

This cart could go! Kids with blurred faces watched me fly by. Some bigger faces whizzed by too. I was in heaven.

My father had several phone calls after dinner that night. I was speeding in the subdivision. A neighbor's wife complained to him and Dad passed on the objection. The speed limit was fifteen miles per hour. He said for me to obey the laws. That phone call almost ended my go-cart career.

When my father finished his lecture (which took a Hellofalong time), it was my turn. Whenever I was catching it, I had to wait for a turn and I didn't get to determine when the turn started.

I explained to my father the problems I was having with the one engine and that the only reason I was going fast was the problem I was having. I looked contrite, sorrowful in my explanation; just as soon as I got the fuel problem worked out I would certainly pay even more attention to the "law." I was apologetic to the nth degree. It worked, but he told me I better resolve any technical difficulties before I drove it again and not to be speeding around while I did. He said he better not hear about it any more.

I hoped he wouldn't.

Pointe aux Peaux Road turns toward Lake Erie at the opening to the subdivision. At the turn, the road headed straight for almost half a mile before it stopped at the water. I did my tuning runs on that road and stayed out of the subdivision altogether. Perfect.

I used that road for one full week before Mr. Neidermeir flagged me down and said he was sick and tired of hearing the gigantic mosquito buzz going back and forth, back and forth, back and forth in front of his house every morning, noon, and night. I was going to tell him somebody else was doing it at night because it wasn't me, but I recognized this was just an expression and kept my mouth shut. I told him I'd quit driving in the morning and he said I better do more than that because I was driving him crazy.

I was running out of places to practice driving which was really a shame because I managed to get that machine really screaming along that straight stretch of road. The go-cart would cover that piece of road in a rush, probably doing fifty miles an hour before I had to slow it down at either end. I sure didn't want to put it in the lake going one way and going back toward Jones's store there was always the chance of a car.

I knew my folks would be mad if I got run over.

The go-cart needed a place to open up and breathe, a long run of highway.

I continued to creep around the subdivision but could never resolve the fuel issue with one engine. Driving slowly caused me to almost always have one hand behind me to work the choke linkage, so much so in fact that the lever cut my finger repeatedly. Maybe the blood would help. It was still great fun to drive this machine, really a superb piece of work. I took it back to Carolyn's garage every night as instructed and told her how much fun I was having every time I saw her.

What I really wanted to have was more speed.

I drove up and down again in front of Neidermeir's two or three times, not long enough for him to have any serious heartburn, I thought. When I got back to the entrance to the subdivision, I headed out toward Dixie Highway even though I knew it was forbidden territory with the go-cart. I don't know why, but I did. I hadn't planned on driving on the main road but I was. I didn't plan on getting caught.

I was going flat out by the time I got past the first slight curve, just about a mile from the store. The buzz of those engines was so sweet. Despite the carburetor problems I'm sure I was doing at least seventy miles an hour. The wind made my eyes blur, but not so much I couldn't see the car approaching.

As the sheriff's car passed me, he turned on his lights and his siren and I slowed down quickly to turn around. I thought maybe I would blast back past him. I thought maybe I could make a run for it onto a side street and lose him. I then thought I'd better just wait. I pulled into the entranceway to the old beach recreation area and waited. The deputy slammed on his brakes and turned around in the road, smoke spewing from rear tires of that big Ford cruiser, siren telling me he was on his way. While I watched his car approach, I could see my go-cart days coming to an end.

He was mad when he screeched to a halt in front of the go-cart and didn't waste any time with niceties. I was still sitting in the seat when he pulled up but he snatched me to a standing position before his car stopped rocking back and forth.

"Whaddayathinkyerdoin? WhatinHellyathinkyerdoin driving this on the street and going that fast anyhow? You're in it now, son! Where'd you get this go-cart? Does your father know you're out here doing this?

Our next-door neighbor, Mrs. Williams, drove slowly by, saw me, and saw the flashing lights. No doubt the adult news network would soon be hard at work.

I wanted to tell him that my mother would know in about two minutes but all I did was shake my head, no.

Damn, I thought. Neighbors were almost as bad as the police.

He asked me other questions, but they and my answers weren't important. As soon as I passed the sheriff's car, I knew what the outcome would be and I wasn't wrong.

The deputy told me to help him get the go-cart in the trunk of his cruiser, but even together we couldn't muscle it in. It was heavy to begin with and I didn't think it would fit anyway. We did try but had to give up. I had to plead with him to let me drive the go-cart back. He first wanted to shove it in the ditch so no one would bother it, but I really begged. It was going to be bad enough as it was, I couldn't imagine telling Carolyn Champion that her husband's hand-built go-cart was lying in a ditch. The deputy said he would follow me.

He added, "Don't try anything."

I don't know what he thought I would try. I wasn't quite ready to leave home yet. By the time this was over, I might rethink the finding a new place idea but not just then. I might as well take the punishment coming my way. I was sure there would be plenty.

I drove the go-cart right over to Carolyn's house. I surely didn't want to but I did. I drove it right into the garage and covered it up with the tarpaulin. The deputy had his flashing lights on the whole way and those lights must have attracted her attention because by the time I walked out of the garage, she was standing on her porch.

The deputy didn't let me talk. In fact, he told me to "Shut Up."

He told Carolyn how serious this event was, where I had been driving, and my estimated speed to boot. She could have been held responsible if I had been hurt.

Carolyn didn't even talk to me. She didn't holler at me, but I saw the look on her face right away. It was fright and anger and sadness.

That look was the last thing she ever gave me.

She was through with me.

Done.

Forever.

She just listened to the deputy tell of my sinning ways. Carolyn Champion didn't look at me the whole time. She told the deputy there was no chance anybody would be driving that go-cart again for a long while. She still hadn't looked at me but turned and went into her house.

The officer told me to get in.

"No, get in the back," he said when I opened the front passenger door.

With the mesh between the seats I felt like a real criminal.

On the drive to my house, the deputy said, "You know, I'm the same law-man who came out to your house when you ruined those putting greens at the golf course. I told you then I'd be keeping an eye on you. I'm telling you again, right now."

I wanted to tell him right where to look for me for the next several years, but I didn't. I'd be right there in that house, right there in my room with the door closed.

My mouth had been a long time problem, and I wanted no compounding of issues right then. Besides, he was the police, and they always scared me a little. Mom was sitting on the porch when the deputy pulled into the driveway. It had taken Mrs. Williams two minutes to get home, and fifteen seconds after that Mom knew the police had me. Mom made up for the talking that Carolyn Champion withheld. I was grounded; I was on restriction; I was horrid; I knew better; I'd be lucky to even ride a bike for the next year, and yes, was I in trouble.

"Wait till your father gets home. You can go right to your room and stay there. Right Now! Close the door tight."

The deputy talked to my mom a while longer, but I didn't need to hear any more. I would be listening to the chapter and verse of this for a long time. I got a whipping that night and it ended up being the last spanking my father ever gave me. It might have been the worst one I ever got from him. He didn't stop until he wore me and himself slap out. I got restrictions that made my head spin and earned me a grounding so long I almost started to like it. I heard lectures about all the things I'd done wrong and the exact activities I would follow to overcome those tendencies in the future. I heard them over and over, morning, noon, and night. I recalled what Mr. Neidermeir said and agreed with him: repetition could drive you crazy. All in all, I received the most cumulative and creative punishments I ever had.

Their penalties were small on balance.

It was nothing compared to the condemnation when Carolyn wouldn't look at me. I tried for the next six or seven months to make up for my betrayal trying to earn a smile right up until she moved away to be with her husband. She didn't ask me to help her pack. She didn't say good-bye but just called the house and left a message with my mother to cancel the newspaper. I don't believe she ever forgave me, but I didn't fault her in that.

I'd never been sorrier for anything in my life.

My brother Chip and I regularly hunted at the farm whenever we had the opportunity.

Much of our hunting was laced with playing at adventure stories, but frequently we did capture something more than skinned knees, cockleburs, and poison ivy. We were always prepared for bagging game, of course, up to and including lions and tigers and bears, except that fantasy often interfered with being quiet enough to not be heard within a half-mile radius.

Perhaps these hunting expeditions contributed to my love of autumn as a favorite season. The first flutter of shed leaves, the tang of an almost frost, and the crackle of just frozen underbrush bring recollections of those hunts in a rush.

Patch, Chip, and I were as at home in these woods as we were in the marsh behind our own house. We'd explored well past the boundaries of my grandparents' property, climbing over sagging barbed wire or pushing aside rotted fence posts and knew the surrounding fields and the small boggy spots of marsh as if we'd been born there. We knew where the foxes lived, the heavier cover where we might find partridge and pheasant, and had every deer scrubbed tree trunk marked well in our mind's map. We also knew which oak

157

and hickory trees were liable to contain a squirrel's haphazard collection of leaves for a nest.

Grandpa Teddy hated squirrels. On more than one occasion, they'd gotten in through the eaves or soffit vents of the old farm house and each time had caused damage to wiring or insulation and their chittering within the walls kept him awake. He once ripped out an attic wall to remove a nest of baby squirrels. Grandpa referred to them as rats with bushy tails.

My grandpa harbored a special hatred for many of the wild animals that populated the farm. He perpetually waged a war with them as if he believed they were put on earth for the sole purpose of destroying that which he had created. Moles dug tunnels through his gardens and lawn. Deer winter chewed his fruit trees and caused poor fruit production. The pigeons that roosted in the barn and spoiled the hay were shot with an abandon that bordered on mania. Skunks, well, everybody feels very cautious around skunks, and Patch had made sure no one in our family ever forgot how horrendous they smelled. Rabbits, field mice, and chipmunks chewed up his garden, too and got into the corn crib no matter what he did to prevent it.

So, squirrels were considered fair game at any time of the year, but the full leaved trees of summer didn't offer many chances for a clear and sure target. But in the autumn when cold nights had turned the trees to a blaze of color and the ground underneath the trees became littered with paint-like splashes, Chip and I had a chance to add to the stew pot Grandma kept on the stove most fall and winter days.

We'd packed up enough gear to spend the night in the oak grove. Blankets and rubber mats were rolled up and carried across shoulders. We had an axe for firewood, full canteens and I carried Grandpa's old, single shot .22 rifle. We always took along some home baked treat, whether bread or cookies or hard-boiled eggs or cold fried chicken. Although we knew we'd never starve to death during those short camp-outs and so did the grownups, Grandma always insisted we take something to eat with us.

We didn't take Patch with us, though. Grandpa was going to an adjacent farm to butcher pigs for a neighbor, and despite his feigned indifference to my dog, when he was selecting the hogs he liked her at his side. Her presence and strength in a hog pen kept even the most unruly animal submissive. She'd grabbed more than one by the snout to bring it under control, and whenever Grandpa was cutting up pigs, he took her along. Chip and I also knew we'd have a better chance at shooting squirrels if her tail wagging and impatient butt wasn't stirring up the leaves all the time.

At the hindmost of the farm property was a wooded area made up by scores of huge and ancient oaks. It was a treasured and magical spot; about ten acres in size, and it smelled musty, damp and held many kinds of promise for two young boys. Leaf litter carpeted the ground so heavily that it was possible to tread soundlessly through the woods, either as hunters or as a make believe Daniel Boone or Davy Crockett. The acorn bounty of these trees also attracted game, and if we were patient, we were often rewarded with at least the sight of some critter. Of course, sighting one isn't the same as shooting one. We were always encouraged to tell of "the one that got away," or "I only missed it by an inch," but to Chip and me, the best tales were those when it didn't get away.

Although we set out early in the morning right after breakfast and chores, we didn't get to the grove until late afternoon. Our meandering through favorite haunts often combined with our imaginative abilities to become pirates or Indians or explorers often caused us to be late for dinner or dusk when at home. It was virtually the same wherever Chip and I went together. We heard many a siren song and were susceptible to the music every time.

In the fading light of Michigan's winter approaching evening, we made a hasty camp at the outskirts of the oak trees. We'd camped here before and already had a ring of stones for a fire pit. There were scads of leaves to cushion our sleeping spot and there was just enough daylight left for a quick hunt through the woods. If we were lucky, we'd have fresh squirrel for dinner. Even though we had supplies, it somehow always made us feel important that we were able to "bag" our own food on those occasions when we did.

From the scattering of leaves in the grove, we knew there had been plenty of activity. Squirrels in autumn spend most of their time burying or digging up acorns in a frenetic scurry. It's almost as if they suddenly decide to change from their carefree summer grasshopper persona to that of the stock-away-for-winter ant.

We quickly settled our backs against a tree trunk, Chip on one side, me on the other so I could pass him the .22 if he saw a squirrel. Even though Chip had turned six just that past summer, I secretly allowed him to shoot at game whenever we were out together and had been doing so for a year. I figured that as long as Chip enjoyed the advantage of a big brother with complete wilderness savvy, he should be allowed to participate much earlier than I had been able to under the restrictions my parents demanded.

Chip and I had spent a lot of time on his training and aside from the Indian rubs he frequently got when I thought he deserved one, he was a quick learner. We'd spent many summer days and nights on our bellies watching the water's edge or the slope of a hill just to see what came there. We tramped countless trails; those of animals or those we made ourselves. I'd shown him how to discern between the wind's play on a leaf with that of an animal's movements in the reeds. I pointed out the sharp smell of an approaching buck and to listen for the distant chutter of a partridge. I showed him the soft imprints of a raccoon down for an evening drink, the mirrored and inverted commas of a deer's hooves, and the bed where a fawn had lain down for sleep.

He could already tell the difference between fresh scat and old and could tell who pooped it to boot. We found owl's bullets under trees and took them apart to see what he'd been having for dinner. For a six-year-old (I was only ten at the time), he was really good in the woods; he had a great sense of an ability to just "be" even then. He also had "eagle eyes," much to my dismay. My far vision was good, but my near vision missed many things. Once Chip knew what to look for, he was much better at spotting movement in fields or forests than I could ever hope to be.

There were several nests in adjacent oaks and once we'd been quiet for twenty minutes or so, the stillness of the woods returned. A failing forest light makes a magic unlike any other, as if an unseen blanket is spread, and a hush unfolds with the approaching night. A jay cried harshly far off and the trees whispered as a night-wind rustled their leaves. We heard the chatter of the squirrels as they questioned each other about the wisdom of making another nut-gathering run before it got full dark. Chip's hand crept around the tree trunk to tap my arm, a prearranged signal that he'd seen a squirrel.

I checked the safety of the gun, slid the butt toward him and heard the faint rasp as he drew the rifle along the ground. I heard the faint click as he pushed the safety off and a murmur of the stiff blue jean sound as he drew the gun to his knee.

Crack! Even the flat sound of a .22 can be explosively loud in a still woods and the sound startled me.

"I got him! I got him!"

Chip kept up a delighted cackle as he rocketed toward the tree where the squirrel had been seen. It would be a chore for him to keep quiet about his success, but I knew who'd catch the devil if he spilled the beans about this shot. I'd remind him about the Indian rub later. Right now he was too excited to hear anything.

The wild crackle of leaves nearby drew us to the spot where the dying squirrel landed and we waited until its frantic writhing stilled. Chip bent over the limp body but didn't touch it,

"Is it dead?" he asked.

I nudged the body with my foot. It didn't move.

"It looks like you got him."

"I just saw that old squirrel and got him right in my sights. I got him, didn't I, Clark?"

"Yup, you did." I bent down to pick up the squirrel. "Way to go. He's a fat one, too. Let's get 'im skinned and cook 'im. It'll be great for dinner."

By the time we got back to the campsite, it was dark enough to warrant a fire just for the light it would provide, but we needed one to cook, too. I started skinning the squirrel and Chip gathered up some grass, twigs, and firewood. He laid the twigs in the pit and asked me for a match to light the fire. Instead, I smeared his face with some blood from the carcass.

"There you are. You really did it. You are now officially a hunter."

This was Chip's first official "kill." Although he'd shot both a rifle and a .410 shotgun when we'd been in the woods together, this was the first time he'd ever produced anything other than a perforated tin can or a shot-off tree branch. And not many of those either. My folks didn't much hold with "wasting" ammunition on target practice. It cost money, and if you shot you'd better have something to show other than an empty cartridge case.

"You've gotta keep this a secret," I warned him.

I saw him puffing up with pride and indignation.

"Nuh-uh, I'm telling everybody. I shot that squirrel right out of the tree. And he was running real fast, too. I'm telling everybody."

I personally thought the squirrel must have been sitting three feet in front of him, but my brother could be bullheaded, so I kept quiet about any possible luck involved.

"You know what Mom will do if she finds out? I do. You won't be able to ever shoot a gun anymore. Not even when you're really old. She won't let you even look at a gun picture. And me? Well, she'll prob'ly kill me for lettin' you shoot. And Dad will whip my butt. No prob'ly about that part. And Grandpa will, too."

Chip pooched his lower lip at me. I didn't add the story about a little bird perching on his lip and pecking his nose would do any good and let him be.

It didn't take long to finish the skinning, but I had to promise Chip the bushy tail in order for him to agree to keep quiet about the real shooter. After all, it was his by rights. I'd probably have given it to him anyway, but it always helped, especially with Chip, to have a bargaining tool. I rinsed the carcass off with a little water from the canteen and spitted it on a long branch, handed it to Chip and went over to the fire pit. It took only a few minutes to kindle a fire, and we sat in silence while the flames sank into coals suitable for cooking.

The twenty minutes or so it took to cook that squirrel were some of the longest minutes of time I'd ever experienced ranking right up there with the last day of school and the day before Christmas. The smell of roasting meat on an open fire in a darkened woods is unsurpassed by any other. We were salivating so much at the end of the interminable wait we could have put out a forest fire.

Most wild game is unique in taste, and squirrel is no exception. It has an untamed taste, tangy, sharp and strong, and musty, as of the woods where it is found. This flavor is not present in domesticated meat. Squirrel is also sinewy and tough, and each bite must be chewed at least forty-seven times before it can be swallowed without fear of choking, but we didn't care. We were ravenous after the excitement of the hunt and the waiting for it to cook, and its stringiness didn't slow down or diminish our enjoyment. That squirrel may have been the best meal I've ever had.

As the fire died down and we settled ourselves on our blankets,

Chip could talk of nothing else but "his" hunt. He went from scarcely believing it himself to being the best shot in the whole world. I let him ramble on knowing that in a few minutes he'd talk himself to sleep and he did. It didn't take me long to follow and the forest sounds put me to sleep, too.

"Hey, boy!" A hand shook my shoulder roughly.

I sat bolt upright, all sleep vanishing in the new dawn.

"I shot it, Dad! Honest, it was me!" I shouted.

A tall, green clad figure was crouched by my blanket. He had a broad-brimmed hat, a uniform, a shiny silver badge...and a pistol at his side. He'd picked up the .22 from the tree trunk where it had leaned the night away and kept a tight grip on my shoulder as if he thought I'd bolt.

And I would have, like a rabbit.

"What're you boys doing back here?"

Before I could answer, Chip woke up. He saw a big stranger crouched over his older brother, and the man must have appeared to be getting ready for something sinister. Chip did something he was already noted for in our family. He screamed.

"Aaaiiiiiieeee!"

If ever a woodland stillness was rent, pierced, torn asunder, and shattered, it was at that moment. I had a quick thought there'd be no more squirrel hunting for us today.

The game warden dropped the rifle, loosened his grip on my shoulder, and lurched to his feet all in one jerky motion.

"Aaaaaiiiiiiiiiieeeeee!"

Chip was starting to get worked up, really finding his voice.

I began crawling toward Chip and the man reached out to grab my shoulder again.

I looked up at him, "Well, mister, you've scared the dickens out of him."

"Aaaaaaaaiiiiiiiiiiiiiiiieeeeeeeeee!"

I managed to elude the man's still grasping hand, scuttled over to Chip, and put my arm around his shoulders.

"It's okay, Chip. This guy's a game warden like a cop, but for animals. He ain't gonna hurt anybody. It's okay."

It took me several minutes to turn his screams into hiccups and urps, but I finally did. The man hadn't stayed next to us for very long but walked several feet away. I thought he did this to allow Chip to calm down and put a little distance between him and Chip's screams, but when I looked back at the game warden he was busily poking through the dead ashes of the fire with a stick. We'd thrown the bones of last night's dinner into the embers enjoying the spit and sputter as they were consumed by the coals.

"Looks like you boys shot a squirrel," he muttered, as if to himself. "Looks like you boys shot a squirrel."

The second time his words were louder and directed at us.

"Yes, sir, we did. We cooked 'im and ate 'im, too. I was the one who shot it."

I squeezed Chip's neck in an attempt to keep him from blurting out that he'd been doing the shooting. For once he kept quiet, although it was probably because he was still blubbering softly against my chest.

"Well, these leg bones look like they're from a fox squirrel. You boys know you're not supposed to be shooting them? Red squirrels are okay, but these bones belong to a fox squirrel. You boys from the Billings place?"

"Yes, sir, that's my grandparents' farm," I said, not liking the stern tone of the man's voice. I didn't tell him about the bushy tail under my sleeping mat.

"Well, we're gonna have to go up there and get this straightened out, right now. It's against the law to shoot a fox squirrel, and you boys ought to know better if you're back here with a gun. There's a fine if you kill one."

"I gotta pee," Chip whined against my shirt. "Really bad."

"Is it okay with you if my brother goes pee first?" I asked. This guy wasn't talking very nicely. I thought he sounded a little like my father, as if he thought he'd put a scare into us with the tone of his voice. Heck, all we'd done was shoot a squirrel.

Chip went pee, and I rolled up the blankets carefully rolling the distinctive tail out of the warden's sight. I went over and stirred the cold ashes to make sure the fire was completely out, shouldered the bedrolls and reached for my rifle.

"I think I'll just keep this," the warden commanded and lifted the little .22.

I balked at this. I'd been taught about gun safety, had to pass a complete and thorough exam by parents and grandparents, and I wasn't about to be marched out of the woods with my tail tucked between my legs. All we'd done was shoot a squirrel. Everybody knew they were just rats with bushy tails. Ask my grandpa.

"No, you won't, mister. I carried it in here and I'm gonna carry it out. My grandpa said I could use it and you are not the boss of me. It's not even loaded if that's what you're worried about."

The warden must have seen the determined look on my face. I didn't think he'd give it back, but after pulling the bolt back and checking the breech, he slowly handed me the rifle.

"Whatsthematter, you didn't believe me?" I asked. "I said it was empty." I made a great show of re-checking the still open breech as if I might not have believed him.

"Come on, let's get going," he said.

We didn't talk to him on the way back to the farm. I took some great pleasure in his struggles to keep up with Chip and me as we scooted along narrow bramble lined paths or burrowed through locust thickets. As we cleared the hill that looked down on Grandpa's big barn and the orchard, I could see the state-owned car parked at the end of the long driveway. It was the same color green as his uniform, had a big golden Michigan state seal emblazoned on the door and a single red light on the roof.

Grandma was sitting next to his car.

There are few people from my childhood who remain as vivid a memory as my Grandma Phoebe. Despite being told repeatedly how she came from poor beginnings in England and had shipped herself off to Canada to escape a life of domestic servitude when she was twelve, I was pretty sure she was somehow related to the Queen. Grandma had an air about her that beggared description, one which reduced every person in her vicinity to respectful silence and instant obedience. She once caused my dog Patch to quail before her onslaught, and Patch didn't do that for anyone.

I was instantly soothed when I saw her sitting on the bench near the barn. I know now that the rickety seat wasn't really adorned with the gilt and jewels I imagined then.

Chip and I ran ahead of the warden reaching Grandma several moments before he climbed the slope up to the farm. We spent hurried moments telling her how badly he'd frightened us, about the squirrel (but not Chip's part) and how he said we were going to have to pay a fine. It all rushed out so fast I wondered if she kept up, but I needn't have worried. She remained seated while the warden walked up.

"Well, young man, you certainly didn't have the courtesy to stop by my house before you parked your car on my property."

"No, ma'am, it was early and I..." he began.

Grandma cut him off. "And here you are following my grandsons out my woods as if they're criminals."

"Well, ma'am, it looks like they shot..." he tried again.

"A squirrel on my property," Grandma finished his sentence.

"Yes, but it was a fox squirrel, ma'am," he replied. "They're not allowed to shoot..."

"Who gave you permission to come on my farm? I don't recall this being public land, and I certainly don't remember the state of Michigan ever doing anything other than making me pay taxes for it. How dare you come in here like some Hun and tell me what my grandsons have done wrong."

The last sentence wasn't a question. And Grandma used Hun for everyone she didn't like. She still hadn't forgiven Germany for the bombing of England during the Second World War.

"Listen, Mrs. Billings, these boys shot a fox squirrel. That's against the law. I'll need their parents' names and address."

"I wonder if it's against the law to trespass on private property," Grandma stage-whispered to us. "I think it's just about time for you to get back in your car, young man. You've done enough damage here today. I wonder if your superiors would like to know how you made this little boy cry."

Grandma pointed to Chip's dirty and tear-streaked face.

"Mrs. Billings, those boys shot a fox..."

"Where is the proof?" Grandma chopped him at the knees again.

"There are bones in the ashes of their fire," he replied.

"And where would those ashes be?" Grandma rose from the bench and walked up to the warden. He took an involuntary step backwards. I thought he might be getting ready to bow, and I couldn't help the chuckle my imagination forced out.

"Why, back there in your woods."

"Exactly. Those are my woods. I am giving you notice that you do

NOT have permission to go back into my woods. I think you really should leave now."

"I'm gonna go back there and get those..."

"If you like," Grandma imperiously stated. "I'll call the sheriff while you do. That way he can be here with the signed trespassing complaint when you get back. He's a good friend of ours as well as a neighbor."

I think at that moment the warden realized just who he'd been talking to all this time. He slowly turned his head to gaze back at the woods, swiveled it to look at Chip and me standing mutely by Grandma's side, and nodded his head in her direction.

"Ma'am."

We stood there while he started his big green car and as he swung it around to drive out the way he came. He shook his head once or twice, put the car in forward, and drove slowly down the rutted driveway.

"You boys go on up to the house and get in the tub. I'll be up there soon. Grandpa will want breakfast."

Chip and I nodded to Grandma and walked to the house. When we climbed the porch steps, I paused and looked back toward my grandmother.

She was seated on the bench royally surveying the fields of her farm.

Chapter 8
Playing with Fire

Our Independence Day celebrations were celebrated with all the fervor of a Christmas.

We began preparation early, as well, most often in May or June because getting ready took a long time. We not only had plenty of fireworks, but the ones we did have were always a surprise. Not because we had scads of money for "store bought" rockets and roman candles but because we made our own, and we weren't limited to firecrackers that went bang.

My father had a little boy love of pyrotechnics as had his father before him. He was inordinately proud of his creativity in putting together explosive devices. Chip and I were allowed to help from a distance, but we were contributors. We got to pee in a jar so Dad could make a "cake" of gunpowder in order to grind it to varying sizes.

My father would begin accumulating the materials: saltpeter, charcoal and sulfur, as well as finely ground metals to produce different colors. At that time, private fireworks were illegal in Michigan, and my father was always a bit paranoid about making them but he always did. He went to different pharmacies each year for the saltpeter just in case someone was watching him, or he'd buy small amounts instead of making one large purchase. Maybe the illegality of it had something to do with his enthusiasm for making them. I could never figure out why it was against the law. Grandpa

Teddy could and did have dynamite for removing tree stumps on the farm, but fireworks, no, no, no.

Dad started by mixing a formula which he kept secret from us. He would add the urine we'd enthusiastically donated and then he waited for the mixture to dry out. When the time came for sizing the granules, Mom did make us move out to the garage. We had a family story of my grandfather lighting up a long ago kitchen with a huge flash of powder while he was grinding it. Fortunately, the powder was loose in a wooden bowl, so there was no explosion, but the legend concludes with a visual image of Grandpa without eyelashes, eyebrows, and with an instantly receding hairline. Mom was adamant about keeping the stuff outside once it had the proper potential, and few folks would deliberately cross her, Dad included.

In fact, our garage was perfectly suited for fireworks. Separate from the house, it was full of all the materials one could wish for: bundles of newspapers that never quite found their way to the local paper-mill where you got paid a penny a pound, strings, rags, and sticks left over from crashed kites, tin cans washed and with the paper removed, empty toilet and holiday wrapping paper rolls, and scorched rocket launchers from last year's party. We even saved our empty coconut shells and glued them back together for really big bangs. Anything that appeared to be of use for the 4th of July was carefully hoarded during the year between.

Dad would soak the cut strips of newspaper in another secret formula and let them dry as well before he began making the fireworks. Small amounts of the metal shavings would go into each tightly rolled cylinder or tube along with undisclosed measures of carefully sized powder, fuses, and wadding placed at intervals known only to him. He'd cover each completed one with scraps of leftover Christmas paper.

As with other holidays, we often celebrated this one several times. If the 4th fell on a Saturday or Sunday, we were at the Grandma Phoebe's and Grandpa Teddy's farm in Manchester. If it fell during the week, we'd go to the fairgrounds for the county display and then delightedly hold another on the weekend following the holiday. Several family birthdays also fell during the summer and we would mix them all together with July 4th and have one big party. Special "mystery cakes" with money baked in them, homemade ice cream with raspberries and strawberries, my grandma's special baked sloppy-joes, early corn on the cob, and new red potatoes were eaten all day long.

Dad's brightly colored fireworks were displayed on a strictly guarded table for the whole day. It had to be carefully watched, too, because all the cousins and some of the adults (my father especially) couldn't resist the temptation to scare the be-Jesus out of someone with an early explosion.

By the time late afternoon had arrived, the waiting was just as fever-pitch bad as Christmas Eve.

It was never quite dark by the time we started. Somehow, fireworks (especially those which make a loud noise) are best enjoyed in the twilight. It must be the pained expressions on a mother's face, the grinning grimaces of children, or the satisfaction of the fuse lighter's face when the explosives made their loud blasts.

Rockets, pinwheels, and roman candles were always postponed until the fireflies added their glows to the get-togethers. My father and Grandpa Teddy would nail the pinwheels to tree trunks or to the barn and scurry about lighting their long trailing fuses. Roman candles were held by Dad (he was the only one brave or foolish enough) and everyone oohh'ed and aahh'ed whenever the flaming balls would shoot up to enormous heights.

The rockets came last in the progression.

My father could make a great rocket. He'd figured out the proper nozzle size for the rocket so that it could attain maximum height, and his combination of powder size and powdered metals was spectacular.

Sadly, our summer celebrations ultimately stopped having fireworks as a finale.

On the last occasion, one of the rockets didn't go up very far before it turned back toward earth and exploded in the field adjacent to the orchard. It had been a particularly hot and dry summer and the burst of flame when the rocket disintegrated set the field on fire. Before anyone could reach the crash site, much of the field was ablaze and it was headed toward the orchard and garden. The grownups quickly organized a family fire brigade carrying buckets of water from the well and stomping and stamping errant flames. All the adults and big enough kids slapped the flaming brush with wet burlap until Grandpa knew we weren't winning. Everyone was exhausted, blackened, and scorched before he called the fire department.

With a clangor of bells and whoop-whoop of sirens, their fire trucks pulled up along Grossman Road. The big red fire-truck couldn't make the turn between the pillars flanking the farm's driveway and the firemen had to fight this brush fire from the road, a terrible distance. The volunteer firemen quickly formed into a line and directed us to join them. We walked down every spark and ember as we went and with the help of the huge hose got the flames under control, but it took a long time. Several distant neighbors who had seen the red glow in the sky came and lent their help as well. The fire chief gave everybody hell afterward for fooling around with fireworks in such a dry month.

From then on, we went to the county Independence Day displays. They were surely more spectacular. Their brilliant starbursts and loud explosions were superior to anything homemade, but they seemed far away and didn't measure up to our family creations. We might have all had a touch of the fire-bug in us, but after the brushfire, the most we kids got to burn was a sparkler.

Our home was invaded by every wandering tribe imaginable. It wouldn't have surprised me to hear my mother say Attila and the Huns were dropping by for a visit.

My Grandma Grace was a child psychiatrist who counseled troubled youths in Wayne County. That meant that she came in contact everyday with thieves, hoods, and punks, all juvenile delinquents. These kids had managed to do everything the adult felons could think of, but because they were under age, Grandma and the county thought there was a possibility of "turning them around." She and Grandpa Clark had kept this one or that one at their home in Southfield any number of times, and for the most part, she'd proved herself right.

Apparently there was an over-supply of these difficult youths in and around Detroit. Grandma often asked the members of her church to help out in the sheltering part of their rehabilitation by having these families open their "stable" homes to the teenagers. Her program of helping these young criminals was such a success that she asked Mom and Dad to house one of them for some indefinite period.

My grandparents came down for what we thought was just a visit, but their reason was to cajole my folks into taking in one of these kids. Grandma Grace explained how these kids were the products of broken homes, abusive parents, gang influence, and bad choices. She painted such a sad picture that just two minutes into her story, I knew my adoption-inclined, Christian do-right, and sympathetic mother was hooked.

My father, on the other hand, started out with a slight frown when he began to see what was transpiring. His frown turned to scowl, scowl to glower and from there his countenance got much blacker.

"Come on, Dad," my dad said to his father, and turned to Grandma. "Grace, there is no way I'm harboring some wannabe gangster in my house. And that's final."

With that he and my Grandpa Clark both walked out into the yard probably to commiserate with one another of the inevitable outcome of their visit. My father, like the rest of the family, saw that Salvation Possible look on Mom's face.

There was only one thing that was final. Mom would decide. Once she took on that beatific smile, Satan and all his imps, let alone some poor teen, didn't have any other than an assured place in a heavenly kingdom. There'd be less room, less food, less privacy and more turmoil in the house, but that didn't deter my mom. She knew there was always plenty of room in God's house and as long as she could find a place to lay down some blankets, her home was as good as His. If Jesus couldn't save this poor lost child, my mom could.

The farewells between my dad and Grandma Grace were pretty frosty. In fact, after my grandparents left, the glares which passed between Dad and the entire universe were cold enough to bring on another Ice Age. My mother retreated into her usual sanctuary singing the hymns, "Shall We Gather at the River," "Ye Who are Weary Come Home," and "Jesus Loves the Little Children of the World." We four kids made sure there was an empty hole in our belts, started thinking of places to hide our personal treasures, and began secretly hoping Grandma would get lost or kidnapped before she brought this kid to our house.

Grandma didn't waste any time bringing Doug to our door; she brought him down to us the very next day probably before anyone's Christian fervor had a chance to die away. He was lank and lean, slouched at the shoulder, had brown, slicked-back hair, long sideburns, and he didn't make eye contact with any of us. He was already big enough to be considered a man by us kids because of the dark stubble on his face which he was shaving already. He had one beat up suitcase and a pillowcase stuffed with clothing. My mother gave him a hug that he accepted but didn't return.

"Hello, Douglas, these are my children," Mom said proudly. "This is Carole, who's fourteen; Clark, who's ten; Chip is six, and little Peg is four," pointing to us in turn. "Let's all go in here and sit down. My husband will be home later. He's working."

We all dutifully trooped into the living room where the Greene family (less my at work father) proceeded to "make poor Doug feel at home" and give him the third degree at the same time. Grandma started extolling his virtues; before getting in trouble, Doug had been a good student, attended church, and played baseball at his school. We didn't find out until later that all these "hads" had happened at least ten years ago when he was in grade school.

The evening before in a kid's only conference, we Greene kids had decided this kid was probably a killer, or at the very least had tried to kill someone. Our first sight confirmed and fed our imagination. He had "LOVE" and HATE" tattooed across his knuckles and "JUDY" tattooed in blue ink on one forearm, something only real hoods and sailors had in the 1950s.

Doug was nineteen, taller than my father, wore dungarees rolled up high to show scuffed and dirty engineer's boots, and limited his responses to "Yes, ma'am" and "No, ma'am" the whole time he sat on the couch. Although I secretly thought he was pretty cool, I didn't dare show any admiration for this obvious sign of past sins. I also thought he was scary.

Mom told us kids to make Doug at home, show him where he'd sleep, and for Chip and me to show him around the neighborhood. Grandma was going to get back to her office right away. The bad kids were lined up at her door.

Despite his silence, Doug was polite and guardedly friendly while we showed him around the house. We put it off to shyness or his feeling out of place in such a God-wholesome and superior situation. Carole had already decided he was cute, and that once he was less a stranger, he would fall in love with her. Why, how great we all felt knowing that our sacrifices were going to save this poor boy from the fiery flames of Hell! I called to Patch and we started walking with Doug down to the lake, convinced that once he saw the wonderful things our family and neighborhood had to offer, he'd be that much closer to God.

He didn't talk to us on the way down to the beach. Chip and I were just a little wary of this newcomer. Even at age nine, I could tell Doug was downright indifferent to the wonders of Lake Erie. He gazed about, but his face remained impassive. Patch had been secretly sniffing him while we walked and gave him a thorough going over once we stopped. He shoved Patch's head away, knelt, pulled up one pant leg and removed a long clasp knife from his boot. He began to clean his fingernails with the knife and spat, "You need to keep that mangy dog away from me, ya hear? So whadda'ya punks do around here for fun?"

"We can skip stones," I said, putting my hand on Patch's neck. "Or we can look for driftwood. My mom always likes us to bring home driftwood for her garden. And my dog's not mangy."

"I don't mean any of that chicken-shit stuff. Where can I get some smokes or a beer?"

"We don't drink beer in our house," I replied. I tried to sound Holy.

Although my father smoked a pipe and cigarettes, my mother barely tolerated it. She was always giving him the devil for smoking and I was surprised he stood up to the relentless pressure. Amazingly, the collision of my father's bulldog stubbornness and my mother's eroding persistency hadn't ever produced much more than several days silence between them. My dad always had a pack of Lucky Strikes in his pocket. But beer and liquor were definitely out at our house. Baptists use grape juice for their communion services but only after they check it to see that not one bubble of fermentation has begun. Doug had about as much chance for beer around us as he did for forming us kids into gang members.

Doug continued to inspect Chip and me almost as if he expected us to produce a beer bottle from under our clothes. I just shrugged my shoulders not knowing what to say to his interrogation. He uttered a sharp sneer and reached into his boot again and withdrew a crumpled pack of cigarettes.

"You twerps don't even think about seeing these smokes. You got that?"

Our heads alternately nodded and shook from side to side not knowing which we were supposed to respond to. It must have been correct because Doug continued to kneel while he carefully kept the cigarette tucked into one side of his mouth. As soon as he finished and flicked the butt away, he turned and beckoned to us.

"Come on, you punks. I'm hungry. You think your old lady's got any food around that crummy house?"

I wondered who the old lady was, but grabbed Chip by the shirtsleeve and pulled him along beside me. I didn't like the way Doug talked about anything so far.

He did all of the talking on the way home.

"You little turds call me 'D' when your folks ain't around, none of that Doug or Douglas crap. You don't say anything about what I do or where I go. You don't give me any crap either. I'll play this stupid bein' rehabilitated game and be all polite while your folks are around, but you guys don't get to give me any of this Holy Christian shit. I ain't interested. I heard it all before. Ya got it?"

Trying to bring the conversation back into something normal, I asked him, "What grade are you in?"

"I got kicked out a long time ago. School's for punks like you two. Those dumb-ass teachers don't know anything. My old man taught me all I need to know. Just as soon as things get settled back in Detroit, I'm goin' back."

"How come you don't stay with your daddy? Where's he at?" I asked.

Doug stopped in the road and whirled to face us, his hands on his hips. He stabbed one finger at Chip and me, his hand moving back and forth to impale us both. I noticed his fingernails were dirty and chewed ragged, and thought my mom would fix that too.

"He moves around a lot. And besides, you don't ask me nuthin'. I'll tell you what I want you to know. My old man's none of your friggin' business. Ya got it?"

Chip blurted, "Where's your momma?"

He lunged at Chip and grabbed his shirt front. "I said you don't ask…"

He didn't finish the sentence. Patch growled deep in her chest and advanced stiff legged toward him. Chip began to whimper and Patch crouched, her front paws extended. I'd seen her offensive posture before and knew what would follow. I'd give Doug a chance although I was pretty sure he didn't deserve one.

"You'd better let him go," I warned. "Patch doesn't like it when anybody bothers us."

"Listen, you shit ass! You keep that friggin' dog away from me. I'll kill it."

I grabbed Patch but didn't call her off attention.

"You better turn loose of my brother. I can't call her off once she gets started and if she does, you sure aren't gonna get to that stupid knife quick enough if that's what you're thinkin'. Let him go."

Doug slowly let Chip's shirt fall from his hand and never took his eyes off Patch. I kept her close by my leg feeling her tremble against my pants. We would have to declare some sort of truce if we were ever going to get to the safety of the house.

"You'd better not be grabbin' anybody when my dog is around. I'll keep Patch away from you, but you'd better be nice to us."

Doug didn't say anything but turned toward our house and stalked away. Once we walked through the door, his demeanor magically changed. He smiled while he told my mother what a nice time he had at the lake and how much he would enjoy his time with us. As soon as Mom turned to make him some lunch, he stared at us daring us to contradict his story.

We didn't.

During the next few days, we discovered how good Doug was at hovering around us. He didn't take much part on our conversations, but he seemed to be there whenever we had one. His presence put a definite damper on our talks. At the dinner table, he was a picture of courtesy, smiling while he ate, asking Mom and Dad all the right questions. He joked with Carole and Peg, made small talk (and huge lies, I thought) about what he'd do when he was restored to the good graces of the authorities in Wayne County. He appeared attentive during nightly devotions, smiling when my mother read, "And every knee shall bow."

He seemed to agree with all the family rules and paid attention to Mom and Dad while they listed acceptable behaviors. These same rules had been plaguing me for years, and I still had trouble keeping up with their changing with the circumstance. I was amazed that he seemed to take them in so quickly.

I secretly noticed he didn't close his eyes during the prayers. While everybody's eyes were shut in devotion, Doug continually wore a small sneer. It never occurred to me that the discovery meant I was doing my own furtive observations.

Doug quickly settled into our family routines at least in my parents' eyes. He was polite, even fawning, to my mother and always seemed to be there whenever she needed some small chore done. He paid particular attention to my father when he came home from work, asking how the day had gone, commiserating with him about the hardships in the Ford factory. Their acceptance of him changed from slightly distant to welcoming him like a prodigal son.

To us kids Doug was surly, aloof, and downright malicious when my folks weren't in the room. Doug bullied Chip and me just short of violence and treated Carole and Peg as if they were expected to attend to his every wish. He was able to change his demeanor lightning quick from one of fondness to one that was distinctly abhorrent. We all had a hard time understanding our parents' automatic trust and affection, but *we* knew what Doug was made of. It was meanness and cruelty, but his behavior did band us kids into a solid defense.

Doug wasn't able to continually torment us because Patch was usually there. The one episode of her loyalty and protection of Chip had certainly given him an example of what she would do. Patch was a formidable and awesome presence. Even a city boy could figure out her coiled and waiting strength. He must have known with an animal cunning all his own that it wouldn't do to cause Patch to act. However, Patch couldn't be with us all every minute. We began devising a strategy to confound and torment Doug and help our folks see the cruel person he really was.

Doug must have brought money of his own when he came to our house or found a way to get it on his own. He sure didn't get any from my folks. They seldom had enough for our own family needs. But Doug still had enough to buy cigarettes for whenever he was away from our house; he kept one dangling from the corner of his mouth whenever possible. I'd seen him hooking a few of my father's when Dad left a pack lying about, but he also kept his own in his engineer boots.

He'd managed to meet a few of our subdivision's resident hoods: Tory and Larry, Ted and Wayne, pairs of brothers whose sole purpose in life seemed to be scaring the be'jesus out of younger kids. "Birds of a feather," Grandpa Teddy would have said. In the 50s, many teens wanted to be a version of James Dean or Marlon Brando; collars up on unbuttoned shirts, dirty dungarees, perpetual sneers and greasy hair. Doug fit right in.

Chip and I stealthily learned their haunts: Orleans' Store where they could strut and spit to their heart's content, and at the sandy beach where they cussed every unattended person who was smaller than they were. We were great at sneaking.

We spied on Doug every chance we got, but oddly didn't share the results with our parents. It seems odd because we all delighted in telling on one another, but it may have had something to do with Doug's well-concealed treatment of us as if we knew we'd have to get irrefutable proof of his transgressions. In just a short time, we knew more bad things about Doug than he knew about himself.

Tory and Larry were old enough to buy beer. They were said to have jobs. No one knew where, but they always seemed to have money. In addition, at Orleans' Store, age was never much of a deterrent to buying forbidden goods. If you had money in your pocket, Mr. Orleans would be happy to sell you something. He had men's (naked women) magazines and condoms (although we only knew them by their proper name, rubbers) right out in plain sight on his shelves, and even little kids could buy cigarettes. The Orleans family lived across the street from their store. My mother referred to Mr. Orleans as low.

His store was a popular place for those people who staggered when they walked, had red noses and rheumy eyes, and were "on the dole" for one reason or another. You could see someone drunk though the dirty store windows almost any time of the day and every second when it was dark. Mr. Orleans had a brother who bet on the horses, played poker for money, and owned a bar. His brother's tavern was across the street from the store and had much the same reputation, although what you could buy was less specific and therefore, more tantalizing. The Greene kids were definitely NOT allowed to go into Orleans' store. We weren't even allowed to look at the tavern.

Mom's law stated that if Jones' Market, our approved country store, didn't have it, we'd live without it until they did.

But Doug took to Orleans' store just as if he were part owner. He and his buddies could be seen outside the store casually inspecting the cars driving by or cat-calling the many tourists that came for the summer. He and his friends made up a pretty formidable group and they soon established themselves among the resident kids as a gang to be avoided. How Doug managed to escape my parents' (especially Mom's) discovering gaze was beyond me. Mom, especially, could tell with a supernatural ability when one of her own brood was even *thinking* about some ill begotten deed. Then again, Doug was good at staying under her radar.

Chip and I, along with some special help from Carole, began to help my parents see the real Doug who was staying with us.

As a stay-at-home mother (almost every mom was in those days), mine had a schedule for every housework chore. Mondays and Thursdays were washing days, Tuesdays were devoted to mending and darning an active family's previous week of destruction and wear. Wednesdays Mom spent preparing for that night's Prayer Meeting and the following Sunday's church. Fridays were spent food shopping and strategizing just how on earth she was going to make my father's paycheck stretch far enough for food, school supplies, second hand clothing, and pay the rest of the household bills. Saturdays were cleaning day just in case Pastor came for dinner. Of course, all this was interspersed with corralling her bunch into something faintly resembling a normal family.

Washing days began with Mom insisting that her family gather up their dirty clothes, sort them, and bring them out to the porch where our washer and dryer were located. Each child was responsible for their own clothes, and if we didn't do a good job and left some article behind, we could be sure we'd have to wear something dirty to school on at least one day. With the grouping came emptying pockets, turning pockets inside out, and piling according to color. My mother insisted on the pants pockets task. She'd been more than surprised, and we'd been devastated to learn that our favorite turtle or a special spider had gone through the wash. We were often beset with a litany of which one we didn't empty or turn out and wished to avoid her accusing looks. But more important still, it didn't take Chip and me long to learn that washing meant certain death for anything left in a pocket.

Mom often got after my father for the tobacco remnants which accumulated in his shirt pockets.

With surprising cunning Chip and I figured Mom would really pester Doug if there was evidence enough. Doug wasn't supposed to be smoking at all. Mom had already challenged Doug regarding the smell of cigarettes on his person and clothing, but thus far he'd been able to blame the other hoodlums he associated with. Despite having to listen to a sermon about running around with the wrong sort of boys, he'd been able to allay my mother's suspicions.

Carole, Chip and I began by picking up one of my father's cigarette butts and pulling a few strands of tobacco out of it. After Doug had added his laundry to the piles of dirty clothes, we put the shreds into his shirt or pants pocket. We accomplished two things this way: planting incriminating evidence and making sure he got sanctioned for not turning his pockets out. Mom challenged him the very same day we did it and right at the dinner table.

Doug was confused at first and insisted one of his buddies must have done it for a joke. Then he made up a story about picking up a pack of somebody's cigarettes after it had fallen unnoticed and putting it in his pocket. He claimed he gave it back to the unnamed person as soon as he could.

I could see the suspicion growing in my parents' eyes. Hot Ziggity!

"Which one was it, Doug?" my father questioned.

"Huh?"

"Which one was it; a prank or you picked a pack up off the ground?"

I saw the indecision and wonder on Doug's face. He was getting the same third degree we did when parental radar went on alert.

"We've told you we won't allow you to smoke while you're here. You're too young and it's a disgusting and nasty habit." Mom made sure she looked piercingly at Doug and my father while she spoke.

"Dorothee, don't start on me," Dad cautioned. "She's right about you, though, Doug. If you're going to stay in my house, you're going to live by my rules. No smoking. All right?"

Everybody in this house knew who really made up the rules. It was a Mom Rule. I thought she was wasting her breath on both of them.

Doug nodded in agreement, but I thought I still saw confusion worrying his eyes.

The three of us did the same thing the next washing day and the next. This incrimination worked every time. Mom gave him the devil. His excuses grew more outlandish and more feeble. He soon gave up trying to invent plausible explanations and retreated into silence.

We kids were delighted when Doug got put on restriction: keep away from those "bad" influences, stay away from the beach. In other words...GROUNDED! We kept our smirks hidden. *Now* he was finding out about life at the Greene house.

Several days later Chip and I were playing outside with some frogs we'd captured in a deep and water filled ditch behind our house. We kept them in an indoor and outdoor terrarium we'd scrounged from somewhere. We usually played with them several days or weeks, feeding them bugs and flies we'd caught for their food. They were always released, either by us or by my mother when she noticed our flagging interest. We knew that if we let them go there'd be more when a "frogging urge" came upon us.

Chip and I didn't notice Doug walk up behind us until he'd reached over our shoulder and grabbed one of the frogs. We whirled to face him.

"I don't know what you two are up to, but I know you did it. I keep my cigarettes in my boot. There ain't no way that tobacco got in my pockets by accident. Whatever you're tryin' to do, it'd better stop." He held the frog in front of my face and squeezed until it eyes bugged out. "This can happen to you two little shits. I ain't screwing around." He squeezed the frog harder and I heard it go croak-squish-pop, a slurpy wet sound. Doug threw the dead frog on the ground in contempt. He grabbed the back of my neck, reached down, and wiped his hand on my face taking his time.

"If you two little ass-holes wanna get hurt, just keep it up."

Doug spat on the ground, turned and stalked away without another word.

Chip and I were ashen, terrified, speechless. We should have been frightened enough to just quit any more attempts at getting Doug in trouble. We probably would have been scared enough if I hadn't been hearing sayings of "don't let anybody push you off your own front porch," and "a man's home is his castle," my whole life. Instead we chose to step up the attack, but why we did I couldn't have told you.

What we needed was an example of a more severe sin (Baptists do think some are worse than others) something which would get Doug in real trouble and convince my mother there was no hope.

It was possible for kids in the 1950s to amass a small fortune with cast off bottles. Beer bottles. Pop bottles. Any bottle found in ditch or field was worth two whole cents at the corner store. Although Mr. Jones would look at us askance when we brought in beer bottles, he always paid up. Chip and I already spent every minute of our rambles with half an eye peeled for some tossed away remnant. There were days when we got as much as thirty cents with our collection of brown or clear glass. In every empty one there was always a dribble or two left over. We started collecting that, too.

While we were planning, Doug was re-ingratiating himself with my folks. He soon was "back in the fold," or so Mom thought. His participation in our never-ending church attendance picked up, and he was soon a "darling" there as well. We'd stopped salting his clothing with tobacco, and he let up on his intimidating tactics but not by much. Although he was full of smiles and pleasant looks for my folks, for us he kept dark looks and frowns at the ready.

There was no further mention of restrictions for Doug although he was frequently warned about the company he kept. These words meant little to Doug, and he was soon spending most of his time with Tory and Larry again. We'd seen them speeding around in Larry's old Ford whooping it up and tossing their discarded bottles out of the windows. They never knew how they'd contributed to the growing supply of stale beer we were accumulating in an old Mason jar. They were also making us two cents richer every time they threw one away.

When Doug came to stay with us, my folks had rearranged the sleeping arrangements for the family. Carole's attic bedroom was transferred to Doug so that he might have a place of his own, a sense of personal ownership to lessen his feeling of being an intruder.

Carole and Phoebe would sleep together in Peg's tiny walk through bedroom that connected to my parents' room. Mom must have thought, when all was said and done, that it was only a short time before Doug was a fully reformed, born again, loving-God Christian. She was convinced it wouldn't be long before he went back to spread the word in his old neighborhood.

At the outset, my sister Carole put up quite a fuss about being displaced. She used her room as a retreat when her two little brothers got to be too much (this was about two minutes after she came into the same room we were in), or when Mom was giving her the dickens for being sassy (the same amount of time in any company). Her fuming didn't do any good. Once a decision was made in our house, it was the same as being etched in stone tablets.

Her attic bedroom had pitched ceilings, a pull-down, wooden fold-up ladder that screeched horribly when it was opened and windows at either end of the room. No one could go up or down without the whole family knowing it. I figured they also put Doug up there so they could keep tabs on him at night.

Several nights later the entire family was snatched from their beds by a heavy pounding on the front door. Mom and Dad slept in the back room, so I got there first. A big sheriff's deputy was standing on the porch. He had Doug by the collar.

"This kid live here?" he demanded.

Before I could say no, my father pulled me away from the door and asked what the dickens was going on.

"Mr. Greene. Sorry to get you up at two o'clock in the morning. This kid…Doug…said he's staying here with you. He and two other punks got caught breaking in to Orleans' Store."

"I told you I wasn't breaking into nothing." Doug looked defiant.

"Yeah," the officer replied. "And I'm *almost* sure that's the truth. Anyway, Mr. Greene, Eddie Orleans caught them at it and a scuffle broke out. This kid cut him with a knife. You ever see him with this?" The deputy held out Doug's big knife.

My father shook his head no.

"Those other two punks say the same thing," the deputy continued. "And Eddie had been drinking."

That knife had already indelibly imprinted on my nine-year-old brain. My little kindergarten aged brother Chip, who was peeking around my side, would have said the same thing. Doug had waved it in front of our faces often enough. I'd have known it anywhere. I silently exulted about his capture but didn't tell about what I knew of his knife. I was too scared to say anything. There was no way anybody would believe Doug's story anyway.

"That guy just came at us," Doug insisted. "*He* had the knife, I told you! All we were doin' was walkin' down the road. I took it away from him and he got cut by accident. All's I was doin' was protecting myself. He had'ta been drinkin' or something."

We kids were hurriedly chased back to our beds by Mom, but Chip and I listened at the bedroom door. Although the conversation went on for a long time, all we could hear was the rise and fall buzzing of angry voices. I heard the deputy's car pull out of the driveway and Chip, and I talked ourselves to sleep congratulating ourselves and sure in the knowledge that Doug was in gigantic trouble. No more Doug! Why, he'd probably get the gas chamber! He was gone for sure!

The next morning I wandered into the kitchen rubbing the sleep from my eyes and happy that we'd only have six for breakfast. I heard voices coming from our dining room.

"Mr. and Mrs. Greene, I'd never do anything like that. I just couldn't sleep last night, so I went out through that back window. Honest to God, all we were doin' was walkin' back here so I could go to bed. That guy came out of nowhere actin' crazy. I tell you, he was drunk!"

I stared open-mouthed. Doug, my mother, and my father were sitting at the table, drinking coffee and having a "parent to son" conversation! I couldn't believe it!

"How come he's here?" I blurted out still not quite believing my eyes.

"Doug says he was wrong to sneak out last night, but that none of the rest was his fault. I'm going to give him the benefit of the doubt. He's promised to stay away from the store." My father looked forgiving. "You know how Eddie Orleans is. He probably was drunk. The deputy turned Doug over to us."

"We've all prayed this morning, Clark. And Doug has just re-dedicated himself to the Lord," my mother chimed in. "He's seen the error of sneaking out last night and wants to do better. I think he will." She reached over to pat Doug's arm.

Man...this was a turn of events, I thought. Every time one of us was even suspected of doing something wrong, we were considered guilty until proven innocent. Mom spouted "My God is an angry God!" at us when we were approaching anything remotely sinful. And when we were at fault, we might have to wait until the last trumpet blew before forgiveness was bestowed. My folks believed in punishment for sins, real and imagined, and the quicker the better. Mr. Orleans got cut with a knife last night, for Pete's sake! How on earth was this kid getting off scot free?

Breakfast that morning was quiet while Mom and Dad told us Doug's version of the story again. Every time Doug caught my eye, I saw a warning written just as plain as day in his. He couldn't have made it any more plain if he'd shouted "Keep your mouth shut!"

If anything, after that episode, Doug became more of a thorn in our sides. He knew he'd frightened us enough that we'd remain silent no matter what. He never had much patience with us and had less afterward. Chip and I avoided him at all opportunities and the only contact we had was during meals or church. While he was back into the graces of Mom and Dad, we were on guard every second.

Several days passed. Doug appeared to be living up to my folk's expectations. One afternoon I heard Patch yelp and ran into the back yard. Patch was growling at Doug and straining at the end of her tether.

"That damn dog is always smelling my crotch!" Doug snarled with his hands clenched into fists.

"What'd you do to my dog?" I yelled.

"I kicked her, that scroungy-ass mutt. I'll do more'n that if she don't keep her nose away from me."

"I'll sic her on you!" I shrieked. "Then we'll see who you're kicking. You don't get to kick my dog!"

The yells brought my mother out the back door.

"What are you hollering about, Clark?"

"He just kicked my dog!" I was still screaming. "He kicked Patch, Mom!"

"She was gonna bite me, Mrs. Greene. She *tried* to bite me," Doug complained.

"I've never known Patch to do that. Maybe you just startled her, Doug. But we don't kick animals around here."

"Jeeze, Mrs. Greene," he said. "Maybe I did startle her. I'm not used to dogs and I guess I just overreacted. I'm sorry. It won't happen again."

"There, son, Doug said he was sorry. Why don't you take Chip and Patch down to the lake? Doug, would you help me with the laundry, please."

"Sure," Doug smiled.

"Doug," Mom continued. "We don't say Jeeze in this house. It's almost cussing."

I untied Patch, but instead of going to the lake, I retrieved the mason jar of stale beer from our hiding place under some boards my father kept behind the garage. Chip and I hid on the other side of the garage where we couldn't be seen from the house. Every once in a while I peeked around the corner. When I saw Doug bring his clothes down from his bedroom, I waited until he'd gone into another part of the house. I crept through the front door hoping Mom's bells wouldn't sound my entry. When I got to the washing machine, I sprinkled Doug's clothes with the beer, made a circuit through the dining room and escaped through the back door. Nobody was in sight. I was careful not to let the door bang shut.

I ran around the garage, grabbed Chip, and we ran toward the beach. We laughed the whole way, but we didn't stay long. The more I thought about the likely scenario, the more I wanted to see it. We got back to the house just in time to see Doug hurl himself through the front door and stalk off down the road.

"Hi, Mom, we're back," I innocently greeted. "Where's Doug going?"

"Smell this, son." Mom thrust one of Doug's shirts under my nose. "What does that smell like to you?"

"I dunno…is that beer?"

"It certainly is. It's all over his clothes. I don't know why I didn't smell this stink before now. And Doug stood right there and lied about it. He said you'd done it although he didn't know how. He swore he gave up on any drinking when he got saved again. I told him not lying about anybody was part of being saved. He still claimed you two were to blame. He's gone for a walk to cool off."

"Me, Mom? I don't know why Doug would lie about me." I pictured a halo hovering above me. "How could I get it? Besides, I know how bad it is to drink beer."

"That boy is troubled. It's bad enough him drinking without trying to drag you into it. We'll have to talk about this when your father gets home. You two and Patch get back down to the lake and play. If you see Doug, tell him to come back home. Be home in time for supper."

If I saw Doug, we were going to run.

We played at the lake for a long time, all the while wondering if Doug was going to be able to talk his way out of this one and hoping not. We wandered over to the base-ball field and waited until we saw Dad's car pull into the driveway before we headed toward home. We could hear the hollering from across the street as we walked up. The whole house was in a rapid boil by the time we got there.

The screaming accusations that flew around the living room could have beheaded someone. Chip and I scrunched down low just in case and scurried to our bedroom. Our door did not muffle the sounds and feelings much. From my father's roars particularly, I thought he might swell up enough to explode.

"Those two are sneaks and liars!" Doug screeched.

"Where'd you get the beer?" Dad countered.

"How could you do this?" Mom implored.

"I told you, those two godda..."

The sound of my mother's hand against Doug's face cut his sentence short.

"We do not take the Lord's name in vain in this house. Ever! You can go to your room, Doug. Right now."

Dinner was strained that night. Everybody wanted to talk about Doug, but none of us kids was brave enough to start the conversation. We could hear him walking around in the upstairs bedroom. I did not feel sorry about him not getting supper. I did not feel sorry for getting him in trouble. I salved my conscience with the thought that he'd already been in trouble and probably would be again. I also thought I might even have been doing the Lord's work by exposing his many sins.

In the morning Doug was gone. With him went Mom's haircutting money, Dad's coin collection and several sterling silver spoons my mother kept polished and on display. We called Grandma to report him missing and the theft. She said she was sure he'd turn up.

I hoped not.

After breakfast Mom read a passage from her Bible: "Father, forgive them, for they know not what they do."

I'd have picked, "As ye sow, so shall ye reap."

Peck Tooman was a shyster.

Today we might call him an entrepreneur, but then we knew him as a guy who was always trying to find an easy way to make money. Easy to Peck meant someone else doing the work.

The Tooman's home happened to have a pear tree growing in the back yard. One summer the tree developed a branch that appeared to be a replica of Christ's Cross. There was a small write-up in the Monroe Evening News entitled, "A Sign of Christ's Return?" After the article ran in the paper, cars lined up on their street to see the miraculous tree. While others might have seen a demonstration of faith, Mr. Tooman saw opportunity. He quickly erected a screen in front of the small tree and tried to charge a quarter to everyone who wanted to see it. He got away with it for a few days until another article accused him of exploiting the heavenly occurrence. The screen came down the day following the scathing remarks, but I heard Mr. Tooman grumble about it when we were visiting.

Our families were friends; they had two boys, Bob and Tommy, about the same age respectively, as Carole and me. My father and Peck had worked together for a time at Ford Motor Company before Mr. Tooman got fed up with hard work. He was now constantly going hither and yon with a better mousetrap or a car battery restorer or some such rot. Peck also had a gift of gab. To my family's financial dismay, he often convinced my father he'd discovered the secrets of alchemy or other get rich quick schemes; his pot of gold was always just around the next bend in the road.

One summer Peck was convinced that onion farming was the certain and sure road to riches. He was going to corner the market of Michigan onions, make a bundle of money, and sit back forever and ever as he rightfully should, enjoying the fruits of someone's labor.

Peck rented fifty acres from a farmer in Chelsea, Michigan. Part of his plan for farming was finding a group of peons who would do the work. Bob, Tommy, and I qualified.

Chelsea was an hour and a half drive from our homes, so we boys would camp out while we worked the field. No sense in wasting gas with a lot of unnecessary trips, especially, with the omniscient Peck to lay out the terms of our servitude. In addition to the terms he gave us, my mother had a plethora of others designed especially for me. Planting would be supervised by Peck, but after that we would be on our own. Someone would check on us three boys, but for the most part we'd be left untended for days at a time. Peck also emphasized the great responsibility we were being entrusted with, becoming real providers for our respective families. He went on long enough about this prospective life changing opportunity as if he were doing us a great favor. He might have thought he was, but his two boys didn't seem to think so.

On the way to Chelsea, sitting in the back seat, Bob whispered that his father would disappear just as soon as he tired of the enterprise. He also said "tired" would take about an hour. Mr. Tooman was pretty vague about the pay we'd get, too, mentioning only that we'd be pleased with all the money we'd make.

We drove well off the highway turning on a dirt and gravel road, past a big farm house, and finally on to an almost invisible farm lane. The field was well away from the farmer's house, adjacent to a sluggish creek. Despite being distant from the farmhouse, we could immediately smell the pigs that obviously inhabited the farm. The prepared ground was bordered by enough scrub woods and trees to provide firewood for our campout with a grassy, rutted lane on one side for access.

During our on-site pep talk, Peck emphasized the requirement of staying out of the farmer's hair unless one of us was bleeding to death and even then to think about it twice.

Peck had purchased an old army surplus tent smelling of must and dust, a battered aluminum cooler for the few perishable foodstuffs we'd have, and some canvas covered canteens. We were allowed to bring a sleeping bag (which I didn't have and substituted blankets for), two changes of clothing, one for wearing while the other dried from its washing in the creek. We were not allowed to bring ball gloves or anything else that might distract us from the "grownup" work we were supposed to do.

Planting onion sets over a fifty acre field by hand is no small task. About four hundred yards wide, the field stretched lengthwise before us seemingly to infinity. Even though the field had been plowed and prepared by the farmer before we got there, Peck insisted that we rake smooth each designated row. Prepared by tractor didn't suit Peck, so we raked, broke dirt clods, and raked again until the undulating ground began to look as smooth as tanned leather.

Peck started out showing us how to do the job properly insisting we follow his great wisdom in the secret science of raking. He was vigorous...at first. Feet properly spread, he'd rake with the tines and twirl the rake over and use the flat bar to level the dirt. I was surprised...Before his expert advice, I was under the impression that garden work was just sweat equity type of labor. Peck made us practice the technique until he was satisfied. His satisfaction just happened to coincide with a blister forming on the palm of his hand. He studied the blister for a while and walked over to his car telling us he'd be back when he sliced the blister.

As soon as he walked through the fence row to his car, Bob held up his hand, fingers outstretched.

"Five...four...three...two," he slowly said.

We heard the car start.

Bob had been wrong.

It took Peck only about thirty minutes to dismiss himself.

We watched the car turn around and pull away.

"Well, shit," Bob, older and more worldly than Tommy and I, spat into the dirt. "We're not gonna rake this whole damn field by hand. C'mon, grab that twine and a couple of stakes. Let's get some rows laid out."

We were interrupted about an hour later by the sound of the owner/farmer's tractor. It came down the grassy lane, Johnny-popping its arrival pulling an old wagon heaped with crates of onion sets. The farmer waved us over as he came to a halt adjacent to the smooth field.

"Mr. Tooman said you boys was to unload them sets," he hollered above the noise of the tractor. He swiveled on the tractor seat looking at the meager accomplishment of our few rows. He shook his head, turned back toward the front of his tractor and waited while we muscled the wooden crates to the ground. The John-Deere tractor continued its rhythmic chug, but the farmer didn't help. Bob sarcastically said the farmer couldn't be all that busy if he could sit around waiting for us and although the farmer must have heard him, it did not influence him to lend a hand. By the time we cleared the trailer, the sun was high in the sky and making us hotter than we were from the unloading. When we were finished, the pile of crates looked even more impressive on the ground.

Just as soon as the man and his tractor had made a u-turn in the lane, Bob motioned to us. Dutiful to our elders, Tommy and I followed him.

"Let's get the tent set up and take a break," he said.

Tommy balked. "Dad ain't gonna like it if we don't get some of this done."

"I don't care," Bobby spat back. "He's always got this great stuff for *someone else* to do. We're the ones gettin' stuck out here in the middle of nowhere while he goes his merry way thinkin' up more stuff for someone else to do. It's a bunch of crap!"

I followed Bobby and Tommy as they walked out of the field. We ended the day down by the small creek which ran through the woods on one side of the field. We set up the tent, laid out the sleeping blankets, and then whiled away the remainder of the day telling one another lies and loafing. It was much better in the cooler woods than out in the field under the hot sun. When evening came we built an unneeded fire, ate a sparse dinner, and went to bed.

The following day we made a mild attempt at getting the onion sets planted, but we didn't get too far. In the late afternoon, Peck showed up and he wasn't very pleased with our progress. I immediately wondered at his sons' deference as compared with their talk during the day before. They sure hadn't been saying "yes, sir" and "no, sir" while we lazed the day away. Now it was all business, and Bobby was doing most of the talking. From his explanation for our lack of progress and without saying it directly, I somehow got the impression that Tommy and I were mainly to blame for the poor output. Bobby was following in his father's footsteps.

Mr. Tooman took over, handing us each a box of sets, pointing us into the field with directions to plant, plant, plant those little onions. He hauled a wooden fold up chair from the back of the car and sat down to better direct us (and to make sure he had enough energy reserved to think, think, think about his next pot of gold).

We planted onions until it was too dark to see the strings laid out in the field. It took a long time for the sun to go down. Peck followed us over to the tent and brought his chair with him. We listened to a lecture about how he was depending on us to "bring home the bacon" and "take care of business" and "do what has to be done." He also helped himself to our scant food and told us he'd be back early the next day to get us started properly. He took his chair with him when he left. No sitting allowed for the peons.

The days that followed folded into one another, indistinguishable in their content. We heard Mr. Tooman's car sometime between dawn and noon. Fortunately, the lane could be seen through the trees from the campsite, and we had a few moments advance warning. The lane was badly rutted, and Mr. Tooman had to drive slowly to the field. We waited each day until we saw the car's chrome bumper and then made a mad dash to the field. The further we got in the field the less like it was that Peck would walk the growing distance to inspect what we'd accomplished. He infrequently replenished our food supplies when he came, and then only after we bitterly complained about moldy bread and dried out bologna. He was even angrier when he discovered that we'd been supplementing our meals with the little onions meant for planting, the litter of which was scattered around the fire pit.

Peck slapped his leg. "Goddammit! You boys are eating the onions! Plant 'em Goddammit! Get 'em planted!"

He seemed to always be disappointed in what we'd done during his absences. I, for one, had started being amused at his continued attempts to get us to do more, but his sons weren't. I thought his pep talks were contemptuously funny because he invariably followed the loud chewing us out by leaving us to our own devices. I thought his logic poor: berate the boys, encourage them to impossible accomplishment...then leave. Just as soon as the car's brake lights winked around the bend in the lane, Bobby threw down whatever he was doing, and we quit. Bobby got so disgusted one hot morning listening to his father's broken record that after Mr. Tooman left, he took several boxes of the onion sets and threw them in the creek. All three of us were pleased at the way they floated down the stream.

Word must have reached our families about our meager production. My mother and Mrs. Tooman showed up one morning after about a week of our being out by ourselves. Neither one of them looked particularly happy as their eyes glared through the car windows. I'm pretty sure our devious loafing had gotten in the way of most things these women considered essential by that time, and we boys knew we were guilty of something.

When our mothers pulled up alongside the field, Bobby, Tommy, and I exchanged worried glances. There was "at fault" etched on the two faces I saw, and I was pretty sure it was also written across my brow in huge black letters. The women sat in the car for long moments ignoring our waves and greetings while they held private counsel. I could see their lips moving and I was betting they weren't saying how proud they were of their sons. After several minutes, my mother and Mrs. Tooman opened the car doors still talking but now their words were directed at us three boys.

My mother immediately remarked that we obviously hadn't used the change of clothes we'd brought, and things went quickly downhill from there with the speed of an avalanche.

But Mom was wrong. We had changed clothes when our originals became stiff enough to stand by themselves with the clay dirt accumulation. Of course, she wasn't far off the mark because we hadn't washed the dirty ones preferring to leave them heaped in a pile "to do," but she didn't know that just then. The ones we were wearing also belonged in the pile, right on top.

There was definitely a difference in an absent father's authority and the authority under the eye of a mother. Both mothers set about the important work first. Although I'm sure they set out from home to help with the planting, there were far more important tasks requiring attention and all three of them were standing in that Chelsea field.

Teenage boys are poor creatures at taking care of themselves. Without constant direction and when left to their own devices, they immediately revert to unkempt, uncouth, and unwashed beings akin to the Neanderthal. The campsite looked slovenly; blankets and bedding were vomited out of the open tent flap and were dirty and smeared. The rolls of toilet paper we'd brought with us lay damp and unrolled in the shade of the tent. The cooking pot and old plates had at least three coatings of Campbell's Pork and Beans encrusted and were scorched black on the outside. We hadn't neglected letting ourselves slip either. Bobby, Tommy, and I had assigned an importance to our personal hygiene that ranked right alongside the pile of dirty clothing.

My mother thrust a bar of soap into my hands. Silently, she pointed toward the creek. I heard her loud and clear.

We boys trooped down to the creek. Both women followed us.

"Strip them off and get in there! Hand those clothes over here!"

My mother made disgusting noises when she saw my underwear. When I looked, I saw why.

The creek was cold despite the heat of early summer.

The observations of both women while we bathed were even more chilling. To our collective mortification, they both called out instructions that would have befitted a two-year-old.

"Lather up your crotch."

"Scrub your ears."

"Make sure you get your bums. You all stink like hogs."

There are few ordeals that instantly transform your psyche back to an earlier age. For adolescent boys, one of them is having your mother observe you taking a bath. I'd been able to shed my mother's attendance during bath time quite a few years before. It was obvious from Bobby's and Tommy's attempts at concealing themselves that they had as well. The creek was shallow, probably eighteen inches deep at most, and I'm sure both mothers enjoyed our turtle-like appearance as we tried to scrub and remain hidden at the same time. Both mothers continued to watch this entire operation. By the time we emerged dripping from the creek, we were about as chastened as it is possible to be. It also proved difficult to turn our hands into fig leaves as we winced our way across the rocky stream bed. But our humiliation was not quite complete.

Mrs. Tooman had taken our clothing after satisfying herself of our outward return to humanity and began scrubbing dungarees and shirts in the stream. She looked very much the washer woman as she beat the dirty clothes against a rock on the stream edge, but she sounded like a Harpy as she worked. It probably took about two minutes after Mom and Mrs. Tooman arrived to change us back into their good, subservient little boys.

"You boys can just sit there until they've dried."

She pointed to the stream bank further down from her washing rock.

"Besides, I'm so disappointed in you boys, I don't want to look at you for a few minutes."

While we were in the creek, my mother had walked back to the campsite and was shaking out the bedding, and cleaning up the scattering of tin cans, utensils, and other boy trash we'd created. She walked down to our wait-until-dry spot and thrust the blackened pot in my direction, shaking her head.

"It's a wonder you boys aren't dead of ptomaine."

It's very difficult to sit naked and receive something offered without revealing what might otherwise be covered with your hands. It was hard enough for Tommy and Bobby, and she wasn't giving them anything. They both squirmed around until their backs were turned to her. I made no attempt to take the big cooking pot, but beseeched her with my eyes to just set it down and go someplace else. Mom eventually got the message.

"I expect to see that clean the next time I see it."

As soon as she walked away, I got up, took the pan, knelt by the water's edge, and began scrubbing the filthy thing with the coarse sand and gravel of the creek bed. The sight of me kneeling naked by the stream must have been funny. Bobby laughed first, but Tommy joined in pretty quickly.

"That's about the ugliest thing I ever saw. You're swinging in the breeze!" Bobby hollered.

I ignored the jibe. My mother was much too close for a proper retort.

From far off, Mrs. Tooman said, "I heard that, Bobby. Of all the things you ought to know about, you ought to know better than *that*, too. I've still got plenty of soap left, and you aren't past the age for it."

Bobby made a face, but we sat the rest of the time in complete silence. We didn't sit for long.

Using the scant long weeds for cover, we crept toward the bushes that held our clothing. We put them on when they were still wet, no easy task with blue jeans. We certainly looked even funnier hopping around with one leg in and one leg out. Once on, they weren't very comfortable, but we weren't allowed much time to think about the chafing.

Once our humanity had been restored to our mothers' liking, they set about the tasks of supervising the onion field. Both women had been raised to appreciate the importance of farm work. My mother was raised on a working, if not profitable, farm and Mrs. Tooman had been raised by her grandparents who were real, honest-to-god farmers. I'd heard stories of the "real life" from Mom thousands of times. I learned it myself first hand on my grandparents' farm in Manchester, Michigan. It took the women all of twenty minutes to set things in motion. They ordered us boys to start carting the boxes into the field placing the crates at each row's end and intermittently leaving some toward the center. While we were doing the lift and carry work, they quickly began staking out the remainder of the field with stakes and string.

It surprised me how quickly the work began to progress but it shouldn't have. We were working in a rhythm, lead by two conductors who would not let us lose the beat. By the time the sun was westing toward evening, we managed to plant a dozen or so straight line rows of onions. If it hadn't been for the heat and the dirt and the work and the scathing commentary of our two supervisors, the job would have been fun.

We had been listening to remarks during the day about disappointment, lost trust, and general disparagement about our quick slatternly slide. There was surprisingly little conversation while we worked, but most of what occurred let us know exactly where we stood in the grand globe of a mother's pride. We boys were not at all surprised when we were told to rinse off in the creek and get in the car when we finished for the day. We would NOT be spending another night, or another minute for that matter, unsupervised, unwatched, and unwashed. Not while one of these mother's breaths still inhaled and exhaled, anyhow.

It took us another week or so to finish the planting. We completed the planting work just in time to start chopping the weeds that had skyrocketed from the bare earth. Mr. Tooman was nice enough to buy new hoes for us. He did not hang around long enough to show us how to use them. In fact, I think their delivery marked the last time we saw him at the onion field. No longer did his big Chevrolet station wagon jounce down the road with him peering through the windshield at any given moment. My mother's old Dodge disgorged us early every day and became the only vehicle assigned to the transport of workers and daily supplies. Peck had moved on, it seemed.

The job had been completely absorbed into the busy schedule of both mothers. It was no mean feat because my mother had two little ones at home. Chip and Phoebe weren't at an age that they could be left at home by themselves and Carole was press-ganged into service. She was sixteen and could be trusted to a reasonable degree. At least leaving the two young ones held immensely more wisdom than entrusting three boys to their own devices.

We spent the rest of the summer tending the onions. The pale first spears of the onion sets grew into green and upside down rocket contrails of mature plants while we chopped weeds up and down the rows. By the time we finished one complete weeding of the field, it was time to start all over again. The perfect early summer days turned blistering hot, and it was a rare early morning that didn't see every one of us sweated through and through. We began to pinch off seed pods from the plants reaching growth, and it wasn't too much longer after their appearance that it was time to harvest, but we were finished. Before August had finished baking the earth with its hot sun, we stopped going to Chelsea.

The farmer would be in charge of getting the crop to market.

Several more weeks passed before Mr. Tooman came over to the house in the early fall to settle up. He made a great production of payoff and spoke at some length about all my hard work, the great harvest he'd had except for the damp rot that infected a third of the field, the additional loss of onions due to mechanical picking, the downright robbery of the trucking company used to haul them to Detroit and the terrible price he received from the wholesaler. He was desolate that he didn't make more than he had.

He extended his hand and offered me two ten dollar bills for the entire summer's work. When I reached for them, he seemed reluctant to let them go and I had to tug twice to get them from his hand. I did not see him pay my mother any money, and I don't think he ever did. Before he released my wages, he asked my mother and father if they'd ever heard anything about a great device to improve television reception called a super antenna mounted on a pole. He knew the man to erect the poles while he sold the antennas. Everybody would want one. It was sure to make anyone smart enough to invest a huge amount of money.

My mother said we weren't interested.

Chapter 9
Deeper Still

When I was a teenager I was great at digging holes. I did have a problem getting out of them.

I was so often in some sort of squeeze or another it's a wonder that I received much more formal learning than that of middle school.

Eighth grade was particularly tough. Bells for this, warning alarms for that, all mixed in with official announcements from the loudspeakers metallically telling teachers that some student or another was to immediately report to the Principal's Office. All too often the student was Clark.

This became problematic for my folks, for the school, and for me.

When I first entered junior high school, I'd discovered a wonderful sometime hiding place, Mr. Zinner's workshop in the boiler room. Mr. Zinner was the school custodian, occasional bus driver, and he owned every key to unlock every secret of the school. He was a tall, lean man with blond hair, always wore his shirtsleeves rolled up and was ever-ready with a grin and greeting to students and teachers alike.

The boiler room had double steel doors and emitted a constant hum. It smelled hot whenever one of the doors was opened. I was instantly attracted to the space. His sanctuary was located in back of the school, a room partly occupied by the big fuel oil fired boiler, floor polishers, huge steam and water pumps and a workbench that held a treasure of waiting-to-be-fixed door latches, school clocks, broken desks, bus carburetors, and pencil sharpeners.

His office desk belied the clutter of his workbench and was in a small closet in the rear of the machinery room. There he kept a neat and precise ledger of repairs and schedules for the "this or that" required to keep the school in up and running condition. Because the workshop held all the machinery for the entire school, its door was locked except when he was there.

For me it had an undeniable allure: the whispered and smelly swoosh when the boiler flamed into action, the whine of the water pumps when they announced the end of gym class and the boy's and girl's following showers, or the quiet thrum of the fans that pushed air down long ducts to each room. It was always hot in the boiler room and it smelled of oil and steam, sharp and pervading, and it had a constant low droning. I liked the jumble of the inner workings of the school.

While Mr. Zinner was often busy with the never-ending tasks of the school, every once in a while I would find the big door propped open and could slip unnoticed into the hidey-hole. Mr. Zinner also took a sort of pleasure in allowing some boys, including me, to truant their time away in his shop. He never failed to greet any student with a broad smile (and I wasn't the only one to seek a safe haven). That I usually brought him a homemade scone or chocolate chip cookie didn't hurt my entry chances either. He listened appreciatively to whatever lie was pronounced as fact for the reason anyone was there. If there was a task at hand, he'd shove aside the clutter surrounding the object and try to let us help in the work explaining what he was doing and why. He was also the source for important information.

Mr. Zinner kept his audiences entertained with a running commentary on teachers or school administrators and his pronouncements were always taken as fact. I also liked it if a teacher came looking for someone, Mr. Zinner would stand in the doorway and swear nobody was there except him even if someone was. It was like a secret society.

I had a flair for sketching, sculpting, and painting, enough small talent to paint a mural for public display in one of the local banks. Previous teachers allowed me free reign to work at any project I chose. While the rest of the class would be drawing fruit in a bowl, I might be working on portraits of classmates. Because of this former freedom and loose knit nature of the class, during other years, art was my favorite class period.

Then Mr. Daugherty came to our school and I had a terrible time with eighth grade art class.

I'd met him the previous summer when he and his family became members of our church. One of the ways to be instantly absorbed into a community was to join a church. Any church would do as an expression of Godliness, but in most of the eyes of the neighborhood, something Protestant would be the best. Mr. Daugherty started teaching a Sunday school class almost as soon as he started attending church.

He was tall with a grim appearance, stood straight and unyielding as a stick, walked fast, and wore his dark hair slicked back. His face was thin and dark complexioned and he had long blade for a nose. When his family came to church, I noticed that his wife and children followed two steps behind him. Mr. Daugherty took over the teenage Sunday school class and he brought a whole new perspective to worship services.

His lessons always included an original chalk drawing. The scenes would portray some pastoral scene or animals frolicking in the woodlands or people going about the everyday tasks associated with life. While he was setting the scene to words, Mr. Daugherty would turn on a black light and amaze his young audiences. Shazaam! The drawing would turn into another picture representing something spiritually important and related to the ending to his story.

In a few short weeks, we'd seen farmyards turned into the Garden of Eden, complete with a blushing Adam and Eve; trees turned into the three crosses on Calvary, and a resting deer turned into a coming forth Lazarus. His changeling pictures were the talk and pride of our church except with the kids who attended his lessons.

Mr. Daugherty was strict.

By the time school started, I already knew enough about him to be disappointed when I heard he would be the new art teacher. His appointment was a distinct departure from the norm. As far as my limited experience went, these classes had previously been taught by women, usually young, a few years out of college, and new to any teaching job. I personally thought the previous strategy had been wonderful. Young women were more prone to allow freedoms in classroom activities than any men teachers. I liked every other art teacher I ever had and I did enjoy the previously laid back classes. I had done well.

Mr. Daugherty changed all that. He was a talented artist in his own mind and spent the first several days of class showing us techniques and styles. Mr. Daugherty *was* well schooled in his field. He introduced us to art history and the styles used by the masters of the Renaissance period. We were led through the development of art as a record of history from prehistoric cave drawings through the impressionists and into modern art. He also quickly established enough rigidity to be the pride of any military installation. Nothing was done in class without approval and even that needed a command to begin. He had a mental schedule in which every student would become an accomplished and publicly lauded artist. He spent one entire day telling us what we were going to be doing starting with line drawings and progressing toward his ultimate goal for us.

No one was allowed to interfere with that schedule.

He should have been in charge of a prisoner-of-war camp.

Just before the end of the previous school year, I'd started creating a life sized bear's head standing almost two and a half feet tall and two feet wide. I'd formed a wire mesh framework and covered this with thick strips and shapes of clay. Our school emblem was a bear and I'd been approached by my former art teacher to sculpt one during class. The plan was to then display it in the school. It would be a symbol for all of us proud Jefferson Bears. I'd spent last year's final marking period working on the bear and I was pleased with the result thus far.

Mr. Zinner had promised to faithfully keep the cloth covered model dampened during the past summer and he'd kept his word. As soon as school started, I took over the wetting duties, relieving the custodian of the promise. All that was left to do on the bear was the final detail, dry it, paint it, and put it in the trophy display case at the entrance of the school where it would be the first thing everyone saw when they entered the big doors. I thought I'd pick up where I left off last year.

Soon after school began, I approached Mr. Daugherty after class and told him about the bear model I'd been working on. I unveiled the head proudly with a flourish, but he said he'd already seen it. He added that it took up too much space on the side table and asked who had given me permission to keep it in his room. He went on to tell me that I could stay after school to work on the clay head anytime I wanted to, but the progressive in-class demands wouldn't allow any time during regular hours. Despite my attempts to explain what I'd been doing last year, he was adamant about what was going to happen in his classroom. He wouldn't listen to my explanation of my paper-route responsibilities and that I didn't have a way home if I did stay late. He made a point of telling me he guessed the bear just wasn't going to get finished at all.

"I'm gonna talk to Mr. Kessler (our school principal)," I rebelled. "I can't stay after school to do it. I've got a paper route at 3:30 every day. My teacher last year, Miss Evans, let me work on it anytime I wanted to."

"I've already spoken with Mr. Kessler," he said. "If I allow you to do something different than class assignments, everybody else will want to do 'special' projects, too. That's no way to run a class. It doesn't matter what you did last year and it doesn't matter to me if it never gets done. I'm the teacher now. Mr. Kessler agrees with me."

Mr. Daugherty had a habit of pushing his lower lip out in a displeased pout whenever he didn't like something. He also inched forward when he was talking to a student, moving ever closer until he was either standing right on top of him or he caused the kid to take a step backwards. I'd observed him doing both to other students and he did both as he was talking to me. I personally thought he did it to talk "down" to someone and to intimidate. I took several steps backwards and retreated from the classroom.

It wasn't until several days later that I had an opportunity to speak with our principal, but it wouldn't have mattered if my chance had been immediate. Mr. Kessler said he didn't want to interfere with the way art class would be handled. He encouraged me to try to find spare moments here and there to complete the mascot model.

I let the whole issue fester for the remainder of the school year. I tried to dismiss the denial of what I thought was my right as a "talented" artist, but I couldn't. My grades suffered in Mr. Daugherty's class. I went from being interested in art to wholly indifferent to anything to do with it. My projects were turned in late or not at all. When I did finish some task, its quality and design were shoddy.

I talked to anybody who would listen to me as I ranted about Mr. Daugherty. My relationship with him went from privately questionable to publicly war-like. I think it was a contest to see who could say the worst of the other. He made sure to write scathing notes on my six-week reports. They ranged from "poor classroom behavior" to "deliberately rude." In the halls during breaks and lunch period, I made sure to mimic his pooched lip and advancing ways to anyone who'd stop and watch. I was the hit of the lunchroom causing huge uproars from my classmates. I was called into the office numerous times for both report cards and behavior. I got double the trouble at home, but neither had much effect on me. As far as I was concerned, Mr. Daugherty had ruined whatever joy I'd previously had in art. Nothing was going to change that.

In the spring, toward the end of the school term, I asked Mr. Daugherty if I could take the bear out of the classroom, where it had continued to stand under its cloth cover throughout each and every class period. I told him I had permission to store it in study hall where I might have a chance to complete it before school let out for summer vacation. He thought it was a great idea to get it out of his classroom. I hoped he wouldn't check in study hall to see if it was there.

Instead I took the bear down to Mr. Zinner's workshop and with a great deal of perverse satisfaction I stripped the clay away in globs and smooshed the wire frame into an unrecognizable lump. Mr. Zinner watched me destroy it but just stood next to his workbench with a bemused look on his face and didn't say a word.

I started on another project as soon as the bear was ruined. Even without a supporting frame, there was plenty of clay left from the ruined shape. This one was smaller but would still be a correctly sized human. I skipped several classes, Mr. Daugherty's included, with as many lies as I could fashion and didn't get caught in any of them. I needed time on task to get this done. I worked hard to get it just right.

Mr. Daugherty's head emerged from the clay. I fashioned his slicked-back hair with precise strokes. I secretly noticed and copied every feature my mind could absorb, the jut of his jaw, the shape of his ears and nose, and his prominent Adam's apple. I featured the frown his face took on when he talked to me. I had an easy time reproducing that look; I'd been the object of his scathing eyes and words repeatedly throughout the year. I found time to work on this project; every spare moment and many study halls, when I could talk my way out of one, were used to finish the bust.

Mr. Zinner had watched the progress throughout the whole time I worked on it. He didn't comment much beyond "Umm" and "Huh," but he did smile when I asked him what he thought.

When it was finally completed, I didn't get as much satisfaction out of the caricature as I thought I would. It was a good likeness, except for the deliberately crossed eyes I had given the head, but my only audience was Mr. Zinner and the few kids who occasionally wandered into the workshop.

"It's too bad there's no place for it to go on display," Mr. Zinner lamented. "It does look like Mr. Daugherty."

"D'ya really think so?" I asked and agreed. "Yeah, but if it was out somewhere, somebody would just throw it away or wreck it. And Mr. Kessler would give me some real grief if he knew I did it. I guess it's just you and me."

"Well, at least you got it done," Mr. Zinner continued. He'd been a good listener when Mr. Daugherty had come down hard on my feelings. "You feel any better about him now?"

I didn't get a chance to answer. Mr. Zinner scooted me out of the workshop saying he had some locks to repair before the end of the day. He told me to stop by at the end of second period the next day if I could.

The following morning, when the bell sounded the end of my second class, I ran down the halls. I only had six minutes between classes and if I didn't want to face a mad-because-you're-late teacher, I had to hoof it.

When I got to the workshop, I was disappointed to see the door closed. I'd thought Mr. Zinner told me to stop by. In frustration I tried the doorknob knowing it would be locked. To my surprise the door opened easily. I stuck my head through the opened space.

"Hey, Mr. Zinner," I whispered. "Are you in here?"

The only sound was the whine of the water pumps, reminding me I had only a few moments before I was supposed to be in gym class. I walked quickly into the workshop still calling a greeting.

On the workbench, next to Mr. Daugherty's bust was the huge ring of keys Mr. Zinner normally had suspended from his belt and several keys lying loose. The notebook he usually kept in his shirt pocket was also lying open next to the scattered keys. Quickly glancing at the neat printing, I saw written next to the day's date;

Coach F. lost his key to the trophy case. Get new one made.
Door to workshop won't lock. Called Marshall's Hardware, ordered new lock
cylinder. Be here in 3 days.

One of the loose keys had a cardboard tag tied to it and written in ink on the tag was "Trophy Case."

I had two simultaneous thoughts: I suddenly knew where Mr. Daugherty's bust was going to go, and I also truly understood the meaning of the word epiphany. I picked up the key, slid it in my pocket, turned around, and closed the shop door softly as I went out.

The tardy bell for gym class matched my dash into the locker room. I changed into my gym clothes and slipped to the back of the group while coach was telling us what we'd do for the day. I got hit during the first few moments of the battle ball contest in gym. I couldn't keep my mind on the game, but I didn't care. Sitting along the sidelines gave me time to think.

I needed to come up with a really great story.

At the dinner table that night, I told my folks that I'd settled my differences with Mr. Daugherty and that he in turn had asked me to help him organize all the left over art supplies in order to get ready for school closing and summer vacation. My folks were so delighted with the supposed reconciliation that Dad readily agreed to drop me off at school on his way to work at 6am the next morning.

In the morning when Dad went to start the car, I grabbed one of the artificial feathered birds my mother used in her springtime house decorations and stuffed it in my coat pocket.

The school was just coming to life when my father pulled up in front. I said thanks and ran into the school. I headed for Mr. Zinner's shop. He greeted me with a grin.

"Well, did'ya find what you were looking for?" Mr. Zinner asked as I pushed the partly opened door and walked into the shop. He had his tool pouch strapped to his belt and continued, "I've gotta get down to the girl's lavatory before everybody gets here. They've got a toilet that won't stop running. I suppose it'll take me about thirty minutes or so."

He was out the door before I had a chance to answer his question.

As soon as Mr. Zinner was gone, I took the bust from the workbench and carefully made my way to the front of the school. Unlocking the glass case and rearranging the trophies and certificates took several nervous minutes, but I was buoyed by the thought of ensconcing Mr. Daugherty in such a prominent place. I was even more pleased knowing I had the only key to the display.

When the bust was placed inside, I took the feathered bird I'd snitched before I left the house. I placed it on the bust's exaggerated and protruding lower lip, right under the crossed eyes. It looked like the bird was going to peck his nose. I slid the glass door shut and locked it, pocketing the key I'd kept.

I went around to the back of the school where I had a view of Williams Road. I waited until I saw my regular bus coming toward the school and mingled in with the crowds of students as they arrived. I had had to wait about an hour in the damp grass. As soon as the long line of buses began disgorging their loads, I joined them.

The crowd that quickly stalled in the front of the school was almost impenetrable. Normally kids went in to their lockers or sat in the open auditorium before school gabbing and fooling around until the first class warning bell rang. Now, everyone was milling around in front of the display case laughing and pointing and hooting. It was difficult to get through the doors as I threaded my way through the crowd and joined right in with the swarm of kids. Comments flew faster than thoughts, and everybody seemed to be getting a big laugh.

"Who did that?"

"Let me see, let me see!"

"Who is it?"

"That's Mr. Daugherty. Look at that lip. I'd know it anywhere!"

"Who did that...? Look at that bird!"

The uproar soon summoned several teachers. The laughter slowly died away as the authority of adults became evident and as they shoved kids out of the way. In a few moments they were followed by Mr. Kessler and the office staff. Silence further descended like a shroud. The noise died completely away and I saw Mr. Daugherty crane his head over the teeming mass of students. A clear lane appeared in front of him as the students parted, and he made his way to the trophy case arrangement.

I scooted to the back of the shoving and pushing mass of kids.

Mr. Daugherty bent forward to stare at the caricature.

Except for the bird and the crossed eyes, he might have been looking in a mirror.

The laughter began again and rose to unprecedented levels as kids saw him staring at himself nose to nose. From my place at the back of the crowd, I saw the glass reflected secret smiles of several teachers, but they were keeping any enjoyments inside. Mr. Daugherty suddenly straightened and whirled on the raucous crowd, and the uproar died as if someone had thrown a switch.

I saw him looking from face to face to face searching and needing and wanting to find someone. I knew who he was looking for and I knew it was time to go. I crouched down, backed away, and made my way to the sanctuary of Mr. Zinner's shop.

As I scurried down the hall, Mr. Zinner and a teacher passed me going in the other direction; they were hurrying toward the front of the school. I didn't look at either of them but I sure felt one set of eyes on me.

As quickly as I could, I went into the shop, dropped the key on the floor and scooted it under the bottom shelf of the workbench. I stood there several moments, triumphant, but vengeful thoughts were erased by what I was already picturing as punishment. I'd automatically deny any accusations, but I knew what the eventual outcome would be. I eased back into the hallway, strolled back to the cafeteria and passed Mr. Zinner and our principal in front of the display case.

I heard Mr. Zinner say, "I don't know where it is. I had it out on my desk because coach lost his and I was going to get another one made. Maybe he came in and got my key. I'll go ask him."

"We've got to get that out of there. It doesn't look good to have our teachers ridiculed," Mr. Kessler stated. "I won't have it. Find the key or break the glass. I want that gone."

Mr. Zinner looked right at me as I walked by catching my eyes with his. His mouth was a straight line, but his eyes were laughing themselves silly. Mr. Kessler had his back to me so he didn't notice my passing among the other students' going this way or that. I picked up speed as I went by and joined the unidentifiable gaggle of kids in the cafeteria. I sat at one of the lunch tables and pretended to study one of my schoolbooks. I tried to ignore the seemingly hundreds of comments and jibes that were whispered, talked, and shouted my way. It seemed like half the student body had already figured out who the responsible person was. I had a fleeting thought that it wouldn't be long before everybody else affixed blame to me.

I felt a hand on my shoulder and stood up slowly just knowing that the other shoe was about to drop. Mr. Zinner was standing there with the same grin he used whenever I showed up at his shop.

"Where's the key?" he whispered. "I sure don't want to have to break that glass, and you don't want me to either. It'll just make things worse and they're already bad enough. I didn't tell anybody, but I heard Mr. Daugherty say that he knew it was you."

I told him I'd halfway hidden the key under his worktable.

"What do you think they're gonna do?" I asked, but I already knew the answer.

Mr. Zinner looked deliberately into my eyes, thought a long moment and said, "I don't know about that, but I think your best bet is to go right to the office and confess everything. Talk to Mr. Kessler and take whatever punishment he sees fit to hand out. I'd also stay out of your art teacher's way for a while. Say…at least until this time next year." He finished with a half-smile. "If you need to, you can tell him I knew about it. You go on now."

He was right. I thought I'd gone well beyond normal prank playing with this situation and probably knew that before I even began. I walked toward the school office trying to guess the number of swats I'd gather. I also knew this was my problem. I wouldn't involve anyone else.

Mrs. Avendt, the school secretary, cut her eyes in the direction of Mr. Kessler's office when I walked into the area used for registration, waiting for a nurse, and for students who were in trouble. I didn't sit on the long bench but marched straight up to Mr. Kessler's closed door, swallowed hard, and knocked softly.

I spent the next hour and a half under his stern gaze and in recovery from an on fire butt. Mr. Kessler could surely swing a paddle when he needed to. Bent over and holding on to the back of a chair, I was shocked by the first stroke, icy and raging fire all at the same time. Up to and including number ten or so, each one was a repeat of the first. I wanted to cry and scream and holler and shout, but I managed to hold it in. I lost count somewhere between whacks fifteen and twenty, but by then I was numb anyway.

I stood up for the first half of Mr. Kessler's lecture on disappointment and potential and trouble makers. It was hard to listen to him particularly because I knew he was right. When the fire in my pants had cooled to a heated glow, I managed to sit in the chair facing his desk, but even that was hard to do. Sentencing wasn't over with the swats. Another portion was that I would get a passing grade in art only on the condition that I never again darken the door of Mr. Daugherty's class.

When Mr. Kessler called my mother, I knew my troubles were just beginning especially the lecturing and swatting parts. I was restricted for weeks at home and received another paddling from Mom, who chased me around the house wielding her broom and hitting any of my parts that were available. She lamented about having to go to church where she'd see the man I'd wronged so terribly and how could I do such a thing; I knew better; I was raised better; what would Jesus think; what would Pastor think; on and on and on. I went through it all again when my father got home except I did not get another paddling from him. Mom called Mr. Daugherty that evening and apologized for her errant son's behavior, but I didn't talk to him on the phone.

The next day all the kids in school were amazed at my deviltry, but many also steered clear of my company for fear they might be thought guilty by association.

Mr. Zinner let me know how much he enjoyed the whole uproar.

Mr. Kessler watched me closely every time he saw me.

Mr. Daugherty wouldn't even look at me when we passed in the halls.

All in all, I thought it was a fair trade.

Chapter 10
Exiled

The result of that transgression was my going to Port Huron to stay with Grandma I.G. and her fairly new husband, Grandpa Merle.

As with most of my escapades, this last one with Mr. Daugherty was discussed with friends, our church congregation, and even remotely-related family. The church held special prayer meetings for weeks in my honor.

I'd been sent hither and yon before, usually out to the farm in Manchester or to Detroit to stay with my Grandma Grace and Grandpa Clark. This time it would be with Grandma I.G. and her husband, Merle Wheaton. It was only because everybody figured Grandpa Merle's physical presence would make sure that whatever was wrong with Clark would get put right.

I used to get sent off a lot. Just as soon as my mother stopped saying "Thank You Lord for letting him pass" and had had time to study the terrible grades on my last report card, I was on my way. This time I was not going to go somewhere comfortable or someplace I was accustomed to. This time I was going to go to WORK. While my folks probably would have preferred some cell that came with leg chains and a heavy iron ball, they instead chose grandparents. They had lots to choose from since my family included many extra grandparents.

My Grandma I.G. was on her third husband; #1 was my Grandpa Clark, and their chaotic family battles when my father was a child were legendary in our family. They didn't stay married much beyond the birth of my uncle Dave. #2, Grandpa Bill, was an Air Force hero in both World Wars, but died 18 months after marrying my grandmother. Husband #3 was Merle, a large, burly, hairy, cussed-tough fisherman. He owned three big lake fishing vessels, a fish market located in Port Huron and he was just the match for my grandmother's fiery Irish temper. I'd only been in his company two or three times since their wedding, but I quickly noticed how much of an influence he had when he was around.

The two made a distinctly disparate couple. Grandma was tiny, barely five feet tall, and she looked positively dwarfish compared to Merle. One didn't have to know her maiden name was Flynn to know she was from Ireland. Grandma had red hair, pale blue eyes, freckles, and enough of a lashing brogue to shine your shoes. Grandpa Merle, as we kids were instantly instructed to call him, was as big and square as a house, had a florid face, and wore his shirts opened two buttons down allowing his gray chest hair to waggle in the breeze. He hurried everywhere as if he were impatient with life itself.

When he came through a door, it seemed he'd materialized out of thin air and was in a contest to see if he'd fit through the opening. A faint odor of fish preceded him everywhere and Grandpa Merle had big knuckled and scarred hands. He used them to emphasize every word he spoke waving them as if they'd hurry his speech toward the intended target. I was always concerned about sitting close to him in case he lost control of his wildly gesturing paws. Even Grandma I.G. said he was as rough as a cob.

The day after school let us out, Grandma and Grandpa came down to get me. Chip would take care of the paper route. My sister Phoebe would take care of Patch. Grandpa Merle would take care of me. My folks wanted me out, out, out!

"He won't need any good clothes," Grandpa Merle announced to my mother. "Where he's going, the older the clothes the better."

"What about church?" my mother instantly countered.

Grandpa waved dismissal to that suggestion. "He probably won't have much time for church-going, but he'll have plenty of chances for baptism if he's not careful," Grandpa said, jabbing a big finger in my direction. "The boats stay out overnight, depending on the fishing. When he's not on the boats, he'll be in the market. There won't be much time for anything but fish."

Mom looked dubious, and I could tell she was torn between no church and her relief of getting rid of me for a while. She didn't do anything to delay my departure though.

My grandmother didn't say much. It appeared as if she was going to let Grandpa do all of the dealing with.

After a hurried goodbye, I was in the backseat of their big, new Oldsmobile (it already smelled like fish). While he'd been very nice while we were in my house, he didn't wait long after we were out of the subdivision until he started telling me what things would be like.

"Well, big boy, half the world's pissed off at you and the other half's thinking about it," he spoke into the rearview mirror.

"I guess," I said mulishly.

"Ha! You don't have to guess. I'm telling you, but don't worry. We'll get that set right pretty quick. You won't have time to get in trouble." He speared the mirror with his finger. "We're gonna fix that smarmy mouth on you, too."

Grandma tried to make small talk on the way to their home. She talked of her new house, cousins who also lived in Port Huron, and some of the sights and sounds of the surrounding area. I didn't do much more than grunt answers her way, and I could see Grandpa Merle's eyes in the rearview mirror. I silently wondered how he could drive and watch me because every time I looked up he drilled me with a look of his own.

When they were first married, Merle lived in an apartment several blocks from the waterfront, his fishing boats, and the market, but Grandma changed that immediately. Although surely she'd seen the apartment before they were married, my father said she took one look at his place after their honeymoon and stomped off and checked into a local hotel. Dad said she got her Irish up, and she was great at that. Grandpa Merle went right out and bought her a house and their new car.

Their home was very nice and in an upper class section of Port Huron, but I wasn't going to get much more than a one night stay in it. Grandpa had told me on the way up that I'd be staying with one of the boat crew's family while I was there, or at least until I'd earned the right to stay with them. That man lived close to the market, right on the waterfront, and I'd have easy access to work.

We had a nice dinner with little conversation, but went straight to bed after the dishes were cleared away and washed. Grandpa said 4am came early. He was right; it was still dark when he rousted me the next morning. He told me to bring my small suitcase when he came in to wake me. Down in the kitchen, he slurped a fast black coffee, shoved a piece of toast in his mouth, and pushed up from the table, motioning me to hurry it up. He tossed me a duffel bag and told me to shove some clothes from my suitcase into it. Grandma did not come down for coffee; Grandma did not come down to make breakfast, and Grandma did not come down to see us off.

Port Huron's waterfront in 1961 was a shabby and blighted area, heaped with cast off crates, old fishing nets and floats, half sunken boats, old engines, and everything else that someone thought to throw away easily. It stank of rotted fish mainly because the boats and fish markets got rid of their fish leavings by throwing them in the waters that surrounded the docks and walks of the harbor. The mixture of gasoline, diesel fuel, fish heads and entrails, decaying nets, and human garbage gave off an odor that overwhelmed the senses.

As Grandpa and I walked down one pier, I thought what a shame it was that Patch wasn't here to enjoy the stinking heaps of fish. She'd have been in her glory, because she loved to roll in dead fish but one part of my sentencing had been the loss of my dog while I was here.

The big ship was moored at the end of a long wooden pier, its engine rumbling in the faint glow of dawn. I'd started getting used to the pervading smells of the dock area, but the ship renewed the attack on my senses. It somehow reminded me of Patch, or at least a Patch returning from one of her forays into dead fish territory. The boat smelled so strongly of fish I might have been buried in them.

The boat was about forty feet long and was remarkable in the spotted appearance it had because of all the rust spots that showed through its dirty white paint. It was broad and sat low in the water. The deck vibrated under my feet and I had a sudden sense it was a living thing unto itself. There were metal stairs that led to the wheelhouse which sat well forward, and nets, floats, and crates were piled and stacked everywhere possible. Two large hatches dominated the center of the rear deck and two huge cable winches were perched directly at the stern. It was altogether an awesome place, and I was not just a little cowed at all the new sights and sounds.

I was introduced to the three man crew of the boat, the H. R. Helen, one of the vessels that belonged to my grandfather. Jay Wheaton was the captain and nephew of Grandpa by his first marriage; Pete was mate, and Bill was deckhand. Jay looked like a captain, wind tanned to a straw color on his hands and face, with dark eyes that were mostly in motion, as if he were constantly appraising the water about him. He was tall and slender and wore a ragged green sweater at our first meeting that reminded me of some of those Grandma Phoebe made for my family. He shook my hand and I momentarily wondered if I'd get splinters. It was like holding a rough block of wood.

Pete was in charge of my "straightening out." He and Bill appeared remarkably similar but weren't related. They were both small in stature but heavy in the arms and shoulders, and were dressed in such grimy clothes they looked as if they were coming home from fishing instead of going. They weren't overly friendly, but then again, neither was I. I was still smarting from the cast out feeling I had when my grandparents picked me up.

The boat was scheduled to leave while it was still dark and we were heading around Michigan's thumb into Saginaw Bay to fish for whitefish. Actually, we were fishing for anything that got trapped into the big purse-seine and gill nets, but whitefish was what we wanted most.

Bill took me on a tour of the ship pointing out the wheel-house, the two bunks, the head, a small galley and lastly the storage areas deep in the ship's hull.

"Two men stay on deck all the time. Everybody's on deck when we're setting or hauling nets. You'll sleep and eat when you can, on shift, not when you want to, and you'll use whatever empty bunk there is. We go six hours on, six hours off, around the clock."

I'd never been a stranger to work. You might say I got personally introduced to work early on, and while I might not have always liked it, I could keep up most any pace that was set. I was pretty good sized for a fourteen-year-old and had finally reached the age where I was prideful of being able to keep up with the adults when the family got together to work on the farm or any other task that loomed in front of me.

"You can start right here," Bill said, pointing to the bulkhead doors that marked the refrigerated and partitioned storage areas. "They've gotta be scrubbed and cleaned and rinsed before we can start the compressors and get them chilled. Pete will be down to check on 'em and he'll want them clean. They'll need about four hours to get down to temperature after you're done. Get to it."

He thrust a long, dirty yellow rain coat in my direction. He handed me a scrub brush with a broad bristled head and about 10 feet of handle and a battered tin bucket, all the while going on with instructions.

"Here's the pump to get clean water through the hull. Don't forget to turn it off when you're through. There's the drain for the compartments. They're all in the center and you've gotta keep them clear of scales and crap. See them strainers? Make sure they're seated in the drain, or there'll be a stinkin' mess below. It'll plug up the bilge pumps. The drains go down into the bilge. Once you've got them compartments clean, come and get me. I'll show you how to get down into the bilge. You're gonna clean that, too."

I went to work with a vengeance although one of my Grandma Phoebe's sayings thrust itself into my head: "A fine kettle of fish..." I smiled with the thought. Oh, yes, it was, and a big kettle at that.

Before long I felt the boat's continuous vibration turn into a deliberate rattle, shaking as she motored away from the pier. The diesel engine's noise increased to a throaty rasp, and the smoky smell of diesel fuel drifted into the compartments through the open door. I felt rather than heard the engine go full throttle as the boat cleared the buoys marking the entrance to the harbor of Port Huron, and the boat took on an up and down galloping rhythm as she breasted the waves on Lake Huron.

The engine fumes mixed with fishy smell and the stench became intolerable. The boat climbed up the short waves and fell into the hollows with a dull thud, also felt but not heard over the blanketing thrum of the engine. The motion of the boat and sickening smell of diesel swirled up into an unbearable maelstrom, overwhelming. It took me about thirty seconds more to get sick as a dog.

I understood the meaning of the phrase completely. I was down on my hands and knees throwing up my coffee and toast, my head low and thrust forward close to the floor. I threw up the previous night's dinner, violently getting rid of everything my guts held. I threw up until my stomach hurt with the paralyzing contractions, on and on and on and on, acrid, sharp and vile. I thought I might have puked something I ate the previous Christmas.

When nothing was left but the drool glistening on my chin, I crawled into a corner, weak with the aftermath and slumped half sitting, half lying on the white floor. The motion of the boat, once nauseating, had become similar to a rocking cradle, and I closed my eyes to enjoy it. I don't know how long I lay there; I do know that it wasn't long enough.

"Hey, boy!" was accompanied by a hand roughly shaking my shoulder. "C'mon, big boy! You've made a bigger mess than you had when you started! We've got nets to set."

I looked up to see Captain Jay towering over me and struggled to find my feet in the once again ragged lurching motion of the boat.

"Get to it. These coolers gotta get cleaned up and we want your sorry ass on deck." He turned and walked through the big white door. "Be quick about it!"

I didn't answer him except with a nod of my head but grabbed the brush and hose and swept the swirling the remnants of my stomach down the drain.

Despite the lingering remnants of queasiness, I managed to get the coolers into what I hoped was an acceptable state. I stowed the brush, pail and hose, and staggered my way up the short ladder to the deck.

While I'd been both puking-ly conscious and sickeningly unconscious in the hold of the boat, we'd evidently made our way well along Lake Huron's shore.

Pete and Bill were at the stern standing next to the big winches. "Get over here, so we can show you something other than how to puke!" This struck both of them as extremely funny. Pete bent over with his hands on his knees, making loud yurking sounds that I could hear over the noise of the engine. Both of them laughed even harder as Pete continued his little show.

I still hadn't found my equilibrium on the rolling and shuddering deck. My path was one of going forward and sidestepping, going forward and sidestepping until I reached the two men. Bill grabbed me by the shoulder of the slicker I still wore and steadied me while he explained the workings of the machinery. It was a complicated process; the ends of the nets had to be anchored, floats attached to lines as they were run off the drum, kept kink free, and done quickly as the boat made a wide flat arc to the final anchor position.

"You just watch, Bub," Pete commanded. "Keep your eyes open, your mouth shut and your hands in your pockets. This ain't a game."

A loud double blast issued from the wheelhouse horn. "Whroop, Whroop!"

I was thrown forward as the boat went full throttle reverse and then came to a bobbing standstill. I lost what small balance I had and ended up face first on the slick deck coming to rest against a wire basket of floats. I rolled over and push-upped myself to a crouch. My stumbling toward the cabin had brought fresh laughter from both men, but they quickly bent to the task of driving the first anchor stake into the lake bed. I stayed right where I was grasping the heavy wire for support and watched the men efficiently feed the big nets off the stern of the boat.

I was mesmerized by their work. One would unravel the net off the winch while the other smoothly clipped the big cloth covered cork floats by their long ropes at intervals of about fifteen feet. The winch whirred and whispered as the net off-fed, and the floats made flat plopping sounds when they splashed into the water. I followed the line of floats issuing from the stern of the boat, a zigzagged, undulating trail marking the position of the net. The indistinct line of land well beyond the far anchor marker showed how far away from solid ground we were. I didn't really need a reminder; the continuous bobbing of the deck was indication enough of just how far away I was from anything familiar.

I'd been on Lake Erie plenty of times in small boats, fishing or just fooling around joy-riding. Pleasure crafting was fun, a time to enjoy and forget, basking in sunshine, feeling the soft rhythm of the waves. My Grandpa Clark had powerboats even after the disaster that befell his sailboat, Gracie. Several of my friends' fathers had boats, power and sail, and I'd been on any number of outings, once as far as Put-In-Bay off the Ohio coast, a day trip well to the south and east of Monroe. My thoughts traveled back to the many great boat rides I'd had in the past.

"Hey, boy! Slide them floats up here! Hey! Damn! You think

you're just along for a ride? Unclip that basket from the gunwale hook there! Slide it up here! C'mon, boy! Time don't wait!"

Oh, yeah, I was supposed to be helping here. I reached for the hook, managed to get the basket loose, and slid it down the runners close to the stern.

"'At's your job! You keep them baskets full when we get 'em emptied! That forward hatch is where the rest of 'em'll be," Pete indicated with a pointed finger. "We'll work one side then th'other. Got it?"

I shouted back at them to let them know I'd heard and walked toward the big flat cover he'd indicated. Neat, serpentine piles of nets were laid out on either side of the hatch, fold upon fold upon fold, carefully placed for the next use. I just had room to put a foot down on either side of the cover in order to raise it.

With the cover laid back and held in place by two small chains, I could see the twisted jumble of floats piled in the well. I grabbed as many lines as I could and began to drag them toward the stern of the boat. I turned and trailed the long lines and floats behind me as I struggled against the continuous movement of the boat. The floats seemed heavy and I slung their ropes over my shoulder leaning against their weight. They kept getting heavier the further I went.

"Hey! Damn! Hey, boy! Lookit what you're doin'! Ferchrissakes!"

The metal clips on the float lines had snagged the big nets pulling them all a'skelter. The once neat piles were stretched out halfway across the deck twisted upon each other as if someone had deliberately done the task.

"Skipper! Stop the boat!" Bill screamed above the noise of the engine. "Stop the damn boat!"

Bill shoved me roughly out of the way as he and Pete rushed by. I heard the engine die to an idling rumble, and the boat lost headway. The motion of the deck increased as it slowed to an almost halt in the water. I saw Captain Jay slide down the wheelhouse ladder without his feet touching the flat rungs and land with a thump on deck. I inched away until my back came against the cabin wall and stood watching the men undo the twists and snarls my "helping" had produced.

"C'mere, boy," Jay said, motioning to me. "This is how it's gotta be done." He grabbed one of the floats and started winding the rope around it. "Grab a float line and wrap it tight around the float as you pull it out. Clip the hook back into the line and toss the package into the baskets. That way, all the men gotta do is hook the damn thing when it goes on the net."

He looked at me full in the face, his mouth set, serious and very, very adult-like.

"Don't ever drag anything around the deck of a trawler. Hell, you might get hooked into a net or an anchor or something that's going overboard. I don't want to be telling anybody something like that, especially your grandma and grandpa."

He walked toward the two men who were re-stowing the nets. "You two better get with the program. That kid's gotta get more boat learning before you ask him to do anything. Got it?"

He motioned for me to follow him and walked back up the steps to the wheel house. I spent the next several hours listening to the do's and do not's associated with the running of a fishing trawler. There were more do not's than do's, just as if my mother had been the one thinking them up.

After his lecture, he relented from his stern character a bit, and I was allowed to steer the big boat.

"Follow the compass heading. It will wander around a bit, but the job just requires that you follow a general direction except when we're working the nets. There's the throttle and shift; don't mess with them at all; we're just going over to another shoal and set some more nets. Now, you'd better turn in for a bit. We'll be coming back here, pulling those first nets after dark. It'll be a long night."

For the next several days, I followed a loose schedule; follow the captain, watch Bill and Pete as they worked the nets, eat a hasty meal of fish something or other, sleep, do it all over again. I quickly learned to grab both food and sleep whenever the opportunity arose. I became adept at peeing over the side (always downwind) from a rolling deck. I also learned to stay well out of the way when nets were being laid down or retrieved. Any interference with the men's work was likely to earn me a shove at the least or a slap on the shoulder if I didn't move fast enough.

Bringing full nets on board was a mish-mash of controlled chaos.

One end of the net was freed from its anchoring point and fastened to the primary winch. The net was in turn draped over a large revolving drum. As the winch wound up the net, the fish had to be pulled headfirst through the mesh as the net rolled over the drum, then thrown onto a tray, sorted, sized, headed and gutted, then slid down the tray toward the refrigerated hold. The fish were slippery, the gill-net folded in on itself, a seemingly endless snake of twitching bodies waving from the heavy cords. Each net pulled meant the deck was soon slippery with fish-scales, guts and heads; the air was full of screaming gulls, and no one dared take a breath until the far end of the net was aboard. The two men had a rhythm, but I'm not sure I even recognized the music.

The gutting tables were even more of a whirlwind. When the end of the tray began to slop over with fish, Bill walked to the table, grabbed a thin-bladed knife and began cleaning the fish. I watched, amazed again by his rhythmic hands, as he made two swift strokes. *Whit-whit.* The head was sliced off, the fish turned on its back and the belly slit open. Without a pause, he raked the entrails out, slid them into the gutter on the table, pushed the gutted fish onto the slide leading to the open hatch and grabbed another fish. Whit-whit-scoop. Head off, belly opened, entrails out. Whit-whit-scoop.

"C'mon, big boy," Bill hollered over the sound of the engines. "You're just beginning to have fun. Grab a knife."

There was nothing smooth about my first attempts to clean one of the fish, but I managed to get it done. Bill managed to do six or so to my one, but at least I was contributing. Pete finished bringing the tail end of the net on board and joined us at the cleaning station. The whirl of sliding fish parts more than doubled, the men's knives flashing and slicing, headless bodies skimming their way to the hold, heads and guts, scaly, a smelly, slimy and blue-gray-green coating over everything. The slickers we wore were soon slimed up, an identical look and smell of the fish we were cleaning. I'd never seen anyone do anything so fast and with so much expertise.

My brother and I fished all the time at home, at least whenever we took time out from our normal ramming about. Whenever Chip or I brought home a string of fish from Lake Erie, cleaning our catch of perch, bass or crappie was always a real chore. When we did it, we usually ended up butchering the fish so much that Mom then made chowder and we spent a long time afterwards cleaning up the mess we had made.

This was nothing like that. There were thousands of fish in the nets the first time we hauled them up. This was "get 'em in the hold, there's more to do" type work.

For the most part, I was able to help out although I was the object of many a jibe and cuss. I heard more "Hey! Damn!" and "FerChrissakes!" than I'd ever imagined existed. Both deckhands must have felt my instruction had to include a healthy dose of belittlement. I'd have had to move at the speed of light to keep them satisfied, and I wasn't so sure about even that. Mostly I stayed out of the way.

Jay was just as stern, but he seemed to take more of an interest in my becoming someone more than a staggering and all thumbs crew member. Maybe it was just the fact that if I did manage to learn something, I could become a helping member of the crew. Whatever the case, whether he just tried to keep me so busy I couldn't get in the way or he had an idea of my contributing something other than a cause for concern, I never knew. He did manage to get me comfortable with several necessary tasks aboard a fishing trawler.

Within three more days and nights, we had enough whitefish to head back toward Port Huron. The trawler sat low in the water; everything was packed up and stowed; the decks were washed after each haul and again during the trip back. As we motored back in the still dark morning, the ship took on a more relaxed atmosphere. There were still plenty of things to do; refrigeration units monitored; floats removed from the nets and stored; nets cleaned and stowed on deck; winches checked and greased, but the sense of urgency dissipated. Everyone aboard (me included) was pleased with the full holds, and Jay had radioed my grandfather of our good fortune.

Grandma and Grandpa were standing on the dock before noon when Jay eased the trawler alongside.

As soon as the trawler was tied up behind the fish market, Captain Jay and my grandfather held a conference while the other two men started the unloading process of the full holds. I stepped off the boat expecting to be warmly welcomed, if not because of the good catch, then at least as a beloved grandchild returning. I did get a brief embrace from Grandma, but it was interrupted by Merle's hand on my shoulder.

"You see them men pushing those carts?" he asked, pointing to a line of men and boxes on wobbly wheels issuing from the back of the market.

I nodded, "Yessir."

"You'll want to get back on board and start throwing those fish on the conveyor. We've got to get them washed up, cut up and packed. Let's get to it."

I started to protest but took a look at Merle. The stern man pointing to the boat didn't much resemble any family member of mine at that moment. He looked more like a picture of General Eisenhower in Germany during WWII. Directing troops or employees appeared to be about the same thing. That's what I was: an employee. I walked back to the trawler, stepped down to the holds, and joined Bill and Pete in the unloading.

With the lower doors open, the holds had spilled fish in a slimy, silvery avalanche. The two men were busily tossing the fish carcasses onto the conveyor, but the heap of fish looked endless. I joined in the work heaving and throwing fish in the general direction of the hopper on the end of the conveyor. It was hard work, bending, grabbing, twisting, throwing, and doing it all again and again.

It took only a few moments before each of us started shedding clothes, and despite the frigid air in the hold, we were soon sweated through and through. I struggled to keep up with the practiced and regular metronome of the men's movements. Their experience taught them economy of motion, but my lack caused me to work harder for less result. The pile of fish in the hold slowly grew smaller, but my careless efforts resulted in a growing heap around the end of the conveyor.

Just as I'd turned around from a particularly poor throw, I was smacked in the face by an armload of fish.

"Hey, Damn!" Bill screeched. "What's the matter with you? Get them in there the first time! Ya just gotta pick them damn things up again! Why do something twice?"

I yelped in surprise and shock. My faced burned with humiliation, but my aim improved considerably. I held in any retort. I was still slightly awed by these men and didn't want a confrontation with people who had been strangers only a few days before. Although there were still piles of fish left to unload, the work progressed. I busied myself cleaning up the results of my indifferent work and joined in with a new appreciation (and thoughts of revenge).

It took several hours to finish emptying the holds. Just before we were done and the men were coming through the door with the few remnants of the catch, I picked up a large fish, and threw it in Bill's face.

"*That* one was yours," I shouted, and ran toward the ladder. I hollered back as I scrambled out of the hold. "Why do something twice?"

He yelled, and his screech made me move faster. I saw him start toward me, but he had to dodge around the conveyor, and I was up and out on deck before he got close. I scurried off the boat, pleased with myself for the first time since I came on board. I was on the dock before Bill got his head through the hatch opening. With a curse, he went back down the ladder.

I found a new face on the dock.

"Yuh ready, big boy?"

He stuck out a hand in greeting. He was short, not much taller than I, and wore a used-to-be white apron. Now it was colored with blood and the drying remains of fish scales and entrails.

"I'm Timothy," he said. "Named after the Timothy in the Bible. I got sisters and brothers: Esther, Ruth, Naomi, Mary, Luke, Mark, Noah, and Solomon. We're all close in years. I believe my mother woulda had kids for every name in the Bible there is if Dad hadn't died in the war. C'mon, I'm gonna show you around the fish market."

I shook his outstretched hand and introduced myself.

"How come you're here?" he asked. "You're a little young to be workin' the boats for the Mister. And you're gonna work the market, too. You got kin? The Mister says you need help. What's that mean? You an orphan?"

I grinned. "Nope, but sometimes I think my folks wish they would have left me on a doorstep."

"Well, that ain't a new wish." Timothy grinned back. "People been thinkin' them thoughts about their kids for a long time. Specially 'bout a boy child when he gets a bit of size. C'mon, let's go see what's what."

I didn't tell him my grandmother was married to "Mister." Timothy turned and started toward Grandpa's market. I noticed he walked lopsided and sort of sideways. His left shoe had a thick sole. He saw my staring look.

"Got one leg shorter than the other. Lots of folks come into this world with a'firmity. Wore braces and special shoes all my life, but its never-mind and get to work around here. Mister gave me a job just as soon as I asked, and I asked a long time ago. A couple of my baby sisters work here. You'll meet 'em shortly."

The fish market opened out onto the dock. There were two large swinging doors scraped and scarred by the thousands of trips through them with carts. Jumbles of trays, baskets, and cartons lay about in profusion on either side of the doors. The market sat slightly higher than the dock and the ramp leading upward was deeply grooved by the wheels of countless cart trips. While Timothy and I had talked, the last of the fish had been trundled through the doors. He shoved one door open and we followed the uneven wood planking up to the market.

"This here's the shed. We gotta unload them fish and get 'em to the women. See them cutouts?" He pointed to four curtained openings cut into the far wall of fish shed. "The women are on the other side. They'll wash 'em and finish cleanin' 'em, fillet 'em and send 'em further on to get packed. It's rush, rush, rush now. It'll be all we can do to get 'em done. We got a truck here this afternoon, and we ain't gonna let 'em sit and wait."

Although mostly open to the air, the entire space had the strong and pervading smell of fish, not exactly unpleasant, especially when I compared it to the stench on board the boat. And the floor wasn't moving like the trawler either. The odor seemed to hang undisturbed despite the breeze that gently opened and closed the swinging doors with its comings and goings.

On the wall directly below the openings were rough and sided platforms that angled down toward the openings. Each chute was lined with shiny metal, smoothed by the countless fish that had been slid over them. The men who had been wheeling the carts from the boat were already busy now off-loading the fish. They chattered and gibed at one another as they emptied the carts, stooping and bending to empty the load.

"C'mon, Boomer, let's get them fish out."

"Hey, Will, don't be tearing them fish up. The Mister ain't gonna like 'em wrecked."

"Gimme 'nother cart."

Timothy shoved a cart up to the table with a bang and started scooping the fish onto the sloping trays. I had just finished loading all these fish and was getting mighty tired of them, but I went to the other side of the cart and started helping. The fish slid down and through the curtains. I could hear the garbled murmur of women talking. It didn't take long before the carts were unloaded and Timothy pointed to a water hose hung up on the side of the shed.

"Get them carts rinsed out. Wash 'em down into the water at the end of the dock. Then come inside and I'll show you what comes next. Make sure you get 'em cleaned good. The Mister liable to look 'em over. Then open them drains and do the same to the tables and trays. Don't be squirtin' the water through the curtains. Them women got knives."

He looked at me seriously, but a grin stole his look away. He started chuckling and ended up in a loud cackle.

"If there's one thing you'll learn here, it's keep them women happy. 'Sides, two of my sisters still live at home with me and my mother, and they're some of the ones I'm talkin' about."

When I'd finished and went in to the other section of the market, the intensity of smell was familiar. It had the same level of odor of the ship's hold. I was surprised at the number of men and women working on the catch. There were four rows of about a dozen people each cleaning the fish. Their respective tables were further separated by two long conveyors, so that rows of people sat facing one another in two long lines. There were upwards of forty-five people as busy as I'd ever seen.

"This here's Clark," Timothy announced loudly. "The Mister said we gotta show him what to do." He pointed at me and laughed. "You can start haulin' them buckets down to the dock. Just throw the leavings off the end. The gulls will take it from there."

With a chorus of greetings, the women resumed their chatter and cleaning. I watched for a few moments as knives flashed, fish were flopped, filleted, skinned and cleaned of anything that had been missed on board the boat. Once complete, the women pushed the filets on to a continuously moving belt which took the fish away from their stations. They talked to one another the whole time, almost as if they didn't have to look at what they were doing, but their hands never stopped moving. Between every other woman were huge black rubber buckets, most of them full to overflowing with skin, scales and slop. Every so often a woman would sweep the results of cleaning the fish into the bucket leaving herself with a semi-clean area to resume her work.

"Right here, boy," hollered one of the women.

I looked down the long set of tables to see one woman waving her arms.

C'mere, you're holding me up. Bucket's full."

I ran down the line of women and grabbed the bucket handle. The woman had to change positions when I took the handle, disrupting her work.

"Slide it on out and get me another one in here." She pointed to a stack of empty buckets next to the wall. "C'mon, boy, there's fish to do."

No sooner had I slid the full one out and put an empty bucket in place than another shout of "Here, boy!" assaulted the constant thrum of conversation. I dashed over to that woman, slid her bucket away and replaced it with an empty. I ran back to the first station and grabbed the brimming bucket. As soon as I lifted it, the flexible sides collapsed and much of what was in went out and spread across the floor. I stood there long seconds wondering what to do.

The woman turned in her seat and started to laugh. Before another heartbeat, her amusement had spread up and down the lines. My face flamed with the thought of all eyes on me.

"You've got to lift 'em easy," she laughed. "Otherwise, well, otherwise, that'll happen every time. And you've gotta keep up."

The rest of the afternoon swirled by with little time for thought. If there weren't buckets to be emptied, there were carts to push; if no carts needed pushing, knives needed to be sharpened on the big powered whetstone sitting in one corner, or the conveyor had to be wiped, or on and on and on. I managed to almost keep up, but it seemed like everyone wanted me to do something well before I finished what it was that I was doing at the time. They seemed to have a habit of needing me when I was the farthest away from the point of need.

At first I didn't notice when they'd finished. As if at a silent signal, the buzzing of the conveyor stopped, and the men and women began standing up and stretching, putting things away. I watched them trundle over to a big circular wash station where they shed their aprons, rubber gloves, and the protective plastic sleeves they'd worn while they were cleaning fish. I thought it was quitting time and walked over to join them. I was more than ready. I'd been up since before daybreak and I was tired.

I didn't make it to the washbasin.

"Where ya going, big boy." It wasn't a question. Timothy grabbed my arm. "We got another boat in early tomorrow morning. We gotta wash everything down, get them buckets emptied, tables wiped, knives all sharpened. There's lots of work to do. C'mon, we ain't leavin' this mess for a while yet."

He kept up a running litany while he led me back to the workstations.

"You get that hose and them brushes. We gotta get this done, almost time for dinner. I'll fetch the squeegee. The Mister stopped by a while ago. Yeah, that hose over there. Start washin' down from the far end. The Mister said your grandma wasn't havin' no fishy, smelly boy in her new house. Grab a couple of slickers off the hooks, we liable to get wet. How come you didn't say you was kin to the Mister? You can get all them buckets dumped, too. The Mister called my ma, and you're gonna stay with us for a coupl'a days. The trawler you was on need somethin'. Cap'n Jay ain't goin' out again till it's fixed."

I wasn't paying much attention until he came to the staying with them part. I stopped and looked at him with my mouth agape. I couldn't believe it! Not only had I been banished from my own home, I was now stricken from the rolls of Grandma's house, too.

Timothy must have seen my astonishment.

"Don't be worryin', there's plenty of room. The Mister said just till the boat's fixed. My ma will have a place set up for you. It ain't the first time we had company, and there's plenty of room at the table. I guess your grandma gotta put up with how the Mister smell, but she don't have to put up with you. Hah! The Mister brought you some other clothes, but I don't know why. You'll just get 'em fishy again tomorrow. Oh, yeah, you gotta be quick when you eat." He chuckled, almost to himself. "Everybody's hungry that comes to our house."

As I followed Timothy's instructions, I couldn't help feeling abandoned. I thought I'd done a fair job of fitting in on the trawler trying to help, trying to stay out of the way. I thought I'd done a fair, although an awkward and sloppy job, working in the fish shed. I'd followed Timothy's directions and listened to the loud calls of the people cleaning fish.

Finally, Timothy announced that the fish shed was completed. To me it still looked in disarray, but now the scramble of buckets and trays was thoroughly soaked as well. I wasn't in any mind to argue with him; my feet were dragging with fatigue.

"C'mon, big boy. It's time we were gettin' out of here. Ma's got dinner on by now. We only live a few blocks away."

I followed Timothy out of the large doors and lingered a few moments staring wistfully at the H. R. Helen tied at the far end of the dock. At least on board the boat, I'd gotten plenty of chances for idle time. There was no such thing in the fish shed, and the flurry of activity had made my head spin. Now that we were finished, I realized how tired I was.

Timothy took my arm once again and led me off the dock. We walked through a neighborhood dotted with houses, a scattering of tattered and rotting boats sitting on timbers, crossed alleys littered with debris and past "Fix-it-Joe" repair shops until we came to an old, imposingly tall house with a wide front porch. Two young women I recognized from the fish market sat on the rusty metal porch swing hanging from the exposed rafters. They smiled when Timothy introduced me. Naomi and Ruth were both chubby, plain looking women, only a few years older than I was, but their eyes held much more experience than my fourteen years had seen. They looked like just what they were, two people who had just finished a long day's worth of work.

They chatted with Timothy, but I was too tired to add much to the conversation until I heard Ruth laughingly say, "I think he spilled every bucket he put his hands on."

I'd slumped down on the porch steps while they talked but when they began to tease I got up and walked over to the swing. My mind was so fuddled with tiredness I couldn't do anything other than grin. They must have seen the weariness on my face, because they both got up and led me into the house.

The front room was lined with old, dark wood; the windows were shuttered against the evening sun, and there was an ancient and worn Persian rug on the floor. The furniture was old-fashioned, over-stuffed and lumpy, and every cushion was overseen by a doily draped across the back. There was a fireplace and on the mantle sat a picture of a man in uniform next to an American flag folded in a neat triangle.

"That's my daddy," Naomi said when she saw me looking at it. "I was just a little girl when he was killed in France during the War. Momma hardly ever comes in this room. She cries every time she looks at his picture…Now, let's get you cleaned up for dinner."

We walked into the kitchen, where their mother was busy preparing the meal. She turned to me when the girls spoke. I saw a pale, dumpling of a woman about ten or twelve years older than my mother, with already graying hair, a worn example of Timothy's sisters. Her face immediately lit into a smile, and the wear and years dropped away. She took several steps away from the sink wiping her hands on the apron she wore.

"Hello, Clark," she said, still smiling. "You're welcome here. Your grandfather's told me so much about you."

I hoped *that* wasn't so.

I was relieved by her warm greeting and it was obvious from her smile that Grandpa Merle hadn't told her everything there was to tell. My well-deserved family reputation was safe, at least for now. I thought that I'd have to be doubly sure it stayed that way. Best behavior stuff.

"Timothy, you and the girls get him cleaned up. Dinner's almost done. Naomi, call upstairs for the rest. Ruth, you call over to your sister's house."

Timothy walked me through the huge dining room onto a small back porch. The table stretched from one end of the room to the other. Chairs of all shapes and sizes were shoved up tight, and they were so jammed next to each other I thought that everyone would have to seat themselves simultaneously in order to avoid accidents.

I heard the call to dinner go up the stairs and next door. There was a thunder of footsteps as whoever was up came down. It was immediately followed by a repeated slamming of the front screen door as whoever was over there was now over here. The whole house was filled with voices, little, big, young, and old.

Timothy and I walked back into the dining room and it was full to overflowing with people of all ages and sizes. His mother went through a declaration of names, who belonged to whom, who was what, and how they got that way. I didn't even try to keep up with the names. There was an uncle who lived next door, a roomer who lived upstairs, and several other people who must have wandered in off the street. Three young children from next door were thrown in to the mix, and they belonged to Mary, another sister and her husband, Matt.

Timothy's mother came in and added platter after platter of food to the full table. She remained standing, and everyone held hands. I expected we were to say Grace and bowed my head.

"You don't have to bow your head in this house, Clark. In fact, I like to look at all the faces gathered around the table. I'll say thank you to Timothy, Ruth, Naomi, Matt and to your grandpa. They had everything to do with getting the food on this table and keeping the roof over our heads. No one else did. I haven't thanked God for anything since June 6th, 1941."

I'm sure the surprise must have shown on my face, but no one commented. I knew people whom I suspected of not talking to God. I knew people who should have but did not. I also knew lots of people who said they did despite their actions to the contrary. Timothy's mother was the first person I'd ever known who didn't and admitted it to one and all.

Yet the family acted like Christian folks. More than that really; they supported one another, laughed frequently and well, and from the conversation as they passed the food, were genuinely interested in the occurrences of each person's day. In particular, my first day in the fish market provided so much merriment that they seemed to not get enough of the stories. Each bucket spilled, each uncoordinated movement was related with laughter, pointed fingers, and what seemed an inordinate amount of enjoyment. From their faces, I determined that it was just a method their family used to make me feel at home. I did. Before the meal was finished, I felt as if I'd been eating meals there forever.

I was so weary after the long day that I could barely keep my eyes open. My participation in their family community grew less and less. Timothy's mother noticed the dull, glazed look on my face and whispered to him that he should show me where I was to sleep. The rest of the family began clearing the leavings of dinner, but Timothy motioned for me to follow him upstairs.

"My ma don't hold too much with churchy things," Timothy related as we climbed the stairs. "She's still so mad at God for takin' my father away and leavin' her to tend us kids by herself. I guess it was hard. We were all little when my father got killed. Noah was the oldest and he was just eleven. The worst part was that Dad didn't even have to go, not with all us kids. I guess he figured it was somethin' he had to do, and so he joined up. I can just barely remember him and Ruth was still at the breast. Now all we got is that picture and a flag."

My little room was located in the attic, two flights up, but I didn't notice much until the next morning. Timothy stood at the doorway and pointed into the dim space.

"There's the bed, big boy. I'll see you in the morning."

I'm sure my last conscious thought was trying to say goodnight to Timothy. I'm not sure I did.

He woke me when the room was still dim although faint sunlight was drifting through a small round window. Timothy was sitting on the side of the cot I'd slept on with an amused look on his face.

"You jabber pretty good when you're sleepin', big boy. You was goin' on about your Uncle Dave, and fightin' a war, and stuff. Then you said a slew of 'Amens.' C'mon, Ma's got breakfast on and we gotta get to it. Everybody will be eatin' by the time you get down there. I ain't waitin'. Bathroom's down the first set of stairs."

I nodded my head in reply trying to clear the sleep away. Initially, I didn't remember anything except the feel of the thin pillow against my face.

The small suitcase I'd left at my grandparents' house was sitting next to the cot. I hurriedly changed the clothes I'd slept in, took care of brushing my teeth as if my mother was watching, and went down the stairs to join in an already noisy, crowded breakfast. If anything, it looked like more people were seated at the table than had been there the previous night. Meals in this house were events. Morning hellos went around the group like I was a prodigal son, and I was more than a little taken aback by their welcome. I barely knew these people, but they all seemed to think I belonged there.

Breakfast was over in a hurry with people leaving as soon as they were refueled for the day's work. Mary and Matt and their children were the first to go, Mary slinging her two youngest on either side, nestling them on her hips. Matt took the third by the hand and grabbed small paper sacks from a line of them sitting on a sideboard as they said goodbye. When I finished eating, Timothy motioned for me to do the same.

"Ma's got us lunch packed up." He motioned to his two sisters. "C'mon, ladies, let's go. That boat liable to be there early. We got a full day today."

Timothy's mother gave them all hugs and smiles as they walked toward the door. I got one, too, as I followed her children out the door.

"You come back tonight, Clark," she said. "Don't let Timothy work you too hard. Or your grandpa."

The walk from their house to the fish market was leisurely, the girls and Timothy pointing out people's houses accompanied by quick stories about the inhabitants. They knew just about every body in every house we passed, and their tales were funny enough to wipe the last remnants of sleep away.

I longed to ask them about the non-prayer last night, but I was reluctant to talk about something I thought to be too personal. I'd been raised to believe that a profession of faith was almost as important as the faith itself. The Greene kids were encouraged to give testimony at the drop of a hat, witness in church, witness out of church, witness to people we knew and those we didn't. Although that was an aspect of the Baptists I particularly loathed, I was confused. All her children were named after Biblical figures, but Timothy's mother had flatly stated she didn't want anything to do with God. I wondered if the same requirement for declaration was valid for people who didn't believe.

That day of work didn't allow any thoughts of conversation beyond the workers' constant summons. They seemed to come at three second intervals. I managed to improve my spill rate, and consequently the laughter and teasing were also reduced. I was mostly out of breath from the running back and forth, so I don't know that I would have had much ability to answer anyhow. Mostly I just grinned a lot and tried to keep up. I saw Grandpa several times during the day, but he hadn't stopped to talk, nor did he appear to look in my direction. I did notice that he waved his hands just as vigorously when he talked with workers as he did when he talked to family. I was busy each time I saw him, but I did feel slighted that he'd not waved or nodded.

Lunch was an on-the-run ham sandwich in the mouth, keep on doing what was needed type break. Timothy and I went through the same end of day cleaning although we finished up much earlier in the afternoon. His sisters waited for us, and we all walked home together.

I kept hoping for a subtle way to ask about their mother's attitude toward God on the way to their house, but the twenty or so minutes were filled up with end of day relief that work was over. Everyone's attitude seemed to be "work hard while you're there, but drop it like a hot potato when you're not." Unlike my father, at the end of the day, they talked about the funny parts of work. My father had a habit of belittling every boss, other workers, and the job itself, as if it was beneath a man of his potential to even have to work. Timothy, Ruth, and Naomi labored with a purpose and took pride in their status as providers. More than that really, they spoke of co-workers with affection and worked as if a job was a contribution to a larger entity.

Dinner that night was a backyard picnic. Their home was backed by an alley. Their yard was open to everyone else's and it appeared that the neighbors were all invited. Long, haphazardly erected tables were full of food, a variety of contributions from Mrs. This or Mrs. That. I'd always considered my own house as a magnet for kids and grown-ups, but it had never been like this. The crowding of last night's dinner seemed minuscule in comparison to the beehive of bodies when we walked through the back door.

Every child I could see was running full tilt boogie between an ill-defined game of kickball and the fully loaded tables, snatching handfuls of food as they made the turn. Most of the adults were gathered in groups that turned when we walked into their yard, and they all hollered greetings. Timothy's mother walked over to us, took my arm and led me through a gauntlet of grownups. I was proclaimed "Clark, The Mister's Grandson," to one and all. I met the rest of Timothy's brothers and sisters; they all lived within the area, and attendance at the picnic appeared to be familial duty. Everyone knew Grandpa, and several of the men, by their familiar looks, must have had a connection with either the boats or the market.

"Just grab a plate and help yourself," she said, still holding my arm. "Your grandfather stopped by earlier. You'll be going back on the boat tomorrow. Timothy will walk you to the docks early enough."

We walked over to the table, and she softly said, "Ruth said something to me this morning. I'd like to talk to you before you go to bed. These get-togethers never last long, and after everyone's gone, you and I will find a few moments."

Later in the evening, people drifted off slowly, waving goodbyes, calling out instructions regarding left-overs, pets, and children. Except for family grandchildren, the back yard emptied of people; the adults carted the dirty dishes and half-emptied casseroles into the house, neighbors there one minute, gone the next. Timothy's mother beckoned to me from a bench in the corner of their yard.

I'd been worrying since she said she wanted to talk to me. I imagined my grandfather filling her in on my transgressions detailing my repeated problems and defiance. I'd worked myself into a fine temper by the time everyone left, and I suppose my foot-dragging approach caught her attention. I sat down next to her but stared straight ahead not wanting to hear a litany of my offenses. She turned on the bench and grasped my hand, but I continued to glue my eyes on the house next door.

"Ruth saw the look on your face last night when I thanked everyone before dinner. Everyone except God, that is." She laughed a sad laugh. "I really must apologize. It's my little speech whenever we get together. I'm so used to thanking my family that way, I forgot about offending someone else."

I turned to her, surprised at her sincerity.

"You didn't…" I started to tell her, but she kept on in her soft voice.

"When Joe was killed during the war, I sort of closed up on myself. It was such a terrible shock. I found out only when two men from the Army knocked at my door, telling me he was dead and that they wouldn't even be bringing his body home. I had nine children to take care of and nobody would help. Not his family, not my family, not our church. I suppose now that it was because of the war that they couldn't help, but I didn't know that then. No one had any money to spare. I got so mad at God for taking Joe from me. I'm still mad at God. How dare any loving God take a man who had so many reasons to live, a wife who loved him and a family that needed him. It wasn't fair then and it isn't fair now."

She was weeping while she spoke, shiny tear tracks following the lines on her face and droplets falling to splotch the dress she wore. I'd never experienced this type of adult confidence and was at a complete loss. Not knowing what else to do, I slid my hand from under hers and patted her arm.

"Your grandpa told me why you're here and about some of the problems your temper has gotten you into. He said you were mad most of the time."

I grimaced and thought, *Here it comes, another lecture.*

She continued. "Those years during the war were so hard. I took in laundry and sewing and watched other children for women who worked in the war effort. I know now that I made it harder on myself than I had to, what with the worry and me spending every moment being mad at the world."

I gave her one of my patented grunts of dismissal and boredom.

"That was just about as good as I used to do," she chuckled. "Almost. Mine were more poor-poor-me'ish, but you've got them down pretty good." She laughed again softly. "Then I started having so much trouble with my oldest, Noah; he was fourteen by then and wild without a father around. I thought it was another example of how God let me down."

I'd met Noah and his family during the picnic. He didn't look very wild to me. In fact, he looked just about like my father; he had a wife and a child.

"The police brought him home one night," she continued. "He and another boy had broken into a store and had stolen some food and things. When they ran out of the store, the police were there to meet them. It was a good thing one of the officers knew my Joe before the war. After the police left, Noah and I had a long, long talk. It was almost too late. The outcome was that I realized I'd been mad so long that it was rubbing off on my children, especially Noah."

Her tears continued and I couldn't think of a response. After long minutes she spoke again.

"Another result of our talk was that I knew that being mad at God didn't mean I had to be mad at everything. I also figured out that loving God had nothing to do with loving my family. I'd been raised to believe that loving God and loving anyone else were inseparable. That's just not true. I'll always be mad at God. He's probably just an old codger with nothing better to do than disrupt the lives of people, or maybe he's just the figment of somebody's imagination. I don't know who you're mad at, Clark, or why. You might consider that you don't have to be. It's such a waste of energy."

She rose slowly from the bench, took my hand, and we went into the house. The kitchen was still full of people cleaning up, kids running in and out, and overflowing with the general hubbub of their lives I'd already grown used to. There was much too much to think about. Timothy offered to whip me in a game of checkers, so at least I was spared the task of sorting out what his mother had said to me. I was still befuddled with the enormity of her declarations when everyone went up to bed.

The next morning Timothy took me to the docks in plenty of time before the boat cast off. He clapped me on the back and turned to go into the market.

"I'll see you when you get back," he called over his shoulder. "Catch us some fish, for Pete's sake. We got a boat in today, but nuthin' for a while after that. The Mister don't pay when there's no fish to cut."

Captain Jay was warming up the boat's engines, but the other two men hadn't yet made their appearance.

I waved a greeting to Jay and went to work cleaning up some debris that had been strewn about when the trawler was undergoing repairs. Hatch covers were askew, rags, nuts and bolts littered the deck, and the float baskets were not secure. I knew Jay would want the boat tidied up before we cast off. He was busy in the wheelhouse and didn't come down to the deck.

It wasn't long before Bill and Pete showed up, but they both looked like the last thing on their minds was going out on a fishing boat. I was on the far side of the deck, partially obscured in the darkness, still busy with cleaning up. They went directly to the wheelhouse with barely a nod. I was a little wary of Pete remembering how we parted when the boat came back into port. I knew I'd have to watch out for any payback from him.

It wasn't long before the men came back to the deck area and began casting off the lines which moored the trawler. Captain Jay eased the boat away and soon we were pushing our way out of the bay. The morning was overcast even though the sun was up. Dark gray clouds blanketed the sky. The air felt moist and heavy and a slight mist was already filling the air. I scrambled up the ladder to Captain Jay. He turned as I walked through the small door.

"There might be some weather today," he said. "It won't be much, and besides, we need the fish." He laughed a loud, flat sound over the noise of the engines. "You might even get another chance to throw up your guts. I want you to help out with the nets this time around, but check out the holds again, clean 'em up. Let's see if you can do more than take up space on deck."

Jay was a lot like most men I knew, particularly my father, spare with any encouragement or praise. My dad just didn't give out a thank-you very often. I didn't mind. Through years of my father's biting comments I'd learned to do the best I could and find satisfaction in an accomplishment aside from what others thought or said.

"You'll want to keep a little clear of the men this morning for a bit." He snorted again. "Looks like they both had a rough time last coupl'a days. Pete in particular. He's in a temper 'cause the Mister turned him down about having another boat. Pete used to be a skipper himself. That was before he let himself get tied up with the bottle." Jay gave me a knowing look. "With the Mister, it only takes once. Pete oughta be glad he's on board anything."

I was down in the holds for several hours. I'd noticed that the boat's motion had increased rocking fore and aft with the traverse of each wave and rolling sideways through each up and down. I was proud of the fact that I didn't get sick. By the time I'd finished cleaning and rinsing each compartment and went back on deck, we were well out into Lake Huron heading north.

I stood alongside the net baskets for a while gazing at the shore, a dim line in the day's gloom. The sky had darkened even with the morning's light. Bulging clouds, blackish with rain, covered the water from horizon to horizon with ominous intent. The wind had picked up as well blowing the tops of the waves into whitecaps. The wind also carried the water the entire length of the boat as it plunged into the undulating swells. I was worried about the approaching storm, but nobody else appeared to pay the sky any attention. Both of the men were busily straightening nets preparing them for the day.

"C'mon, big boy," Bill hollered. "We're gonna show you how to be a fisherman. You just watch us."

And that's what I did. I watched. When we began setting the nets, one or another of them would run the big drum winches while the other fed them on to and over the bid winch drum. The nets looked like big snakes as they came out of the hold turning this way and that. They had to untwist and fluff the nets as they went overboard straightening them as they were laid. The speed of setting was amazing, and the nets slithered over the drum with a blur of motion. It took all the strength each man had to feed them properly, attach the floats, and reach for more. I was kept busy just shuttling the floats back and forth to the stern. Pete kept up a running litany as he worked.

"Don't grab the nets so your fingers get tangled; hold *around* the net."

"That net'll suck you straight over the side."

"You gotta guide it out of the hold and over the winch."

"Hook them floats on the top rope.

"Fer Chrissakes, watch where you step."

"That net'll tip you ass over teakettle."

"Keep your hands away from the drum."

"You're on a boat. This ain't a car. It takes a while to get it stopped if you get in trouble."

"That drum'll smash your arm in a skinny minute."

"Pay attention. This ain't no game."

He'd said the latter many times before. I knew it wasn't a game and I did pay attention. Once the net hissed over the side, the only evidence remaining was the line of floats extending out from the stern of the boat. Everything else slid out of sight, down, down, down into the water. The practiced work of the men amazed me. I doubted whether I'd ever be able to be of any use and said as much.

The weather got heavier, and the boat mimicked a huge teeter-totter. It was necessary for me to keep both legs spread apart to maintain balance. The pitching grew to such an extent that it was also important to have a hand clutching something to stay upright. As I pushed a basket to the stern, Bill watched my sliding, indirect effort.

"Don't worry, big boy. You're gettin' it. One hand for you, one for the boat." He thrust his face close to mine and chuckled. "You're out here to fish. We're gonna teach you how. This's how we do it. The Mister said you gotta learn."

I finished that day just watching (and being sick to my stomach). I had a hard time suppressing the urge to vomit. I suppose the only reason I didn't was pride. I couldn't bear the thought of the teasing I knew I'd get from them.

Both men worked as if there was nothing out of the ordinary.

Although each man was slight of build, they were very strong in the arms and upper body. Even so, I could see their necks bunch and cord up with the terrific strength it took to lay out and haul the nets. Their synchronized exertions at the winches convinced me that the only thing that could happen if I lent a hand was disaster. I dreaded being told to help them. One of the traits I picked up from my father was a terrible dislike of criticism in any form or fashion. Both Pete and Bill had kept after me mercilessly after I'd been sick in the hold. I knew there'd be plenty more comments if I had to get involved with this aspect of the job.

I also finished the next day mostly watching although both men would frequently motion to me to put a hand here or there. I still had to do the peripheral duties for them: keeping the float baskets full, helping out when fish came aboard, sluicing the deck clean without end, and stacking the fish in the hold. When there was work, it was frantic and difficult. The idle time aboard this fishing trawler was little and infrequent, except for sleeping and eating. There was mostly just work.

We had several more days of murky and unpredictable weather. The fishing wasn't good; nets that had previously bulged with their load now came up lamely sporting few fish. All three men grew surly and morose over the poor catch. Meal times became a hard stare silence, each man seemingly trying to outdo the other with their lack of good humor. More than once when I passed by or ate with Bill, I smelled the sour odor of alcohol issuing from him. The last day we were out, I wondered how anyone could miss his foul breath and uncoordinated movements about the deck.

Neither grandparent was waiting to laud their triumphant fisherman grandson home that time. The dock was almost as empty as the holds of the boat. No hustle of carts, no bustle of people scurried about the wooden wharf. The dockside of the fish market looked forlorn without its normal activity. Jay signaled numerous times with the air horn as we coasted up to the dock. Finally, Timothy came stumping out to greet us.

"Ha! The Mister sent all the women home a'ready. We gonna have to unload 'em and cut 'em up. There's still a few packers here. They'll stay if we hurry."

I groaned with disappointment, but the men's reaction was completely different. Excluding Captain Jay, who didn't appear particularly pleased himself, the sounds that came from Pete and Bill were just shy of outright mutiny. They cussed and ranted for long minutes before Jay shut them up.

"You men! It's okay with me if you don't clean 'em. We can dump 'em off the dock. I don't give a damn. 'Course, that means no pay for the last four days. I can stand it if you can. Now, we can either get to it or get out. 'Course gettin' out means I'll have to find another crew on top of unloadin' these fish by myself."

The scowls regarding the poor fishing were hard while we were on the water, but those were nothing compared to the granite eyes of Pete and Bill when Jay finished his speech. I thought they'd both walk off the boat. Instead, their loud curses diminished to mumbling and they turned away. They tore open the hatches throwing the covers across the deck. Jay's eyes, a mirror of theirs, followed them until they walked down the short ladder. I chased after Timothy to bring the big wheeled carts while Jay lowered the conveyor into an open hatch.

Although this catch was scant by comparison, the thought of doing the extra parts made it seem the larger. There were lots fewer hands to get all the work done. I just knew we'd be here half the night. As the carts were filled, their size grew and grew in my mind. I

241

pictured myself laboring unappreciated, lonely in my thankless task. I could hear the men's continued complaints from the hold every time we went back with an empty cart. My mood grew to match the men's.

Timothy didn't seem to mind. He went about the work with the same cheerful doggedness he did everything else. He couldn't help but notice my sullen attitude.

"You jus' makin' it harder, big boy," he said with a laugh.

I didn't answer him but gave him a good imitation of the angry looks I'd seen over the past few days.

He laughed again. "If you keep on fumin' like that, this here pile of fish gonna get so huge we can feed a bunch. Jus' like Jesus." He chortled at his own wit, and I couldn't help but smile. "We ain't lookin' to do that. Don't you know it's just work. It ain't the end of the world. When we get done, we get done. It ain't no never-mind."

His good spirits didn't have much of an effect on me past the scant grin. I continued to look at the dark side of the tasks during the next several hours. While we were pushing the carts back and forth, the number of fish being thrown on the conveyor diminished steadily. I thought we were finishing up, when I heard Jay holler.

"What the Hell's going on down there?" He crouched by an open hatch, peering down below. "Fer Chrissakes! WhatinHell you doing?"

Timothy and I walked onto the boat and took positions alongside Jay peering into the dim space below.

Both men were asleep, slumped next to some remaining few fish. Between them lay an empty bottle.

"Damn a drunk!" Jay spat. "The sonsabitches are drunk!"

He picked up a hatch cover, carried it back, and slammed it down with a crash on the opening.

"Let'em lay there till morning. Hell, let'em lay there forever! Timothy, run home and see if your sisters can come back. C'mon, Clark, let's finish this up and get to them fish."

I was right. We did work until late into the night. Timothy's sisters came back, along with another woman who worked there. The three women led the charge, and their speed put us all in the back seat. We did the job though. Bill and Pete stumbled in around midnight, just as we were finishing, but took one look at Jay's face, turned, and walked right back out. We all cleaned up after the last of the fish had been sent down the conveyors to the people packing them up. The last hour or so I'd been plagued with incessant yawning. I just couldn't stop even though I noticed secret smiles from the rest of the group. In parting, Jay told me we wouldn't be going back out the next day, and Timothy added that there weren't any other boats scheduled in either. Their announcements suited me fine. I'd been on the go since 5 o'clock that morning. I was numb with weariness, barely able to comprehend the fact that we were finally going to stop.

I didn't register much during the walk to Timothy's house. I didn't remember getting up the stairs and climbing into bed. The sun was well toward its zenith when I did manage consciousness. I heard the noises of a busy house from below, but I didn't get up, instead I chose to review the past night's work lying under the coverlet. It hadn't been so bad after all.

Everybody worked. Everybody helped. Everybody got done.

The rest of my summer exile went by in similar fashion. I stayed with Timothy's family, never once enjoying the imagined luxuries of my grandparents' home. My summer was work, work and then a little more work to balance things out. I managed to hold up my end of the load despite having to work with new crew members when my grandfather fired Bill and Pete.

I metamorphosed into something similar to a deck hand and gained ten pounds or so of muscle, bronzed into a semblance of careless coordination on deck and off. The physical segment of growing up came despite my efforts to hold it at bay. If the sensibility that should have followed would have come with it at the same time, I'd have been better off.

I was never what you'd call a frugal person. I guess it was because I never had much money, and in some perverse way I thought it better to spend what I had quickly. I might have been listening to my Grandpa Clark's words: "Spend it before it disappears all by itself." In fact, if compared with the old fable, I'd have been the grasshopper. I had a history of spending whatever I had in my pockets. I learned that my paper-route money would purchase forbidden cigarettes (if I believed my mother, the scant money, by default, additionally purchased eternal Hell-fire). Later, my earnings from the gas station went toward the family when my father disappeared, my old junker of a 1939 Pontiac, and anything else I managed to earn was swallowed up in teenage spending.

The only attempt I ever made at savings was what my Grandpa Merle had paid me for working in the fish market and on the boats, and that was because the government bonds couldn't be cashed in when I got them. Even that small egg was eventually lost when my parents' money woes took precedent over my earnings, and they cashed the bonds in to pay household bills.

Chapter 11
Friends and Enemies

Phil and I had been sort of friends since the fifth grade.

But from the very first our friendship was strange. As young boys, we could often be counted on to deliver the other a black eye, a bloodied lip, or at the very least a grass stained knee, but when the fights were over, we ended up curiously side by side. Perhaps it had to do with the fact that Phil was moody and that there was overwhelming evidence that I was unpredictable. Our curious loathe/like friendship carried us through adolescence and into our teens, and we still battered each other frequently. Why we were friends, I couldn't have said, but we were.

We lived in the same neighborhood, went to the same school and played together, but playing changed as we progressed in age. When twelve was a memory and thirteen was a goal, we'd quit "playing," a milestone for boys when games transform themselves into a singular activity called hanging out. Idle minds and devil's workshop more closely fit the description of our relationship. By the time1962 rolled around, Phil had turned sixteen, had quit school (or was kicked out) and he'd become off-limits to me. Phil had been held back several grades in school. He'd gotten to the point that he couldn't and wouldn't make the effort, a snowball effect that I'd experienced myself. His being sent into the banished lands by Mrs. Greene put a slight quash on our friendship, but it didn't stop our relationship altogether.

According to my mother, Phil came from a broken home, whatever that meant. The phrase was ill-defined in our house although there were several families in Pointe aux Peaux that caused a distasteful downward curl of my mother's lips. My mother had also hung the tag of sullen on Phil. His home was well shattered; he lived with his aunt and uncle and never revealed to me where his parents were. He spat a few well directed epithets whenever he referenced his folks but never told me more. He wasn't happy about living with relatives, and I didn't blame him. For one thing, he wasn't too much younger than the adults he lived with. For another they both seemed put upon that Phil was with them. Phil was big for his age, and auntie and uncle didn't really show any interest in his raising. Maybe they didn't know how. They sure weren't inclined to learn. Phil grew up wild: wild at home, wild at play and wild at school, which was why he didn't attend any longer.

I actually envied his no school status. My fervent wish was to be free of school. I'd have much rather been running through the marsh with Patch exploring for lake treasures or whiling away the time doing any one of hundreds of different activities. There was plenty for me to learn and know in my wilderness despite the intrusion of Fermi's atomic power plant construction. Patch and I had become adept at keeping out of sight of their security people, and there was a vast area that we could still ramble about in comparative safety. I was most at home away from home in the sanctity and solitude of the marsh. My parents, of course, had other designs on my time, and seeing as how I was living under their roof, eating their food, and wearing the clothes (albeit second hand) they paid for, I didn't have a great deal to say about the matter of education.

But Patch and I saw Phil almost every day on my paper-route. He could be counted on for a chat and a coke (as well as a forbidden cigarette) just about the time I needed a break, and I often stopped in. Every once in a while he'd even hook a couple of bottles of beer out of the refrigerator. His aunt and uncle both worked, and he was left to his own devices from Monday through Friday. We'd banter about the degrading aspect of school (me), being stifled and sickened by adult authority (both of us) or girlfriends (him). Phil was much, much, much older than I in girl years. He'd been "going steady" with the same girl for a year despite her parents' best efforts to keep them apart.

He was the first boy my age who openly admitted an intimacy with a girl. My naïveté wasn't unusual in the early sixties; sex education had just been introduced into the public schools and every teacher I ever had was embarrassed to be talking about it. Growing up under a Baptist roof did nothing to further my knowledge of things carnal. Delightfully I was forced to learn details on my own but had never spoken of them to anyone. Phil's declaration wasn't boastful or proud but he was thorough; he was in love and had plans to marry the girl at some dreamy, distant day in the future. Phil always could be counted on for a detailed account of his latest discovery, flight, or escapade.

He wasn't happy about their relationship's peripherals either. Ginny's father couldn't stand the sight of Phil and had "escorted him" off their front porch every time he visited. Ginny's mother started muttering whenever he knocked on their door. If I thought my association with Phil was combative, it was nothing compared to the one he had with his girlfriend's father. They'd been involved in any number of fist-fights and yelling matches resulting in Phil's spending considerable time in the juvenile home in Monroe. His troubles did nothing to raise him in my mother's eyes, and she would pointedly remark about any mention of his name in the newspaper.

Phil and Ginny had been making plans to run away, and their plans were growing more desperate; Ginny was pregnant. That declaration was earth shaking for me. As that summer progressed, I was privy to more and more of their guarded secret. I listened as his schemes grew more and more wild. Phil was going to "borrow" his uncle's car, and they'd head out west. He'd find a good job somewhere but wasn't clear about what it would be, only that he'd make lots of money. Phil had been hoarding and borrowing money from everyone he could. He'd also been stealing a few dollars here and there from his aunt and uncle whenever there was opportunity. I donated several paper-route dollars which Phil swore to repay when he got settled.

One late night, after everyone had gone to bed at my house, I heard pebbles being thrown against my upstairs bedroom window. My bedside clock said it was almost midnight. I looked onto the front yard. Phil was standing under our big maple tree. He motioned to me and I raised my hand in a wait-a-minute gesture and told Patch to lie back down. After dressing quickly, I slid through the back yard window, slithered over our peaked roof, listened a moment to make sure I hadn't awakened my folks, and joined him in the yard.

"I just beat the shit out of her old man," he hoarsely whispered.

Just as he told me that, we heard sirens. Toward the front of the subdivision, I could see the reflection from the lights of the sheriff's car as they sped through the gates. We backed into the shadows along side the house. Two sheriff's cars their lights flashing roared by my house.

"I got to hide. Her old man caught me in her bedroom. I got out the window and ran at first, but I heard him hittin' her when I was outside. I went back," Phil gasped. "I kicked down their door and busted his ass."

In the dim light, I could see that he was battered; his shirt was torn and a scrape dribbled blood from his cheek.

I started to tell him he should tell the cops what happened but didn't get to finish.

Suddenly he bolted, running off into the night. I called after him, but he didn't stop.

"I'll see you later!" he yelled back to me.

Screaming sirens and flashing lights were a sure fire way to awaken the whole neighborhood. Lights began to go on in my house and most of the other homes along Goddard Drive. Although as good Baptists, we pronounced indifference of other people's business, we paid better lip service to a discussion of their perceived faults.

My father stepped out onto the porch.

"Whatareyoudoinouthere?" he demanded. "What's going on?"

He walked out in the front yard and stood by my side. I told him I'd heard the sirens.

"I didn't hear your stairway pull down," he interrogated. "Somebody was talking out here. How'd you get out here so fast?"

I made up some lame excuse; the sheriff's cars had parked down the road for some time with their lights flashing before they turned on their sirens; their whirling red lights had awakened me, and I came down to see what was happening but didn't know any more than that. I did not respond to the "someone talking" part. He must have been groggy from his interrupted sleep because he seemed satisfied. He gave a snort of disgust and turned to go back into the house.

"Get back to bed," he commanded. "Nobody who's up to any good is up at this hour."

I watched him walk into the house but didn't follow him immediately. I saw him through the front window as he walked toward the bedroom he shared with my mother turning off lights as he went. I waited just long enough not to be blatantly disobedient. I'd spent years gauging this time period and had it down to a fine art. Not too soon, to avoid seeming completely subservient and not too long, to cause him to find out why I hadn't obeyed more quickly. When the house was dark again, I went in and pulled down the fold-up staircase to my bedroom on the side porch. I'd inherited the bedroom when Carole went off to college and the secluded spot suited me just fine.

The screech of its springs told my folks that I was a good, mindful son after all. I went through the entire dumb-show of re-folding the stairs and pushed them back up and allowed them to slap against the ceiling frame. I listened for a few moments and heard nothing in the still house. I slipped out the front door, muffling the bells my mother had hung up as an early warning system.

I walked toward Ginny's house, knowing Phil would be somewhere close by watching the commotion.

He was hiding in the shadows next door to Ginny's. I'd made my way to a vacant lot adjacent to their house and stayed well hidden as I approached. I didn't see him at first although I was pretty good at picking out places to hide. I'd had plenty of practice myself, but I sure didn't see his. I whispered his name several times into the darkness. He grabbed my arm when I crept by and almost scared me to death.

"Get over here. Scoot back in these bushes," Phil whispered. "Whatthehell you come down here for?"

I backed into the hedge, watching the lighted house as I scooted. The lights played over his partially hidden face when I turned toward him. I told him I wanted to see what was going on.

"They're in there with that asshole," he sneered. "As soon as they're done, they'll be lookin' for me."

I asked him what he was going to do.

Phil didn't answer me but kept looking toward the house. We crouched watching in the dark for long minutes. He pulled me by the arm and we abandoned our hidey hole. We walked down to the lake, still not talking. We sat by the pillars for a long while.

"What I ought to do is take my uncle's shotgun back there and shoot his ass."

Phil continued to rant a while more and I just let him vent his anger. I thought he'd tire himself out and go home to wait for the sure call of the deputies. I also harbored a worry that any attempt at dissuasion would lead to a more violent discussion between us. While I wasn't afraid of Phil, I was concerned that if we did scuffle, it would only lead to a discovery that I was out in the middle of the night. After listening to the sound of the waves breaking on Lake Erie's shore, Phil walked off muttering to himself.

I didn't see Phil for several days after his fight with Ginny's father. In fact, no one knew where he'd gone, least of all me. The sheriff's cars cruised up and down the subdivision and everybody knew why. My mother had new fuel for her "he's not good for you" arguments. The story of Phil's unprovoked (as the father's side of the story was told) attack on a good providing man was condemned across the board. Unfortunately, I'd put myself in a position that didn't allow any defense of him. Not that any would have done much good. In those few days, Phil had taken on the label of someone who was bad clean clear through and speeding toward worse.

All of a sudden, he was home sitting in his aunt and uncle's kitchen when I slid their paper inside the screen door. He looked tired. He looked angry and he was dirty as if he'd been sleeping outdoors.

I asked where he'd been.

"WhatinHell do you care?"

I started to say something but was taken aback by the ferocity of his question.

"I'm waitin' for the cops," Phil growled. "I'm gonna let 'em take me to jail, and when I get out, me'n Ginny are gettin' the hell out of here. Her old man ain't gonna do shit. Ginny told him she's pregnant. Her dad wants her out of the house before anybody else finds out."

Phil's tone was dismissive and I could tell he didn't really want to talk. I put my hand on his shoulder, but he immediately shrugged away my touch. I told him I'd see him later.

"Yeah..."

I heard from my mother that the sheriff had come for Phil later that evening. Mom was triumphant.

"See what happens when you don't stay in school."

Mom continued to re-run her stay-in-school speech for me and the rest of the family over the next two weeks. I'd stopped in to talk to Phil's uncle several times after I delivered papers, and he'd told me that Phil got only two weeks jail time. I didn't mention Phil's plans to his uncle. He didn't seem very pleased with the short incarceration that Phil had received.

When I next saw Phil, he was sitting on the small porch outside the house. He was hunched over, elbows on his knees looking miserable. The patio was littered with empty beer bottles, and his hand held one that was well on its way to joining the dead soldiers at his feet. He didn't respond when I said hello. He did look up when I sat down next to him.

"The sonofabitch sent her away," he spat. "The sonofabitch sent her away to have the kid and he won't say where. The cops told me if I bother him anymore, I'll get six months."

He reached behind the chair he was sitting on and slid a shotgun across his knees. I startled at the sight of the gun. I understood sad; I understood mad, but this distressed deliberation was completely new to me. The situation had black-magically changed into something I wasn't able to deal with. With a show of bravado, but only a show, I reached for the shot-gun and slowly pulled it toward me. Relieved that he didn't snatch it back, I laid the gun on the patio well beyond his reach.

I told him that there'd be a way to find out where Ginny was and that she would get in touch with him somehow.

Phil emptied the beer from the bottle and tossed it to the ground.

"I'll make that asshole tell me if she don't get in touch with me."

I took the shotgun with me when I left. When I walked down the driveway, Phil was still sitting in the chair. He had another beer in his hand and from the tilt of his head was trying to see what was in the bottom.

I must have surprised Mrs. Nelson when I dropped the newspaper inside her door. It wasn't everyday that a paperboy delivers the news armed with a shotgun. She did a double-take at the gun causally stuck in the crook of my arm. Although I felt anything but casual in the aftermath of Phil's dark mood, I laughed it off.

I said I was sorry and that I'd borrowed the shotgun and was just taking it home to clean it up.

From her alarmed look, I figured I probably shouldn't carry the shotgun much farther on my route. Besides that, I had to pass my house on the way down Goddard and I knew certain-sure if Mom saw the firearm there'd be an indefinite delay in delivering the remainder of the papers. She'd have had all sorts of questions that I couldn't answer. I stashed the shotgun in some scrubby bushes alongside a summer cottage used only on the weekends. I'd come back for it later and return it when Phil's aunt and uncle were home.

After dinner that evening, I told my folks I was going down to the beach. I whistled to Patch and we ambled off in a direction opposite that of Phil's house and for good reason. My mother's parting shot was: "you stay away from that Lore boy."

Patch and I doubled back, retrieved the shotgun, and were approaching Phil's house when we were greeted with the sounds of a screaming session. From Goddard Drive, I could see that the empty beer bottles hadn't been picked up. I skirted along the border of their long driveway, and the noise of argument grew louder with every step I took. Patch started growling as we closed in on the house and I had to order her, "Down! Stay!"

The open screen door did nothing to muffle the hollering that was going on inside. I stood for several moments at the corner of their garage and quietly ejected the shells from the shotgun. I tucked the casings in my pocket, leaned the shotgun up against the garage, and slowly backed away from the conflict. There was no way I could have gotten involved in this, and the last thing I thought his aunt and uncle needed to see was me bringing back a shotgun. I hoped one or the other would see it if they came outside or when they left for work the next day. The furor paused and I hoped that they'd run out of shrieking points to make, but before I got back to the spot where Patch was waiting, it began again. I couldn't make out many words, but the ones I heard weren't allowed in the Greene house.

I made my meandering way home troubled about Phil, troubled about Ginny and even more troubled at the whole situation. I knew I couldn't see through a brick wall any better than most people, but I knew first hand where Phil's dark moods often led him. I had the scars to prove it. I hoped the whole set of issues would somehow dissipate but didn't know if there was anything I could do to help them mist away.

I was distracted throughout the entire next morning. Mom had a barrel of chores for me to set right, and before I knew it, I had to pick up my papers for delivery. The walk along the route further shoved all thoughts of Phil into some recess and I lost myself in the task at hand. Garty's, Sims's, Labeau's, White's, Maus', Brown's, Neidermeir's, Adams', their houses came and went, their papers folded just so with a twist, deposited in doors or boxes marked The Monroe Evening News, all in a line next to mailboxes. Patch was up to her normal investigations of everything and anything on the face of the earth turning back again and again to see if I was interested, too. I made my way down the beach, past the water treatment station, Burrer's, Moody's, Worrel's. I'd put away Phil's problems until I found myself walking down the drive to his house.

Patch began to growl ominously. The weight of the situation collapsed in on me an extra burden to the newspaper bag over my shoulder. I picked up my pace to a trot. I hollered Phil's name as we walked onto the patio, and I noticed that the beer bottles had been picked up. Patch's growl deepened and she walked stiff legged, muscling herself into the lead, her hackles raised into a lion's mane. I hollered Phil's name again. The rhyme from a children's book came to my mind: "Something is not right, said Miss Clavell into the night." I chuffed myself for being silly.

I opened the screen door and started to toss paper into the kitchen.

From the doorway, the brick wall disintegrated. I know for certain time stopped. I saw everything clearly.

Phil was lying on the kitchen floor, the shotgun still clenched in one hand. The back of his head was splattered on the white cabinets, an obscene and scarlet exclamation. He lay awkwardly, sprawled in an unholy pose, his arms backlit by a pool of blackish blood staining the floor. The collar of his madras shirt was soaked down to his shoulders. A chair was overturned and lay next to him on its side. The kitchen was suffused with a smell, sweet and acrid all at once, cloying and thick.

I tasted coppery bitter spit in my mouth. My stomach gave a violent wrench. I moaned and my legs buckled. I almost caught myself as I went all the way down, but my muscles betrayed me and I found myself kneeling in the doorway, close to collapse. Patch was barking furiously; more startling punctuations, but the sound was distant and dim. I knelt in the door for long minutes, etching this, imprinting this, trying to understand this.

I'd failed miserably in my perception of what could happen and immediately knew I'd been mindless in returning the shotgun. I had the sickening feeling that understanding wasn't the only thing I'd failed at.

I knew about death; I'd lost friends and family to it, had seen it up close, and had been brought up to understand that there was something after we shucked the mortal coil. I was taught to believe that there were rewards to be expected, treasures to be gained if we had faith. I'd heard stories of people being borne up to heaven in flaming chariots and lifted up into the hereafter on wings of angels. But this, this obliteration, this was way past my reckoning.

I wobbled up, turned and stumbled out of the doorway. I tossed their paper onto one of the chairs.

I don't remember delivering any more newspapers, usually a short two hour task for me. I do remember that by the time I got home that summer evening, it was full dark and the paper-bag was empty, but I cannot tell you where the news went. I vaguely recalled the distant sound of sirens as I'd trudged along the memorized trail of paper delivery. I don't remember Patch following me although she always did. My house was lit up like a beacon as I walked across the baseball field toward home. It was a goal that I didn't really want to reach.

Mom's bells tolled my arrival, a knell for Phil. My mother and father were sitting in the living room when I hung the paper bag on our homemade hall tree. I heard my brother and sister in there, squabbling about something. I went directly to my bedroom stairway and pulled it down without my normal "I'm home" greeting.

My mother came into the porch doorway and watched me as I unfolded the stairs.

"The Lore boy...

"I know, Mom. His name was Phil. *Phillip* Lore. I know more about it than I want to."

"You see what happens..." she kept on.

I took a step in my mother's direction, and she stopped in mid-sentence. I aged as I stood in front of her facing her close up. My father got up from his chair and stood behind her. My eyes traveled between the two.

"I don't want to hear you say anything about my friend, Mom."

I turned, pulled the staircase down and climbed up the stairway.

Teenage boys are great at remembering some distant but audible call to long ago tribal gatherings.

During my teen years, I may have traded my childhood feathers and war paint for Old Spice and Vitalis, but I felt the thrumming of Indian drums in my veins just as if I'd lived half naked in a teepee on the western plains. Other kids joined groups of wandering and nomadic savages, seeking safety in the numbers and following a mysteriously selected leader. Different tribes huddled together at basketball or football games, hunted their elusive prey (girls, of course) through the halls at school, and generally made fools of themselves at every opportunity.

One of the rights of passage ceremonies were dances. The only difference was that these didn't have a fire to dance around. During the early 60s, we had any number of dances to choose from; chaperoned school dances, which my mother considered only moderately immoral, sock hops at Dixie Skateland (closer to Lucifer, but also close to home, and therefore, reluctantly agreed to), dances held at one of the beaches and considered more suspect. They required excellent behavior on my part for several weeks before and after. Finally, in the distant city of Monroe (8 or so miles away), were street dances, held every other Saturday night for the duration of the warm weather. They started while school was still in session and lasted throughout the summer. My mother must have felt her influence diminished with distance or she liked knowing that she could save my sins more quickly if the need arose. Unfortunately, the far-off dances in Monroe were judged to be the very bowels of Hell, and I couldn't attend those, unless I resorted to deception, which of course, I did.

These street dances were curious affairs. The city fathers cordoned off several blocks, hired the evening away to one or another disc-jockey, and then watched nervously as kids did what kids have done for centuries. Boys looked for girls to seduce and girls looked for boys to enchant. The temporary enclosure was packed with overtime working police, sheriff's deputies, and nervous parents trying to prevent the prevalent opposite-sex attraction. The music provided was carefully selected; successive loud rock and roll records were prohibited and had to be interspersed with some soft and soothing tune from previous eras lest the boiling liquid in our veins skyrocket.

The police officers had two jobs; first, to insure every girl went home as chaste as when she arrived, and second, to prevent those aforementioned boy-tribes from beating the hell out of one another. Knots of hair-slicked teens, clannish to the extreme, puffed out their chests and sneaked cigarettes between each other, exuding a fearful bravado among the other like-minded boys. They were identified by high-school jackets or rolled up jeans over engineer boots. Skirmishes between tribes were inevitable, if brief; some were settled quickly by a rough shove, while others lead to promises of retaliation after the streets had cleared of dancers or postponed to some other night.

The perspiring parents were kept busy estimating the distance between groins during slow dances or the amount of jiggle in a particular bosom. All the while they peered into the inevitable shadows of alleys and store-fronts. The music was infrequently interrupted by a father-daughter march toward a waiting car or in a beeline to a lighted home. Just as often a former swaggering teenage hoodlum was escorted through the crowds by some cop who vice-gripped the kid's arm. I'm not sure parents or police were completely successful on either count.

The street dances required a carefully planned fraudulence on my part. My Baptist mother did not approve of dancing or any other physical contact with the opposite sex. None of my friends had a car so we were forced to beg or borrow a parent's. In my house borrowing a car was out of the question so I never bothered to ask.

Fortunately, Bernie's father had a dim memory of being a teen and would occasionally allow his son to use the family car. They had a 1959 Oldsmobile 98, a huge boat of a car with a powerful engine, and it had enough room for two other guys besides Bernie and me. His father used to joke about their big car; "It's better to have that big engine and not need it than to need it and not have it." The car also had plenty more room for the hordes of willing young females we were sure to pick up during the evening.

But getting transportation to Monroe was only part of the issue. I needed to come up with a valid reason to go out in the first place. Often I used Dixie Skateland as the destination; it seemed like my mother was getting used to my excursions there and had come to accept them a part of her growing son. She might check my pockets for a ticket stub and for sure sniff my clothes for the tell-tale smell of cigarettes the next morning, but at least she'd let me go.

So it was that Bernie, Don, Harley, and I found ourselves surrounded one summer evening by the hostile aborigines that inhabited Monroe. I don't recall the reason; it could have been that one of us that cut in on a dance. Most likely it was Harley. Music of any sort turned some switch in Harley. He could become wild with the throb of rock and roll. He'd proved it many times wherever we went and had been chased out of the skating rink on several occasions. He was also good at swooping down on an unsuspecting couple inserting himself into their precious moment and whirling away with the girl before the astonished boy could react. Whatever the reason, we were soon playing "your turn, my turn," a shoving match in the middle of Elm Street surrounded by a half-dozen bristling kids wearing Catholic Central jackets and about three hundred encouragers.

Harley had a mouth to match his manner; brash and bold, he'd let fly with whatever came to mind, Devil take the hindmost. He was quick to offend whoever was close at hand and he did his usual great job.

"You can have her back!" Harley sneered to the boy in front of him. "She's got socks for titties!"

I next remember being flat on my back in the middle of the street with one or two or three people trying their best to pummel me to death. I saw Bernie out of the corner of a quickly swelling eye and he wasn't doing much better although he was still standing. The crowd must have smelled our foreign scent; we were Beach Kids, definitely outsiders, pariahs to be stoned. Or worse.

Of course the swell of noise attracted the police. The fight didn't last long, but it did leave marks. My eye was swelling shut, Bernie's lip was split and Harley had a torn shirt and reddened cheek. I didn't see Don just then but knew he'd been in it. The cops shoved their way through, separated the combatants, and marched us away from each other and out from under the eyes of the screaming crowd. I thought they were taking us to jail and briefly wondered how I was going to explain that to my mother.

Instead, they shoved the four of us against the alley wall of a store while they decided what to do.

They began questioning us. I thought surely Harley's smart mouth would get us in deeper trouble and it almost did. One officer asked where we were from.

"What's it matter to *you*?" Harley asked.

From the reaction of the officers, I thought Harley must have questioned their parentage. They began shoving us around, jerking us this way and that until they got tired of the sport. Finally, one of us said we were from Stoney Pointe. I could hear the music in the background. At least we hadn't disturbed the dance for more than ten seconds or so. Finally they took turns shoving us out of the alley.

"You boys head on home now," one said. "What is it with you beach kids? You come back to another dance here and you'll have to get your daddies to come get you. Understand?"

We walked toward the parking lot by River Raisin, lamenting our poor luck, assigning whatever demeaning names we could to those "at fault." Someone (it might have been me) came up with the idea to play the incident to our advantage,

"Let's tell everybody at school how them CC punks ganged up on us. The cops, too!"

From that beginning, our plan took on a fuller glory. We would borrow any bandages, gauze, iodine, etc. and get together before school on Monday.

I told my folks I'd fallen and bashed my head at the skating rink, a story they accepted. I'm sure the others came up with similar stories to explain their bruises and scratches.

It was a fine Monday morning. We all showed up at the bus stop early. Bernie had a crutch that his father used when he'd fractured an ankle several years before. Harley had enough bandages, splints and slings to outfit a WWII MASH unit. I'd brought along Mercurochrome, Bag-Balm and old sheets I'd torn into strips. Don brought catsup. Perfect.

We looked terrible…as long as no one looked closely. Harley's head was bandaged to the size of a small pumpkin with plenty of catsup gore leaking down the side of his face. We tied Bernie's leg up off the ground and wrapped an old sheet around his foot to make it appear like he'd stepped on a land mine. Don's arm was in a sling, his bandaged hand peeking out, soaked in Mercurochrome. He had bandages on one side of his face, and we used Harley's mother's make-up to blacken both his eyes. I was done in similar fashion: bandages wherever appropriate, small trickles of iodine and catsup as little exclamations. We didn't use make-up on my battered eye. It was quite sufficient all by itself.

The bus driver almost didn't let us on the bus. It might have been better if he hadn't.

We couldn't control our laughter as we climbed the steps onto the school-bus. It wasn't long before the entire bus resounded right along with us.

When we got off the bus, the pre-homeroom bell crowd in front of the school parted like we had communicable diseases. Nobody wanted to get too close. Gasps, ooh's and ahh's followed us like enchanted children after the piper. We played the story to the hilt; Bernie especially, struggling to maintain his balance and composure, Harley limping and hunched over holding his head, Don and I groaning with every step. We cut sly glances at one another as we prepared for school accepting pledges of loyalty and retribution from the guys and soothing words of concern and pity from the girls. We told of our battle emphasizing a despicable ambush on the part of the Catholic Central kids, maintaining our innocent behavior, that we'd done nothing to provoke them or the cops. We also made sure everyone knew we were hard pressed to uphold the honor of Jefferson High School, but we managed to do it despite horrific odds. It might have been a performance worthy of Broadway, but it didn't last too long. Carrying tales is popular in any age group and in every era.

None of us made it to our respective first hour classes.

I was at my hall locker when the "Hand of the Lord" descended. Mr. Kessler, the principal, must have sent his henchmen out as soon as he'd heard about it. I looked over my shoulder slowly (still in character) and found Mr. Sakel, my government teacher, looking closely at the trappings I wore.

I saw "the look" on his face. There was no mistaking the grim, narrowed eyes and thin lips. I'd been seeing them on people's faces for years from parents and teachers and neighbors. I began unwinding the bandages.

"Oh, no, *Mr. Greene*," he said. "I'd think you'd want everyone to see how ridiculous you look. Let's leave them on until Mr. Kessler gets to see you."

He led me away from my locker toward the front office firmly holding my arm, ignoring my protestations of "just fooling around" and "having some fun."

"Do you really think anyone is going to be thinking about school this morning? This 'innocent' escapade will disrupt classes all day."

Bernie was already sitting on the guilty bench in the front office, where we'd both awaited sentence several times before. Mrs. Avendt barely glanced at me as I walked through the door, but I saw a badly concealed smile on her face. I brightened considerably. If one adult thought it funny...why, any adult might see the humor in it.

Don and Harley shuffled into the office, followed by two teachers, Mr. Rath and Mr. Kinner. I'd heard Harley and his escort coming down the hall. Harley's cackle was unmistakable echoing through the halls. Bernie sat next to me defiantly but looking pleased with the prank. Don was silent like I was. I think he knew what came next.

"What's up?" Harley chortled to no one in particular. "Ya think Mr. K's PO'd?"

I watched as Mrs. Avant slowly perused our makeup. She shook her head with a smile that said she didn't quite believe what she was seeing.

"You boys..."

She turned and knocked on Mr. Kessler's office door.

When the principal came to the door, he stood there long moments. The look on his face was so dark I had an errant thought that it appeared bruised. I tried to stifle the thought he'd been fighting, too. I couldn't help the snort of laughter escaping my lips, but no one else thought it was funny. I didn't either, not really. Mr. Kessler continued to stare at us silently. My hope of adult appreciation vanished.

"You boys follow me."

He ducked back in his office but returned almost at once. He was carrying his paddle. It was one of the legendary devices at a school that had many such implements, smooth and sinister, with holes drilled in the face to reduce air drag and improve the effect. I'd had several meetings with Mr. Kessler's hand-held associate before and didn't relish another one. For me, however shocking the impression it had previously made, the effects didn't last long, only until the next application. All four of us began to try to talk him out of the whacks. We knew it wouldn't do any good, but occasionally during times of desperation, hope is all that's left, even if slight.

"We were just playin' around."

"We didn't hurt anybody."

"It was just a joke."

"C'mon, Mr. K."

Mr. Kessler pointed the way out of the office. Mr. Sakel led the way into his vacant classroom and stood by the door as we filed through. Mr. Kessler followed us through the door and began swinging the paddle back and forth warming up. It made a wicked swishing sound as it sliced through the air. Mr. Sakel cleared the papers and books off his desk, making room for bent over bodies.

"You boys ought to know better than to come to school like that," Mr. Kessler began. "You might think you're clever and funny, but I don't. What did you think you'd accomplish?"

There was no answer to the question, and each of us knew not to bother. We stood silently, awaiting sentence. He reached toward Bernie, who stood closest to him.

Bernie pulled his arm away from the clenching grip.

By the time we were juniors in high school, Bernie had reached his full height, tall and ropy-lean like his father, B.C. Pierce. Bernie was about 6'2", angled and broad shouldered and had a confidence that came naturally to him. I'd seen him in action during a number of teenage scuffles, and he never shied away from a conflict. Not once. Although he and I sometimes vied for the informal leadership of whatever group we were in, I knew who the real chieftain of our tribe was. Although at that age I couldn't say it, I loved Bernie and was more than a little in awe of him. If he said go, I looked for the way. I'd have followed him anywhere.

"You can call my mom. You can call my dad. It was just a joke, for Pete's Sakes! You can tell them all about how much we disrupted school today. You can do anything else you want to; keep me after school, suspend me, even,…except! You ain't givin' me a paddling."

Mr. Kessler was so startled he dropped the paddle. Mr. Sakel moved forward as if to grab Bernie but stopped short when Bernie whirled to face him, his fists clenched. Mr. Kessler laid a delaying hand outward to stop the teacher from escalating the situation. Bernie quivered with rebelliousness, the veins on his arms distended, almost at the point of no return.

I decided to follow Bernie's lead whatever the consequence. I knew it would mean even more trouble but didn't care.

The two men withdrew slowly to the door of the classroom and held a brief conference. Mr. Kessler turned to face us.

"Three days!" He pointed at each of us. "You boys are suspended. Now get off school grounds, I don't want to have to look at you. I'll call your folks."

My three day suspension only prefaced the two week grounding and the loss of privileges I received at home. The entire story of street dance somehow came out under my mother's stern inquisition. Bernie's folks were upset about the whole thing as were Harley's and Don's. We each got much more than we realized we would when we'd hatched the whole thing. None of us got a paddling at school or at home.

The incident might have been a high-water mark for all of us.

Nothing short of an atomic bomb could have been more devastating than the departure of my father.

When my father was late one evening, none of us kids thought much of it. He'd been selling insurance for some time and late night sales or collections weren't unusual. His route for weekly premium collections and selling appointments after regular working hours were just a part of the job. He'd been fairly successful with the sales position garnering some award every once in a while and going to recognition dinners, and the like. The following morning when we were greeted by Mom's reddened eyes, we should have known something was amiss, but we didn't. Retrospectively, we should have realized it sooner. Stony silences, deliberate indifference, and tempers shorter than usual were even more a part of my father's makeup in the months that preceded his leaving.

It wasn't until after school Mom made the announcement, and even then it took her some time to admit it to us. She initially attempted to downplay my father's absence, telling us that he was away on some conference or training seminar. Eventually, the magnitude of it caught up with her emotions, and she let us have the whole story. He'd called my mother sometime the day before to say he wouldn't be home that evening...or any other.

My parents had been having financial issues and the accompanying marital woes for some time. It was (and is) seldom easy to raise four children without some money woes unless one happened to have been born with the proverbial silver spoon handy. Both my mother and father came from households where financial success was an erratic circumstance. They also had both experienced the desperation that accompanied split marriages when they themselves were growing up; our lineage was made up of ugly divorces and absent fathers.

For this family, it was catastrophic. For me particularly, it took some time for reality to set in. For a week or so, I was heady with the thought that my activities would no longer be subject to my father's stern gaze. I just knew that my life would be easier; Mom's judgments could often be eased by some attempt at charm. My father's never were.

Reality came with the visit by the Monroe County Welfare official. My mother had called the agency in Monroe shortly after my father left, yet it was several weeks before they got around to coming out for an "interview" that would determine the truth of the claim and our eligibility for any benefits.

He was a balding and blustering man, full of self importance and carrying enough papers and forms to document the Magna Carta. He showed up one late afternoon to review the case with all family members (those of us who were left) in attendance. Carole had by this time left for a small Bible college in Tennessee where she'd been awarded a small scholarship. Her departure was expeditious to the review, one less mouth and body for us (and them) to be concerned with.

It took the man some deliberate time to shuffle through and arrange the forms and papers required for the approval session. He appeared to enjoy the neat little piles when he was finished. The process then did not take into account people's feelings, nor did I think it cared to. He started out with the interview by asking us how old we were, if and what school we attended (a heavy emphasis on if), and whether we knew where our dear departed Dad had gone. He got up from the couch and searched through cupboards and pantry to see if we had food. He looked through closets and bureaus to see if we had clothes. He wanted to see bank statements and asked for tax forms from previous years. I think he even shook the pink-glazed piggy-bank in Peg's room.

He asked my mother if he (Dad) was the father of all of her children. If the question wasn't bad enough on its own, he required that my mother show him birth certificates to prove it.

I expected my mother to rise up in a self righteousness fury at that, but the abandonment's aftermath had pretty much eliminated her ability to fury at anything. By the time the welfare man got there, the entire family had been through enough days of head-hanging experiences to insure an indelible imprint of what our feet looked like. Church people, grandparents, aunts, uncles and neighbors, well-wishers, gloaters and rumor carriers had all taken turns delving into the private and public lives of the Greene family.

Like magic (or the scouring effects of an ill wind) we went from okay middle class to on-the-dole poor people in the eyes of everyone we knew.

After the welfare man left, our little marooned group sat down to some serious planning. My mother had been busy finding more children to take care of (as if her remaining three weren't enough) for the extra money they would bring in. Chip and Peg would take over my paper route while I looked for some after school work. I offered to quit school as my part of the survival strategy, but Mom would have none of those thoughts. Saturdays would be spent with us children scouring the neighborhood for extra work: lawn mowing, weed pulling, leaf raking, dog-poop scooping, whatever we could do. Sundays (much to my dismay) would still be considered Holy and my mother insisted even more strongly that we attend as a family unit to show that despite all, our faith was still intact.

Talking Marvin (Shorty) Vore into letting me work at his gas station after school may have been one of the best things that had here-to-fore happened to me, but the job had another consequence that I never saw coming.

I'd grown up with my dog Patch. From the age of three and a half, she'd been such a constant companion, mentor and confessor that I remembered few times without her by my side. I'd slept with her, bathed in Lake Erie with her, and shared my food with her. I'd seen puppies issue from her body, carried their tails in my pocket, wiped their butts, and cried when they were sold or given away. We'd had adventures and escapes that would have filled a book; Patch had saved me from a number of spankings, serious injury, and maybe even death on several occasions. But the then present took place of the then past, and our trails diverged.

Overnight, just as surely as my father driving away from his family shattered his family, my relationship with Patch crumbled.

It wasn't deliberate and it wasn't overnight, but school, work and age-choices deliberately wore away the time and ability to commune with my friend. There were no longer opportunities for marsh explorations. There was less time for walks down by the lake. Hours that we normally spent idly whiling away a summer day were taken up with my meager attempts at supplementing the family's financial status. Weekends that we camped, fished, and hunted together went the way of all things; they became memories. I didn't realize what I'd lost until it was too late.

Patch's amazing ability to be in the present moment may have delayed my inevitable awareness. Her hind-end wriggling dance had slowed by 1962, but my casual glance didn't catch the significance. She was always there to greet me after work or a Saturday sock-hop or when I returned from hanging out with friends. We went fewer places together and no longer ran full tilt boogey when we did, so I didn't notice the loss of her powerful speed and amazing endurance. My lack of perception dismissed her graying muzzle and that she didn't seem quite as concerned when a stray dog wandered into our yard. She was still ever-present at dinner times and evenings, but unfortunately became just another household fixture.

It could have been that the progression into my teens dulled my senses. Possibly my blood was being used to nurture something other than brain cells. Maybe I was caught up in my own private Hell, or maybe I just didn't want to acknowledge Patch's aging, but I completely missed the change.

My mother, with the indefatigable ability of many mothers, picked up the tasks associated with Patch and keeping the family together.

Except for those required to keep an adolescent boy on track.

So many people thought they knew what was best for our family after my father left,

Of all the people who helped, the one who seemed the most insistent was my nemesis Mr. Daugherty. He was on a mission from God.

My mother began babysitting for the family and their five extra children running around our house did not help the situation. The manner in which he began treating our family hurt the state of our relationship even more. He was a pompous member of our church, thought our fatherless status allowed him to treat us as he would his own kids, and as a deacon of the church, he doubly felt the need to keep Dorothee's children in line. His self-importance was always present at school and church, but never more so than when he addressed me after my father left.

At first it was suggestions for all of us to "make it better" for my mother. The suggestions inflated into orders. The first two or three times he directed me to do something I just did as he instructed. Following his commands was easier than butting heads, and my mother showed no inclination to step in. He took my agreement as a sign of submission and his orders became more and more forceful. He also made sure to "visit" each day, insuring me of a new set of goals and making sure that I paid proper homage to him.

He must have felt success with my chore and task compliance because he soon started working on my soul. Gently urging at first, "for my mother's sake," he soon resorted to bullying. He told me I had to go to church at every opportunity or I'd be damned.

I stopped responding to him. I tried not to be there when he picked up his kids in the afternoon. When that couldn't be avoided, I just didn't answer. I was forever astonished by his overly sanctimonious nature. Those spirits who feel obligated to enforce their will on others were beyond my understanding. Mom's zealous behavior toward me, at least, came from a profound wish that her son follow the faith that had proven true for her. I thought her sense of conviction strange, and as hard as I tried, I couldn't understand it, but I still felt some loyalty to her; I felt I had to try despite personal doubts.

But I didn't owe Mr. Daugherty anything. When I continued to remain silent in the face of his questions, he thought to reinforce his words. He put his hands on me, grabbing my arm as if he were tending a six-year-old, but I wasn't his kid.

In that moment I might not have even been a child at all.

I broke free from his intimidation, turned, and ran to the front door where we kept coats and hats and gloves and our baseball equipment. I picked up a bat and turned around while he was still discovering I wasn't there anymore. He took a step toward me, and I raised the bat just a little, just as a bit of a show. He was used to dealing with his own children and he thought he was obliged to handle me, too, but I was equally sure he wasn't.

He pooched his lower lip out at me but didn't do more than clench his hands. I tried to look maniacal, but it must not have been convincing. He started to spitefully bluster and talk about what a bad example I was for my brother and sister and that I didn't appreciate what Mom was going through.

Then he said, "You're going to turn out just like your father."

I'd been mad before but I wasn't used to this phenomenon. My heart literally froze up.

I flatly told him, "Carl (his first name and I knew he'd hate for me to use it), from now on you have your wife pick up your kids. If you ever come in this house again, I'll take this bat to you."

He opened his mouth to say something but I didn't let him.

"I mean it, Carl." I raised the bat higher. "You need to get the Hell out of here."

I was mad enough now to crack him and he knew it. It was a very good thing he stopped.

But true to form, just like many grownups when they feel an ordained right to talk down to children, he wouldn't stop. His face hardened and he started right in again.

"You better get right with God! *Boy!*"

When he sneered the word boy, he just had time to duck.

It was a good thing he did. The bat struck the molding around the doorway going into the living room, level with where his head had been. I was going to swing again but in a quick moment, he backed away, ran out the back door, and speed-walked to his car. Mom wasn't too happy about the woodwork but didn't say a word as she surveyed the paint flaked dent. I put the bat back and walked out on the porch and watched Mr. Daugherty drive away. He came back about twenty minutes later. I was relieved not to see the police follow him in. His wife opened her door and came in to get their kids, but she would not look at me when she did. Carl never came back into the house when I was there.

We struggled for more than a year on less than forty dollars per week. I tried in vain to convince Mom to let me drop out of school and find full time work, but she wouldn't hear of it.

"The Lord will provide. Have faith, son."

I wasn't so sure about the Lord but I knew all the grandparents, Grandma Phoebe and Grandpa Teddy, in particular, were doing a "Hellofalot" of providing for our family.

Grandma Phoebe had never cared much for my father and had always treated him with contempt and dislike. Contrary to our many farm visits, while the rest of the family was made to feel welcome, my father was seldom included in the reception's sentiment. During the year prior to Dad's departure, Grandma must have had conversations with Mom about the family's status because after Dad left, she completely took the veil off her feelings. They now visited us regularly always bearing food, clothing, and money, but Grandma also came to gloat. I overheard many a "told you so" and "he's not worth another single tear, Dorothee," through the heat vent after I'd gone to bed.

While my mom had always miserly shopped at second-hand stores for the most of our clothing, we started a new phase of Goodwill and Salvation Army visits. I began to believe I was the only person in the world who was my exact pant-size. Every article of clothing Mom brought home or that was delivered by some well wisher seemed to need alterations before I could put it on, but that might have been my perception. I do remember my mother tirelessly sewing something virtually every night as I pulled the stairway down for bed.

By the time spring first peeked at Michigan in 1963, I'd had plenty of the humiliation that went with county assistance, continual prayer meetings in our living room, and Grandma Phoebe's visits. I also hoped some kid didn't recognize an article of my clothing their parents had donated the previous month.

Chapter 12
Not Really a Date

I won two boxes of frozen pizzas and a date with Little Peggy March.

Friday night Sock Hops at Dixie Skateland were mostly community approved events. They had to be. Jim Burns, the son of the owner and general manager of the skating rink, had many parents to answer to whenever boys became a little rowdy while skating was in session. He ultimately bore the wrath of a few smoldering people when a daughter (and there were several) came home much past the appointed hour after having been dropped off for a supposed chaste and virtuous night of skating. During the following Saturday general skating, it wasn't unusual to see this father or that mother speaking in not altogether friendly tones at the counter where rental skates were handed out.

Jim had his hands full as a tacitly approved guardian of chastity and sobriety. There were alarmed exit doors all around the roller-rink, and they were put to good use by whoever could talk someone into sneaking out side for a speedy tryst. They had alarms that were supposed to announce any entrance or exit, but most likely no one considered the teenage mind when they designed the activators. It was easy enough to trick the switches and that technical information passed to otherwise non-technical minds with the speed of good rumor. The side doors were used as a pathway to settle disputes, fix lover's quarrels or encourage embraces, and were a handy place to stash a six pack of beer if someone had been lucky enough to previously find a buyer.

But despite some weeping girl's or battered boy's irate parents, regularly scheduled dances were a normal event at Dixie Skate Land. Jim was a good businessman and held the dances after skating so they cost another price of admission. I had a difficult time convincing my mother that sock hops were almost the same thing as roller skating. Eventually she must have grown weary of my pleading, for by the time I was sixteen, I'd become a regular.

Infrequently, Dixie Skateland put on a special dance complete with an honest-to-God disc-jockey all the way from Detroit. One weekend there was just such an event complete with sound equipment on a temporary stage, plenty of 45's and 78's stacked up on a table, and enough sweating, shimmying, and bobbing bodies to fill the smooth skating floor. There were dance contests and name-that-tune competitions with prizes from local and Detroit merchants. Teens took these events seriously, dressing as if for a modern day Easter Parade, and everyone took great pains to show up in full party regalia.

I was a moderately good dancer and tried to look the part for these events. I had the requisite tri-color, wide-striped, button down the front sweater, and due to my job at Shorty's Gas Station, had been buying my own clothes for some time, all carefully selected at Penney's or Diamond's Men's Store in Monroe. I no longer looked like I shopped at second hand establishments like The Salvation Army or Goodwill. I even owned a pair of blue suede shoes, although chance encounters with rain puddles turned my white socks and feet purple-y.

The night of the dance I was sharp enough to cut (or so I thought). I managed to win the Limbo contest, "How Low Can You Go? Let's Limbo Now." I went lower than anyone else did, or maybe the disc jockey just got tired of watching a bunch of sweating kids writhe their way under a stick. At any rate I won two prizes. The first was a carton of frozen mini-pizzas.

Frozen pizzas were something special. Our family had never gone in for the new wave of frozen foods that developed after World War II. Mom canned everything she could lay her hands on, split the cost of a steer with relatives when we could and still kept rabbits in the back yard for extra meat. Frozen, prepared foods were considered a luxury, and the Greene's didn't get many of those.

The second prize I won was a "date" with Peggy March at the teen night spot Walled Lake Casino located north-west of Detroit. When I went up on the stage to get my awards, I didn't even know there was such a place as Walled Lake Casino, but I was pretty sure I'd have a problem getting there. My mother was certain to shy away from giving permission for anything that had the word "casino" in its name.

I was astonished when I received her blessing for the trip. Perhaps she was overwhelmed that I'd brought home news of being first in something and carried the box of frozen pizzas in the door as proof. Maybe I substituted something about Church Gathering for the word "Casino." Possibly she thought my date with Peggy would lead to an eventual path to fame and fortune. From the very first, Mom was all in favor of the jaunt, as long as I found my own way there and back.

That took some planning. Few families had two cars in the early 60s and the one they did have was meant to get the father back and forth to work and the family to church or whatever familial duties were required. These duties did not include getting teenage sons to some den of iniquity sixty plus miles from the safety (and watchful eyes) of parental protection. I knew better than to ask for our car. At the time we were a fatherless family, and the old Dodge Grandma Phoebe and Grandpa Teddy had given us was absolutely necessary as a Greene family support system. It got my mother back and forth from the baby-sitting jobs she took to keep our house afloat, and there was always just enough gas to get us to Sunday morning services, but that was it. Had I asked to use the car, the answer would have been no.

Bernie's dad came to the rescue. Bernie, Harley, and I had to endure a long lecture regarding the use of his father's big Oldsmobile, but we were all used to lectures. B.C. Pierce ended his with a prediction about what would happen if we so much as scratched his green and white "98." He emphasized his warning with a vise-like grip on each of our shoulders. We believed him.

Bernie and Harley picked me up early on the Saturday evening of our trip. I'd called the radio station that sponsored the event requesting three tickets and received them in the mail from the disc-jockey shortly after the dance contest at Dixie Skateland. As soon as I got in the car, Harley told Bernie that he'd forgotten something at his house and had him turn around to go back to Stoney Pointe. He told Bernie to park at the end of his block, and we watched Harley scurry around the back lot to his house. He came back with a brown paper bag that clinked as he got in.

"Beer..." he said. "I hooked them from the fridge on the back porch. My old man will never miss them. We gotta do this right."

It took us no time to consume the six beers, and we spent the next several minutes after they were gone throwing them at the mailboxes that whizzed by along Telegraph Road. As we reached the outskirts of Flat Rock, we realized that we were already slightly sloshed. Flat Rock boasted a State Police Post, and Bernie slowed down well below the speed limit as if they would have someone outside just waiting to catch three underage drinkers. It was always good to be prudent, and despite completely ignoring Mr. Pierce's warning, we thought to behave as if we were just three innocent guys on their way to a party. Fortunately our fears were unfounded although each of us put some magical method of sensing beer/teens high on a reality list.

We had a hard time finding the place despite the map that Bernie's father had drawn out on a sheet of paper. The trip was a new experience for all of us, and with Harley doing the navigating, we did get lost. We'd never been allowed to go so far from home without a parental influence close at hand. This was also before expressways were commonplace in Michigan, and we'd taken many twists and turns along the way.

Eventually we made it; the glittering lights of Walled Lake Casino beckoned us like a magnet. The place was jam-packed. Kids wandered in and out, others congregated by parked cars, or stood in knots smoking cigarettes beside the doors, and they all looked older. They also looked different than we looked, the boys wearing black leather jackets and engineer boots, and most of the girls had hair that looked like giant beehives perched on their heads. We were eyed suspiciously as soon as we got out of the car.

Every time the doors opened loud music poured forth a siren's call to the three kids from Monroe. This was not a skating rink that catered to all ages and sometimes converted to a sock-hop. This type of entertainment was focused completely on satisfying the urges of teens, and teens flocked there from all points. I'd never seen so many teens congregated in one place. I thought we might have been on a different planet.

Some of the boys standing around the parking lots must have thought we looked like aliens. We hadn't made it through the milling kids before someone said something or pushed one of us. How they knew we weren't regulars, I don't know, but they did. It might have been the way we appeared in the gleam of the neon lights. It might have been our wide eyed wonder as we approached the doors. We might have walked differently. We might have smelled differently. I don't know. I briefly wondered whether we'd done something to inadvertently cross someone, but I didn't have much time for wondering.

Whatever it was, the resulting confrontation in the parking lot was quick and violent. Somehow we found ourselves herded around the corner of the building where the lights weren't bright, defending our honor and our body parts. I remember swinging wildly connecting with someone and being knocked to my knees for my trouble. I heard Bernie cuss and Harley hollered another cuss. Someone punched me again.

Just as quickly as it started, it was over. Bernie's shirt was torn down the front and was missing buttons. Harley had a bruise forming on one cheek, and had scuffed both the knees of his pants. My lip was split and blood dripped down the front of my sweater. The side of my head felt lumpy and my left eye was starting to swell shut. We stood in the semi-darkness gasping for breath. Once they'd marked their territory, the other kids disappeared, gone like smoke. If I hadn't been directly involved in the fracas, I'd have sworn I had imagined it all.

When we approached the entrance, I saw one of the ticket takers motion to someone inside, and several more men came out to stand next to him. We three did look rough. If we hadn't looked out of place when we walked through the parking lot, we certainly did by the time we got to the door. The guys at the door almost didn't let us in. I had to repeatedly show him the complimentary tickets, because every time the door opened a blare of music interrupted my explanation, and I had to start again. I had to plead with him and state over and over again how we'd been waylaid in the parking lot. We begged them for a long time, all the while being scrutinized by the kids going in and out.

Harley, always argumentative, started hollering in a guy's face. One of the numerous attendants (a better word is bouncers) told Harley he smelled beer on his breath. The accusation did not slow Harley down. He said one of the guys who attacked us had swung at him with a bottle and probably splashed some on his shirt. Bernie pulled Harley back out of the smelling zone. We stood there more long minutes explaining our being there in the first place, about winning the Limbo contest and my promised date with Peggy. Even after our pleadings of innocence (although I was still uncertain who had started it), the men manning the door were reluctant, but they finally stamped the back of our hands with a red smear and let us in.

Inside was a different universe. Every human sense was bombarded in quick succession. There was a mixture of Old Spice and English Leather after-shave, twirled up with Shalamar and Emeraude perfume whenever some group of guys or twittering girls walked by. The entire area was lit by glittering, revolving globes that reflected red, blue and green lights as they spun. The music was deafening, the songs coming in quick succession, one after another, running up and down the Top Ten list. The pheromones that swirled in and out of the air were palpable, and it wasn't long before I'd forgotten all about the gauntlet we'd been forced to run in order to get in.

There was a large concession area along the entire front of the building and kids were packed three and four deep at the counter, each trying to be the next served, hollering out their orders. The dance floor was enormous and had more bouncing kids than I'd ever seen in one place. I saw Bernie boogie away with some girl toward the dance floor. I made my way to the stage where the disc jockey was surveying the swirling crowd. I had no idea where Harley went, but I was sure he was busy chasing the closest skirt.

The guy with the microphone ignored me for a long time and as I surveyed my clothing, I knew why. In the flashing lights surrounding the stage, I looked even worse than I thought. I looked like something the cat dragged in. I had to mirror his movements walking back and forth across the stage several times before he acknowledged I was there. Finally, during a song, he leaned over and asked me what I wanted. He looked very dubious as I explained who I was, what I wanted and how on earth I came to look as beat up as I did. He pointed to an area set up on the other side of the dance floor.

"She'll be out there when it's time. Peggy's pretty particular, though, and she'll have chaperones with her. You're gonna have to get yourself cleaned up a bit, son."

I mumbled some reply and made my way over to the table he'd indicated. A life sized picture of Peggy stood along side the table, and there was a stack of publicity photos on one end. I went up to one of the people seated at the table and introduced myself. There were forms for me to fill out and sign. I finally found the dee-jay who had visited Dixie Skateland, and although he claimed to remember who I was, he didn't look like he did. He eventually told me what my responsibilities were, and when I was meeting Peggy. As he went on, he told me what to do when I took my turn dancing with the singer.

"But I'm supposed to have a date with her!" I exclaimed.

"Listen, kid. You are going to have a date with her…and it's going to last exactly for one dance. She's a star, kid. She's going to dance with four boys besides you."

He leaned in close, as if to share a secret.

"You really look like shit, kid," he chuckled. "I'm not sure Peggy is even gonna dance with you."

I don't know what I thought, but I must have appeared crestfallen. The DJ continued to talk to me. Of necessity, he'd been speaking loudly over the sound of the music. Just as he spoke his dismissal, there was a pause in the thunderous sounds booming from the speakers.

In the relative silence, he seemed to holler. "Whad'ja think? That you were going to make out with Peggy March in your car?"

There were twenty or so kids within hearing range when he said it, and every one of them laughed. Within several moments the guy's cynical question was making the rounds through the crowd.

What I thought at that moment was that I should be someplace else. I backed through the crowd of kids as the music swirled up again. I wove in and out of the crowded dance floor losing myself among the noise and writhing kids. I made my way to one of the restrooms thinking I could wash out the blood which spotted and stained my sweater. The little room was so crowded I had to wedge my way in pushing and shoving until I got to a sink. I let out an audible groan when I saw myself in the mirror. My lip appeared grotesquely split and swollen, and my eye was a blue-black balloon. My sweater looked like I'd inherited it from someone who'd been wounded in a war. I'd previously tried to wipe the blood off my sweater and had only succeeded marvelously in rubbing it in.

I stripped off the sweater and held the stained portion under the water vigorously rubbing the bloody spots. I watched in dismay as the stain spread pinkly in every direction. I continued to scrub it, even though it appeared to do little good. Like most kids, I'd only ironed the front and cuffs of my shirt, believing that the rest would never be seen under my sweater. Most of my shirt looked like my mother's cats had used it for a bed.

I finally gave up cleaning. My sweater wound up very damp, stretched out on one side from the twisting, wringing part and was now two-tone where once it had been cream-colored. The side I'd scrubbed sagged limply hanging down almost to my knee. I looked just great, swollen, lopsided, and off-color. Nothing was going to help this.

It would have to do; I'd heard the disc-jockey announcing Peggy's appearance on the stage as I finished up the last attempt at getting the water wrung out.

I quickly doused my face, combed my hair and hurried through the press of kids surrounding the stage. Peggy was already there. She looked good, bouffant hairdo, pretty dress, almost shining under the spotlights focused down on the stage. She and the dee-jay were involved in some patter about her career, how honored Walled Lake Casino was to have her there as a guest, and what great good fortune five boys from the audience had to have won a "date" with her. He called the names of four boys in succession, explaining how they'd won this terrific prize.

"And the last winner, Clark Greene from the little town of Newport, Michigan. Clark won a Limbo contest several weeks ago down at Dixie Skateland, and he's here as a result. Clark, come on up here!"

Peggy took an involuntary step backwards as I walked up the steps of the stage. I watched her appraisal of me. For me, the time passed in slow motion. Her eyes quickly scanned my face and her mouth pursed into a small "O" when she saw my swollen eye. She continued her evaluation and I watched her glance dart to my sagging and stained sweater. She leaned over to the disc-jockey and whispered something. I saw him nod in response. She held her hand straight out when I walked up. She swiveled her head again and spoke to the dee-jay but quickly recovered her composure and turned back in my direction to shake my hand when we were introduced.

"That must have been some Limbo contest," she giggled. Her laughter was soft and melodic.

"Yeah, well, we do things differently in Newport." I smiled back at her. I was never the one to pass up a chance to charm someone, so I continued. "Besides, when I heard what the prize was, I beat up all of the other guys. They look worse than I do."

I'd continued to hold her hand as we spoke. I saw a flicker of doubt cross her face when I said "beat up," but then she laughed again.

"You can tell me all about it when we dance, as long as we don't have to scoot under some stick."

I laughed right along with her. Along with her delightful laugh, she had wit.

"No, if it's all right with you," I smiled, "I want something 'Moon River-ish.'"

Once the introductions were over, we five boys had to exit the stage. We huddled around the steps as if we feared losing out on our awards. I wanted to dance with someone, but I was reluctant to leave right along with everybody else. There was no way I was going to forego my turn. Peggy sang several songs to the eager faces milling about the stage. She finished up with, "I Will Follow Him," her current number one hit. The girl could sing.

I got my wish for a slow dance although it wasn't "Moon River." Peggy and I waltzed to Andy Williams singing, "The Days of Wine and Roses." We chatted about this and that and the other. I told her about the fracas in the parking lot. I asked her if she enjoyed touring to different places, singing before the public, and what it was like to be a recording star. She asked me how I really came to look so disheveled as if she didn't believe my story, and if and where I went to school. All too soon the music ended. Her publicity people made sure I hadn't inflicted any damage during the dance and pulled her away for an autograph session at the little table that was tucked off to one side of the stage. I followed along behind her entourage, a sort of hanger-on who didn't want to go away.

"I had a nice..." I'd started to say thank you to her for the dance.

"Beat it, kid."

The disc jockey had been all smiles up on the stage but now stepped in front of me, barring any further conversation.

"You're all done. You had your date," he sneered. "And you were lucky to get that. If it'd been up to me, you'd never even got close to Miss March. Now, get outta here."

Peggy had turned back to the knot of kids waiting for autographs. I lifted my hand in a final wave goodbye (that she didn't see) and went out on the dance floor in search of Bernie and Harley.

The remainder of the night was full of music, girls, and dancing. Surprisingly my battered appearance didn't seem to bother any of the girls I asked to Pony or Watusi or Twist. Maybe they took pity on a kid who had been so obviously misused. At any rate, I didn't lack for partners and spent the rest of my energy in hot pursuit of anyone that looked willing. I was still slightly overwhelmed by the size of the crowd and wandered around intermittently dancing or trying to find out where my two buddies had gone.

Harley, Bernie, and I finally met up at the front doors as the evening came to a close. Harley had scored a half bottle of wine somewhere and looked as pleased as a treasure hunter when he flashed us a peek from under his sports coat. Bernie had some girl by his side and she didn't seem to want to let him go. We stood around as kids pushed and shoved through the doors, reluctant to find ourselves at the end of the outing. Bernie managed several slobbering kisses as he said goodbye to his newfound true love.

We walked out into the parking lot and stood outside while traffic thinned. The night was punctuated with kids spinning the tires of their Daddy's cars through the gravel and down the road. Car doors slammed and horns blared; goodbye, goodbye to one and all; see you next weekend, see you sometime, see you never again. Harley pulled the bottle of wine from under his coat and passed it to me. The crowds of kids around and through the doors thinned, and the accompanying roar that traveled with any large group quieted. The lack of constant blaring music and teenage noise made the relative silence seem absolute.

In the diminishing noise of the parking lot, I thought about the night. Peggy seemed like a nice girl, and I silently wished her good fortune with her singing career. I wondered if she ever would come to Newport. I wondered if I would ever see her again. I wondered if…

As we got to our car, a horn blared and a dark shape pulled alongside. I thought it might be the cops and hastily shoved the wine bottle behind me as I turned toward the passing car. The car rolled to a stop.

The rear window rolled down and I could see Peggy's face in the parking lot lights.

I heard her speak to the driver. "Stop here a minute, Chuck."

Peggy must have overheard the disc jockey earlier when he told me to leave. She leaned out of the car window supporting her torso with her arms, and kissed me on the cheek.

"I liked our dance," she laughed silkily. "It's the only time I ever danced with someone who had to fight for it."

She smiled, pulled herself back in, rolled the window up and settled back into the seat. I watched the brake lights flicker briefly before her car turned and headed off into the darkness.

All in all, the night had been memorable, although questionable in the middle part. I had my date with Peggy and I had the black eye to prove it. I'd had fun and would remember the evening for a long time, or at least until my split lip healed. My Grandma Phoebe would have said, "All's well that ends well."

I agreed.

Chapter 13
Clash of the Titans

There are few schools that don't boast and claim great athletes, boys who, by favor of heredity or genetics or desire, have just a bit more than their counterparts.

Jefferson High School in the early 1960s was no exception. Jefferson was a new high school; in fact, 1963 was the first ever graduating class. Prior to '63, students were bused into Monroe to finish grades ten through twelve.

We had many athletes; boys who could run track; boys who could play basketball; boys who could wrestle; boys who sparkled under the lights of a football field, and a few who could do it all.

Bill was such a competitor. He was dark complexioned and had arms and legs that corded with muscle. Naturally graceful, he possessed a physique well beyond the build of other gangling teenage boys. He ran explosively, like a startled deer, and he ran often. He ran track in the spring, played football every autumn and during the winter spent his time running up and down the basketball court. He wrestled, and swaggered, and walked on his toes as if he was poised for the starting gun or the snap of the football.

There is grace in track, the smooth extended forms of boys and girls speeding or jumping or throwing or vaulting. There is excitement in basketball, the hurry-up pace, the passing, fluid shooting and defending. Baseball...well, baseball just is, an

American icon even in the name. But there is nothing that compares to high school football.

Perhaps it is a beckoning from ancient fields of Peloponnesia, or Waterloo, or the invasions by the Huns and Goths. It could be a recollection of blood soaked Roman arenas or the killing fields around castles that have long fallen to dust. Whatever it is, it causes young athletes to sweat and all ex-players to remember how it felt.

Football is a complex ritual, from the modified armor to the physical and moral expense at which it is played. Except for war, football may be the only contest in which groups of young men are licensed to wreak injury upon another group. Locker rooms are filled with encouragements to "Kill 'em," "Get out there and hurt 'em," and "Tear 'em up." Football inflames every pore of the participants. From the beginning preparation, each contestant helps another with protective pads in a rhythm and delivers a synchronized slap of shoulders so that the juice flows freely. The adrenaline surges before the first helmet is donned and the smell of anticipation rolls among the young men when they kneel to hear a coach's orders. By the time they attend the field, they are more likely to be frenzied than at any other time in their lives.

I'd played football in junior high school but quickly learned I had only minimal talent and none of the required discipline. By high school, I was not among those who participated in the school's athletic programs beyond the required gym class, calisthenics, and intra-mural sports, but my lack of involvement did not stop my admiration of those who did.

Bill had an exceptional position in school and it just wasn't on the football team. Several other talented boys approached this status, but none so completely as Bill. His place was special. He was followed around the halls by a cluster of cheerleaders and others who fervently wished they would gain some celebrity through association. He accepted this adulation as if it was his due.

The special treatment didn't end in the noisy clangor of the halls or cease with the school bell. Bill's natural ability accorded him a special place in classroom activities. He and I shared gym and several academic classes. On more than one occasion, I'd heard the coach talking to this teacher or that regarding our student from Mt.

Olympus. These intercessions were another acknowledged part of taking care of those special people attending Jefferson. Bill ranked right down in the lower middle percentile along with me. In any case, good grades or not, special privilege or none, Bill owned the ground he walked. The areas crowded with his admirers were considered much sought after real estate. I never saw him without a trailing group of kids in his wake. No one thought it anything but proper that he maintained this revered place. After all, Bill was *our* athlete.

Our coach thought so, too. Coach had a certain influence among the other teaching staff. I wouldn't say Bill got special favors for his participation in sports. On the other hand, I wouldn't say he didn't.

My grade standings might have been due to a poor character and probably were. Bill's were due to his being so busy maintaining his place on the pedestal.

Every student knew…Our Hercules was hands off as far as other teachers went. If anyone had an issue with Bill, they had better to talk to Coach first.

But even demigods have to worry about their place on the mountain. As we entered our junior year, we had a transfer from another school. I knew him because his grandparents lived in the house behind ours. He was a boy who had earlier gone to Jefferson public schools with all the rest of the beach kids but had transferred Catholic school during junior high. Now he shifted home again to Jefferson.

From the day he walked back onto Jefferson property, Al looked the part of usurper.

He'd spent the years away from Jefferson to his advantage. He grew into a man, and no one could deny it. He was big in the shoulders and Big Bad John narrow at the hips and stood about six feet tall. Al had the same easy grace that other athletes displayed, but even more than that he was completely at home with his physical stature. There was no hint of the awkwardness found in so many growth-spurt boys gawking toward adulthood. He also didn't spend much energy trying to fit in to any previously formed cliques; he knew a brand new one would form around him. He was right; the first day of school after the buses unloaded, but before the doors opened, the whole dynamic of the school began to change. Clusters of girls whispered and gaggles of boys speculated about his place in the pecking order. There was an audible hum that punctuated the first-day furor of school.

A separate species gathered as well, identified by their "J" blue and gold letter-jackets. They were further distinguished by thick necks, burly chests, bulky thighs, and they all sweated profusely even when they stood still. They quickly encircled Al. They were the football team and needed to measure this new boy in school. They needn't have been concerned. They didn't find a boy. If ever someone fit the bill as a man and a football player, it was Al.

All school years begin with the remnants of summertime squalor. Kids have to revert from being wild and being free to being studious and focused. They have to learn to learn all over again. It was (and is) a challenge for their new keepers. That year was no exception; tardy slips and lack of hall passes kept teachers and students busy. There were long lines of shuffling students in front of the principal's office who awaited punishment or detention. Romances renewed and blossomed fresh as hormones got in the way of disciplined study. Audible sounds of the paddle came from Mr. Kessler's office and the small enclosure adjacent to Coach's gym class. Kids had red faces and took wincing steps toward their next assignment. All in all, it was a normal start.

Except for the pedestal.

The barnyard scratching that accompanies every new rooster began slowly between Al and Bill. There was no evident animosity at first, but there was wariness among the football players. It seemed as if they had to pick sides despite being on the same team. I heard about it from the periphery that surrounded the letter jacketed kids. Although barely discernable at first, their dissension grew markedly when practice began.

Al was a halfback, and a very good one.

So was Bill.

It should have been an easy problem to solve.

School gossip was centered on football practice. Word came down to us mere mortals that practice had quickly gone beyond the normal contest for first string assignments. The team grew smaller as this or that aspiring boy found he couldn't keep the pace and was cut from the squad. The hangers-on slimmed down or put on muscle and marched the school grounds as if on parade. When coach was satisfied that his team was coming together, he began to scrimmage. Coach Fletcher favored hard fundamental workouts followed by mock battles that lasted well into the dusks of early autumn. He seemed to be determined to first exhaust the football players and then see how they performed during competitive play. Blue squad, Red squad battles soon ended every workout.

Previously, football practice had tacitly been a closed session discipline. Few students and even fewer parents showed up to watch their sons or boyfriends soak themselves in sweat, batter and bruise the tackling dummy into submission, or stagger to the sidelines after wind sprints to vomit the remnants of their lunches. Coach didn't encourage audiences for his practice sessions. He didn't even like the cheerleaders sharing the football field for their work-outs.

The contest between the two big men on campus changed that. Word spread that the workouts were more intense than normal, and then Coach couldn't keep the watchers away. It took only a few weeks before everyone knew of the rivalry. Buses pulled away from the school at day's end sparse of homeward bound kids. Each day a sinuous trickle of students meandered out to the field after classes clamored their conclusion. Once word spread in the community, the school's small parking lot (few students had cars in those days) was packed with plenty of the cars of parents who watched practice. There were parents who waited for practice-watching students and even some mysterious strangers who were suspected of spying for opposing teams. The sidelines quickly became crowded each day and didn't empty until the worn out boys dragged themselves into the locker room.

Coach usually assigned Bill and Al to opposing squads believing that the competition would help them peak to perfection much more quickly. The normally spirited scrimmages became more aggressive. Coach was right; both boys excelled beyond expectations. They were personifications of athletic excellence. If Bill ran through a tackler's embrace, Al would run through two determined defensemen. If Al jigged and jagged his way to the end zone, Bill jagged and jigged at the expense and peril of a first-string tackle. Instead of Gung Ho, it was Give 'em Hell. This team would have dinner early every Friday evening when the real games began. They'd be eating up the opposing teams. Coach walked around with a perpetual grin on his face.

It became easy to determine football players in the halls as well, even if the rest of us hadn't known them. Blue Squaders and Red Squaders were scraped and sore beyond imagining and were easily identified by their bandages, swollen eyes, and limps as they passed between classes. They formed into two distinct bands of brothers before school, during school and after school. Instead of Blue Squad, Red Squad, it would have been better to label them Bill Squad, Al Squad.

One morning before school started, there was a shoving match in the foyer. It was over before it began, with no one but students the wiser. There was a definite athletic code of conduct to be followed, and no fighting was the first on the list. The rumors about the Bill and Al almost-fight reached a fever pitch by the time practice began. The other guy got the blame depending on which squad was talking.

There was a newer fable at field-side during practice, equally hazy as to who did what, another shoving match when the boys were donning their equipment. That workout session turned particularly vicious. As one of those kids fascinated by the increasing brutality of the workouts, I often hitch-hiked back to school after my papers were delivered or if I wasn't scheduled to work at the gas station. I saw elbows thrown, fists plunge during pile-ups and tactics that surely would have earned a yellow flag during regulation play. Coach Fletcher used his whistle almost continually and no one seemed to be paying attention to it. He stopped practice early that day and marched the boys into the locker-room.

The team stayed sequestered for more than an hour. Most of the audience lingered mingling outside the gymnasium or sitting in cars. When the boys finally exited the school there seemed to be a collective inhalation of breath from the onlookers. The boys who came out weren't swinging gym bags or their football cleats in their normal after practice way. There was no distinction between Blue squad, Red squad, and little joy in the whole crowd of boys. The team seemed subdued and smaller in a way, and they stood in a group not getting into the waiting cars. Bill and Al weren't to be seen for long minutes after the team emerged. The team parted as Coach came out followed by Bill and Al. Coach said several words to the team and they went their ways silently into a waiting car or trudging across the fields toward home.

As far as I knew, whatever happened in the locker room remained a mystery. Despite the fact that high-schools are the most fertile spot on earth for tales to grow, this one remained the property of the football team. Their silence didn't stop the "what really happened" whispers. The student body had plenty to talk about and the burgeoning secret fed the gluttons full.

Jefferson's first scheduled game provided an additional respite. The pep rally held in the gym was noisy and boisterous to the point of frenzy. We'd been so expectant of the in-school rivalry that it seemed normal to transfer our excitement to the *other* team. When the cheerleaders ran onto the floor, they looked like the female version of a windup Monkey-Chase-the-Weasel toy. The fold-out bleachers along the basketball court thundered and thudded with the feet and voices of every student. Books were tossed into the air, jackets flung in whirling circles and pompoms flashed like semaphores signaling the upcoming battle. All that happened before the team appeared, before the heroes came out. Coach was dressed to the nines; his normal athletic shorts, whistle and Jefferson t-shirt replaced with a suit and tie. He walked to the center of the gym, erect, solemn and important, the man responsible for this barely-contained horde.

When the boys ran onto the floor dressed in jackets and ties, the gym exploded, brilliant and hot. They lined up behind the coach pushing and jostling one another in excitement.

Coach tapped the podium a signal for silence, but nobody quieted down. He went with the swell of noise raising his arms in supplication, a conductor bringing the William Tell Overture to a measured detonation. It took long minutes before the students ran out of breath, but it was a worthy tribute to our gladiators.

Coach read the starting line-up roster.

The hammering sounds stopped as if a switch had been flipped. The silence was more deafening than the uproar had been, sudden and absolute. It was as if someone had struck every student dumb.

A low murmur swelled as Coach read off the names. He approached the backfield assignments and the buzzing took on distinct sounds when he announced halfback. The undertone of cheers was punctuated with equal groans of disappointment. His selection did nothing to quell the camp fever that had struck the school. The arguments and loyalty re-bloomed as the pep rally was dismissed, but somehow the frustrations were aimed at the opposing team. We'd kill 'em.

The roars of the pep rally were just a vocal-chord warm-up to the visceral shrieks of the sideline crowds that afternoon. The crowd that showed up for the game was immense, "Go Bears! Go Bears! GO BEARS!" Throats vibrated chests and bellies and shook the bleachers in an earthquake of sound. The team gathered in a mass for a final screaming session, but despite their rampant testosterone and adrenaline, no one could hear them.

Al received the opening kick-off and trampled uniforms, theirs and ours, to score the first touchdown. One of the opposing boys didn't get up and the injury fired the crowd more than the quick score. Muscles pumped, sinews strained, the game plunged into a struggle of wills, physical, mental, and spiritual. Boy opposed boy. Helmets cracked and bodies smashed each other with audible thunks. Cheers and grunts and muffled curses accentuated the cadence of the quarterbacks. The liquor of contest reached up in the stands, intoxicating, palpable, and heavy. Above the contest, above the excitement, parents and cheerleaders and players and onlookers melded together into a roiling, boiling mass of raw emotion.

By halftime the teams weren't the only ones that needed a rest. The bleachers were scattered with people showing signs of exhaustion. Where the band got the energy to play and march on the field during the half, I never knew. After their dervish of game activity, the cheerleaders urged the crowd to hold onto their pinnacle of exhilaration. The crowd didn't let them down.

The second half play was a storm, a competition of arms and legs and jerseys and cleats, thrusting and shoving, blurring back and forth toward rival lines. Bill galloped for a score or two and Al produced another. Players panted toward the sanctuary of their sidelines to rest and gather themselves for another attack. Defenses dug in and offenses carried their flags into opposing territory. Helmets were scarred and numbers smeared with grass and mud. Stabs of effort swirled with growls of exertion and finally the clock ran out.

We'd won! We'd won! Nothing could have stood in the way of a Jefferson victory, a predestination written by a higher power. Coach had had a plan to use both Bill and Al but had kept the strategy secret in order to bring them both to fever pitch. He'd alternated Bill and Al during the game, or played them together, one at halfback and the other at fullback. They'd appeared to be able to do no wrong, selecting the perfect gap in the line, breaking tackles, galloping like mad, runaway horses, away, away, away from the opposing players. There were two perfect human beings who played football on that warm autumn afternoon. They were beautiful.

Everybody stood on quivering legs as the two teams formed up to shake hands with a former enemy, and no one was surprised at their instant transformation. Hands that seconds ago sought to annihilate stretched forward in friendship. Coaches who'd prayed for the other's death and doom met in field center and praised the other's efforts and wished each other good fortune.

The audience gave the team a lusty roar of approval standing and applauding them as they strutted into the locker room.

"Bears! Bears! Bears!"

When our warriors trooped by, every head was held high; every face glistened with the sweat of victory. Bruises, scrapes and sprained muscles were forgotten, and they looked ready to play another sixty minutes of football. They were boisterous and proud, each thoroughly in charge of their own destiny. Everyone went home completely satisfied with the first game.

Except for two people.

The pre-school crowd Monday morning was still inflamed with the excitement of Friday's game. Each time any of the football team exited a bus the groups of students screamed a greeting and began a migration toward the latest appearance. Knots of students shoved and pushed their way into the shadow of Eddie or Dennis or Bob or Don or Rob, just to be close.

The eruption was quick. Bill and Al had been anything but satisfied about Coach's selection and order of play. They denied the brotherhood of the football field. Their resentment had festered over the weekend, no balm of victory for either of them.

I don't know who threw the first punch in the slug fest. Blows were brutal and unexpected and furious. For sixty seconds, feet, fists, and ferocity were a hurricane of violence that engulfed the pair. The sheer violence of the fight startled those nearby and the crowd of kids edged back to give them room. They whirled and blurred and fought on as if locked in a death struggle. If their splendor had been collective on the football field, it was magnified ten thousand times more so when they fought. For some brief seconds, they were a clashing, terrible force, two gladiators locked in horrible embrace. Then it was done. The fight was over so quickly that only those few nearest the blast were aware that it had happened.

No one was the winner. No one was the loser. By mutual agreement (or their realizing it wasn't proper for mortal view), the fight stopped as quickly as it began. Their guttural gasps for breath rasped the air and they broke apart. Al's shirt was torn and Bill had a bloody nose. They drew away tentatively, cautiously circling to see if this was what the other wanted.

Other football team members pushed their way into the hasty arena and hurried Bill and Al through the side door of the gym. It would not have done for Coach or some other teacher to find out about the fight.

Over the next weeks or so, Bill and Al became, if not friends, at least warrior figures who put up with one another. They'd proven themselves in singular combat and had measured up equally, so it was easier to accept one another. They each held on to distinct groups of followers, but there was no longer any animosity between the camps. The 1962-63 football team ended the season with a winning record, no small accomplishment for a new high-school. In 1963-64, the tally was better still. Students came and went, got good grades or failed classes, and caused trouble and skipped school. Everything was just about right for a school that had more than its share of heroes.

We learned an undeniable fact that year.

There was room for two up on the pedestal.

Chapter 14
Behind the Curtain

It was his first year at school and no one knew what to expect.

He was burley and broad shouldered, with a weathered face and gray hair at his temples. He wore a tweed coat with elbow patches and had cauliflower ears. His eyes had crinkly lines radiating from the corners, as if he spent a lot of time laughing. He moved about the front of the class with purpose as we trooped in, as if eyeing up an adversary. He looked like he wasn't someone you'd want to cross. Basil Rath was my first male English teacher.

Surprisingly, instead of English, he began his first day with a monotone delivered story of how easy we kids had it...blah, blah, blah. He told of having to haul water from a well and that even the well...blah, blah, blah. He told of having to travel great distances to school through all weathers...blah, blah, blah. He said that one particular winter was epic with the cold and snow...blah, blah, blah. He'd been forced to borrow a neighbor's horse...blah, blah, blah. One evening, as he was riding this particular horse back from his classes...blah, blah, blah. He couldn't stay for a long time, because...blah, blah, blah.

I'd had high hopes when I first saw him, but moments later I thought this was taking shape as my most boring class. He'd lost me when he started in on how hard he'd had it. I'd personally heard of my father's struggles at least seven thousand times; blah, blah, blah at the dinner table, blah, blah, blah during trips in the car and blah, blah,

blah any other time I'd asked for something he didn't want me to have. Mr. Rath's sonorous voice sang the same tune. I looked around furtively. Most of the class had yawned out.

Silence in the room brought me back from wherever I'd been. Mr. Rath had paused in his speech and walked behind his desk. He stood in front of the room leafing through the pages of a tattered volume. He removed a slim pair of reading glasses and slid them on his head, but then closed the book softly. He held the book to his chest reverently, and his eyes traveled across the faces before him.

With a soft voice he recited.

The well was dry beside the door,
And so we went with pail and can
Across the fields behind the house
To seek the brook if it still ran;

He timed the poem's cadence to the tramp of feet finding their way through the woods.

Not loth to have excuse to go,
Because the autumn eve was fair
(Though chill), because the fields were ours,
And by the brook our woods were there.

I felt the sharp coolness of an autumn twilight and the pride of forest ownership. I heard my feet scrunch through old snow and felt the pail bang against my leg as I walked.

His voice had turned melodic, measured and had metamorphosed a dreary chore into a tableau of sights and sounds and senses. I stayed right there with him. He leafed through several pages and smiled, but again closed the book.

I'd lingered in the woods while he found his new place. Mr. Rath's voice urged me to look more closely and I did.

Whose woods these are I think I know.
His house is in the village though;
He will not see me stopping here
To watch his woods fill up with snow.

My little horse must think it queer
To stop without a farmhouse near

All of a sudden I was on the back of a horse feeling its withers shake to the tinkle of bells.

Between the woods and frozen lake
The darkest evening of the year.
He gives his harness bells a shake
To ask if there is some mistake.
The only other sound's the sweep
Of easy wind and downy flake.

I was bewitched by the stillness and the slowly falling snow flakes on my cheek. The night was dark and cold and perfect.

The woods are lovely, dark and deep.
But I have promises to keep,

I got the feeling I couldn't stay. I had someplace to go.

And miles to go before I sleep,
And miles to go before I sleep.

Mr. Rath paused for a long moment watching us. The entire class was hushed, submerged in the romance of the trip we'd just taken.

His voice collected the class.

"Now, I've interpreted the same story in verse by the poet, Robert Frost," he went on when he'd finished. "The first stanzas were a part of 'Going for Water' and the second was his entire poem, 'Stopping By Woods on a Snowy Evening.' Essentially, between my boring childhood story and the poet's two poems, I've conveyed the same idea. Which one was better?"

I was hooked. Although I'd been a voracious reader for longer than I could remember, I was astonished how the second presentation had turned the mundane into the exotic. From that moment on, I paid attention in his class. There was so much to be attentive to.

The students found out more about Mr. Rath as the weeks passed. He'd been a wrestler during high school and four years of college, which explained his ears, while his nose had been broken three times and hence the slight skew. He had a genuine passion for poetry, which was a trait that took many of the teenage boys by surprise, me in particular. Here was a man who looked like he could kick an ass when it needed a kick, but tears ran from his eyes when he recited poetry. He recited powerful sections of Shakespeare, Milton, and Keats with contagious emotion. He treated us to meter and free verse and limericks and was particularly enamored of Virginia Wolfe. For me, he opened a door I hadn't even realized was there. His sense of drama while he read was more compelling a reason to listen than any other.

I'd been practicing the dramatic for more years than I could count. Sly glances, appealing heavenward looks, outrageous extremes of gesture or countenance; I'd mastered them all. It was a matter of survival. What with my many scrapes with parental and school authority, I was especially competent with one I thought of as confused innocence. I was also adept at assuming Christ's position during crucifixion, but I kept that one hidden until I was sure of a favorable audience. It seemed only natural that I could parlay these talents into theatrical success. When Mr. Rath started looking for students to fill the production requirements for the junior class play, I jumped at the chance.

It was one of my rare good choices in high school. I did have flashes of brilliance, but they were few and far between, distant somehow. They might have been the announcements of a remote thunder storm, whose lightning dimly portrays a cloudbank or a vague tree line, pretty to look at but of no real use.

When the cast was chosen and plans were being made for the play, "Hobgoblin House," we all took on second jobs in order to bring the play to fruition. Set construction, costuming, backdrops, furniture, lighting, publicity, and music lists were developed and tasks assigned to one and all.

The set was one of an old and neglected mansion which was supposedly haunted. We needed shabby furniture, painted windows dimmed with decades of accumulated grime, a flickering chandelier, and a fireplace. As part of the set crew and because of my long, long, long association with fireplaces at home, I got to build it.

When I found out how easy it was to get excused from other classes because of "having to work" on the play, I didn't waste any time in enlisting other students in my task. Mr. Rath seemed surprised at how many buddies I'd brought along when I asked him for additional passes, but he signed them just the same. I was great at making up reasons for the additional kids and soon had my own band of Forty Thieves. We were very good at accumulating the necessary supplies.

Bernie and I borrowed Mr. Rath's car (Bernie driving) to pick up some lumber for the fireplace and we stretched the foray into a day long, full blown expedition. Once we'd picked up the building materials, we used our freedom to gather stones from the shore of Lake Erie for the fireplace. It wouldn't have done to construct a "regular" fireplace; we had to have an authentic old one and only stone would do. The time did get away from us; the heady intoxicant of being out of school *with* permission must have caused time to speed up. When we did get back to school, Mr. Rath was waiting outside the by then vacant building, tapping his foot. He also had his arms folded over his chest, but they didn't remain folded for long.

As soon as we got out of the car and had walked up to him, he grabbed us both by the back of the neck.

"You boys are a little late."

I couldn't hear him very well. The pinched nerves in my neck were dying. From the look on Bernie's face his were already dead. Mr. Rath squeezed harder. I felt mine follow Bernie's beyond the pale.

"You boys are *very* late," he repeated. "It's not going to happen again, is it?"

I tried to shake my head, but it wouldn't follow instructions. I'm sure Bernie and I looked exactly like Edgar Bergen's dummies, Charlie McCarthy and Mortimer Snerd, as he walked us around to the back of his car, our shoulders hunched against his vise-like grip. We probably acted like the dummies, too, not being able to do much more than silently walk tippy-toe under his control. He didn't let us go when we got to the laden trunk. Instead he stood there with his two marionettes at arm's length.

"My father was a country lawyer." He gave us a little shake. "He had a client whose dog bit some passerby, but he got the judge to find the farmer innocent by pleading that the dog had probably been startled or was just defending the owner's property. After the trial he took the client off to one side and told him, 'The first bite is free, Amos.' You've got to decide whether keeping the dog is worth the risk of him biting someone else. If your dog bites someone else, it will cost you dear." Mr. Rath chuckled. "Now you two don't want me to risk a second bite do you?" He gave us another shake.

I got it almost immediately and shook and nodded my head in succession. I wasn't sure I knew the correct response, but his pincer grip convinced me to cover all the bases. I silently wondered what eventually happened to the dog, but Mr. Rath didn't say.

He finally let go of us.

I was pretty sure Mr. Rath had won his weight division in college.

We unloaded the supplies warily, both of us unsure if we could bear a repeat of his emphasis. He did not help us but waited behind the stage curtains until we'd finished. Bernie and I stood next to the stairs leading down from the stage. I wondered what came next.

"Come on, I'll give you two a ride home."

When he pulled into the driveway and got out, I was sure he was going to tell my folks about the extended use of his car. I was surprised when he introduced himself to my family and apologized for keeping me after school for so long. Bernie was a regular at the Greene house and had followed us in. Mr. Rath said there had been some things to take care of but that they couldn't be delayed and he'd asked Bernie and me to take care of them. I saw his eyes dart in my direction. I played it straight-faced jokingly saying that Mr. Rath had worked us beyond reason and that's why we were late.

He looked directly at us. "Yes, but we know that's not going to happen anymore, don't we?" he laughed.

Bernie and I laughed with him, but ours was uneasy. I knew Mr. Rath was really saying, "There'd better not be another."

We settled into the tasks of producing the play, rehearsing lines every afternoon going through the paces, and scene changes. We moved furniture around until it was just right and taped location spots for items and for people to find. I'd borrowed several items from our house: a settee, our mantle clock, and an old rug that was on the porch. Bernie and I had hammered together the fireplace from two by fours and covered it with plasterboard. Weeks passed and the set and cast started to take shape.

We did have a few problems. My "girlfriend" in the play was Sandra, but the one I wanted for a partner was her cousin Sharon. I'd have been much happier during the kissing scene if Sharon's lips were mine to have, but even knowing my preference, Mr. Rath decided against romance.

And Bernie and I couldn't get the damned rocks to stay glued in place.

We tried every type of glue and adhesive known, but nothing would work for long. When we stood the fireplace upright, the flat stones would slowly slide off the plasterboard with a resounding thump. Not only had the rocks been impossible to fix in place, their weight had frequently pulled chunks of the plasterboard out when they did fall off. Our esthetically pleasing fireplace looked like someone had used it for shotgun practice.

I'd been banned from anything resembling art class since my bust of Mr. Daugherty days, and he and I still avoided each other's company. I still thought he was deliberately controlling, suspicious and mean, while he thought I was an ungovernable smart-assed heathen. We were both right. However, some of my buddies still painted and sketched under his watchful art class eyes. Harley, a friend and another smart ass, was barely tolerated but was still a student of Mr. Daugherty's. I asked him to look around in the art supplies in the cabinet that was kept locked.

Harley made a great reconnaissance, but his brashness made discovery a sure event. He got caught while he was rifling around in the cabinet but not before he saw many precious items. There were all sorts of good things squirreled away in that big gray cabinet.

Harley recited the list of goodies: paints galore, brushes of every shape and size, multi-colored paper, ribbons, and bright strings, easels, canvas. I perked right up when he said something about plaster-of-paris gauze, the kind of material doctors used to make casts for broken limbs. That might prove a good way to keep the rocks in place. All I had to do was figure out how to get at it. Given the warm place I held in Mr. Daugherty's heart, it wasn't going to be an easy task.

I first tried the direct approach; I asked him outright. He frowned when he saw me standing in the doorway. I tried to appear contrite, sorry for any past sins, and willing to make amends when I went to his class. I said I'd heard that there were some art supplies that we could especially use for the set of our play and wondered if he would let us have some of them.

"Those supplies are for art class," he replied. "Your play has a budget. Use it."

I tried to talk to him about the problems that we'd been having with the fireplace, but he was unmoved. I told him there wasn't enough time to send away for supplies and that this was an unexpected problem. He pooched his lip at me as he spoke.

"I've got grades nine through twelve to worry about all year. Art class is always under-funded. The supplies run out before the end of school. I'm not going to shortchange everyone else just so you have some *grand* fireplace for your play. You go along now; I've got a class to prepare for. You're probably absent from some class as it is."

I was tardy, but I walked to Mr. Rath's classroom instead, morally certain that I'd been denied just because my name was Clark. I motioned to him from the doorway; he had a class in session. I thought I'd get Mr. Rath to intercede, to talk to Mr. Daugherty one on one, man to man, teacher to teacher. I went through the whole spiel again even though he knew of the problems Bernie and I were having with the fireplace.

Mr. Rath said he'd talk to him about it, but he didn't seem very enthusiastic.

Several days went by and although I pestered him about it, he only said that he hadn't got around to it yet but would. We were running out of time. The play was set to open to the high school in a few short weeks, and after opening, would be put on for two nights for the community. I wanted the fireplace to be a show piece.

After school during rehearsals, Mr. Rath told me that he had spoken to the art teacher, but, alas, we'd have to do without the supplies I coveted. He went on to tell me that he understood Mr. Daugherty's reluctance to diminish the other student's quality of class. Mr. Rath suggested that we cover the fireplace with a painted sheet. I thought the sheet idea was lame.

I waited only another day.

I'd always been of the opinion that it was better to know your enemies; the art teacher was an enemy. I'd noticed that he didn't arrive at school until just before the first bell. I was sure he and his wife had a chore getting two of their four children ready for school and their two pre-school kids ready to be dropped off at our house for my mother to baby-sit. At any rate, he usually roared into the teacher's parking spaces just as every one else was coming to grips with the necessary drudge of another day at school. He'd usually unlock his class door and then go down to the office lounge. Furthermore, the first hour was his free time, a time he spent in the teacher's lounge drinking coffee (and I thought thinking up new ways to stifle art students).

My buddies had to work fast.

Harley and Bernie showed up behind the stage curtains with their arms loaded. The plaster-of-paris came in large, 6-inch wide rolls and was wrapped in cellophane bags. We unwrapped each of the packages and put the rolls in pails of water to soak. Bernie and Harley began laying out the stones on the fireplace, and I started cutting the strips into manageable lengths. We had quite a few done when Mr. Daugherty flung open the curtain. He was followed by our principal Mr. Kessler and Mr. Rath.

He stood in the opening with his hands on his hips.

"You stole that!" he screeched. "You broke into my room and pried the cabinet open! You're nothing but a thief!"

I looked up at him innocently.

"We found the rolls here when we came to school. Gee, Mr. Daugherty, I thought you changed your mind and had someone bring the stuff down here to us."

Mr. Daugherty's face turned a dark scarlet. For a second or two, he couldn't catch his breath.

"That's a lie! You know that's a lie! You're a liar and a thief."

"No, I'm not, Mr. Daugherty. I just thought you finally realized how important this play is to all of us, to the whole school, in fact. I thought you decided to do something just because there was no good reason not to do it. Listen, if someone misunderstood you and brought the plaster-of-paris down here by mistake, we'll take it back."

I held up one of the soaked rolls, dripping whitely across the stage floor.

I looked among the three men's faces. Mr. Rath was thin lipped, but I thought I saw a hint of merriment in his eyes. Mr. Kessler appeared non-committal and didn't say anything. Mr. Daugherty continued to rant.

"What are you two going to do about this?" he asked the other men. "They're thieves and liars, the bunch of them!"

Mr. Kessler definitely smiled.

"They said they'd take it back to your class, Carl."

Mr. Daugherty let out a screech of disgust, turned, and shoved the heavy curtains out of his way. I heard him muttering as he stomped down the stage steps.

Mr. Rath and Mr. Kessler stayed there for a long time, their faces vacillating between troubled and barely suppressed hilarity. Mr. Rath murmured something in our principal's ear, but I didn't catch it. He turned back to us; we were working feverishly before the plaster of paris set up.

"It's a good thing you boys had study hall this morning. Who knows what might have happened if you'd had a class to go to. It's also a good thing you had everything soaked, or who knows what would have happened."

"Yeah, we didn't want to waste any time," I said. "I was afraid that Mr. Daugherty might think better of letting us have the stuff. You know he and I don't get along so well. He might have changed his mind again."

Mr. Rath held the curtain open for Mr. Kessler. He looked back over his shoulder as he followed the principal.

"He might have indeed."

The play met with huge success. The fireplace was as authentic as all get out and fit the scene perfectly. Jim and Sharon were great as college-age boyfriend-girlfriend, as were Sandra and I. Diane, as the old auntie, and Roy, as her faithful but hunch-backed servant were both spooky. The fake bats fluttered across the stage realistically and the moans and groans emanated from the suspended speakers when they were supposed to. Sandra acted perfectly horrified right on cue and kissed me when she was supposed to, fortunately, it wasn't at the same time.

I stumbled only once on the rug when I went center stage and barely flubbed the line; "Oh, Jack, don't be facetious."

Chapter 15

Vengeance Is

To add to my problems, my father returned from his self-imposed exile in the late summer of 1963.

I'd purchased my first car, a Chinese red 1939, Pontiac since working at Shorty's gas station. Just before my senior year, one Friday evening after closing the station and driving home, I saw a strange car in the driveway of our house. When I pulled in, I also noticed the out of state license plate on a dilapidated old Chevrolet parked behind our Dodge and thought, "great, now we're getting do-gooders from out of state."

I went in the house and took off my work boots on the porch. I saw my mother walk into the living room carrying a cup of coffee and hand it to my father. He was already ensconced in his favorite chair.

"Your father's back, Clark," Mom said cheerily, although I could see that she'd been crying. "Isn't that wonderful?"

My father and I had had a strained relationship for several years before he left. He didn't seem to like the fact that I was growing up. He didn't seem to like the fact that I was becoming independent. He didn't seem to like my earning my own money. He didn't seem to like my refusal to respect his every wish. We were about equal in our studied disregard of each other. I thought he was a deliberate bully, quick to take offense, and distant when it came to family participation.

I didn't like him much as a person or a parent.

Mom looked like she'd just witnessed the Second Coming and was all open arms and smiling face, but I was determined not to allow him the faintest glimmer from me of any pleasure at his return. I reluctantly went in to the living room.

"How long is he going to be here?"

I was pretty sure that was the wrong thing to say even before I said it, but I didn't care a whit about my father. I avoided his eyes and looked at my mother. I'd watched my mother age and cry and work and cry and sad-smile and cry for about eighteen months during my father's absence without leave. I hadn't understood my father's abrupt departure. I'd only seen the resulting chaos. I'd seen my brother and sister go without new clothes and suffer through the gibes of friends and family while he was gone. I'd listened to my mother's practiced explanations. I'd listened to my Grandma I.G. swear she didn't know where her son was and learned later that was a lie. I'd listened to Grandma Phoebe rub it in when she said over and over again, "I told you so, Dorothee, I told you so, I told you so."

I walked over to my mother and handed her my week's pay from the gas station. My father had been stewing in his chair since I opened my big mouth, but when he saw me hand the money to my mother, he shot out of the chair like he had a spring tied to his butt.

"I'll take that," he said and grabbed for the few bills in my hand. "Until I can get back to work, I'll take care of any money that comes into this house."

I snatched my hand away and held the bills out in my mother's direction. My father caught my wrist in one hand and tugged at the bills with the other. I held on for brief seconds but then turned the money loose. The battle was only beginning.

My father added some fuel. "You heard what I said."

He quickly fingered through the bills, stuffed them in his pocket, and sat back down. He picked up the cup of coffee, smiled at me (although there was nothing friendly in the smile), and told my mother he was hungry. He also said he wanted to talk to me while Mom was fixing dinner.

"You go on, Dorothee. Clark and I are going to have a talk."

I waited until Mom had gone into the kitchen then turned and headed toward the front door of our enclosed porch. I stopped long enough to grab my car keys and started putting my work boots back on.

My dog Patch hobbled in from her day-bed to get her usual welcome and I gave her a good petting. Although the time I spent with her had diminished, she always greeted me with the same quivering anticipation she had for thirteen plus years. Although I'd refused to admit it Patch had aged during the last winter. Her once tan muzzle was fully threaded with gray; she was going deaf and had arthritis. She still slept in my room when I could coax her into a shove up the attic stairway, but her running days were over.

The pause for Patch resulted in my father following me out to the porch. I hadn't laced the second boot when my father loomed over me.

"I said you and I were going to have a talk."

I continued stuffing my foot in the boot and waited until I got it tied before I answered. I stood up facing him and saw that I was taller than he was. I think he did too.

"I thought we just did. It was the same way you always talk to me. You told me what to do and you expect me to obey you."

I moved toward the door. My father grabbed my arm when I turned to leave.

"We're going to get some things straight before you go anywhere."

I slowly pulled my arm from his grasp and went out the door. When I got in my car, I saw him standing in the doorway staring after me. He was still there when I backed out onto Goddard and drove away.

I spent the weekend sleeping in my car until body odor and hunger birthed a realization. I needed someplace to stay. I continued showing up for work at the gas station and drove by my house over the next week hoping the car my father showed up in was gone. Mom's Dodge was absent from under the Elm tree every day, but from all appearances, my father was sticking close to home. My mother came up to Shorty's every other day or so to plead for my return but I was so caught up in disdain for both parents that I was belligerent every time she did. I was disgusted with Mom for letting him back in and my father for leaving in the first place.

Eventually I found my way to Mr. Rath's house in Toledo. He and

I had developed a very close approximation of friendship and had had numerous talks during my junior year. We'd hashed out my feelings about my father's abandonment although I never quite found the right words to say. Mr. Rath was a great listener and often interspersed his commentary with literary quotes to support his remarks. He'd always allowed full freedom of topics even though my side of the conversation usually ended in rants and raves.

I wasn't disappointed with Mr. Rath's reception when I drove down after work. We sat on the porch of his house long into the first night I showed up. He was attentive and understanding but told me that I could never understand the workings of other people's hearts, my folks included. Mr. Rath also said it was important for me to get my own feelings under command before I devalued anyone else's. For some reason, his words were weightier than other adults and I listened to at least half of them. The end result of our talk that night was that I could stay with him as long as I thought necessary, on condition that he call my parents to tell them where I was. He only smiled when I said my stay would be forever.

It took my folks less than a week to disrupt my new found sanctuary. I hadn't noticed their car when I parked on North Haven Street, but when I went in the back door, I heard their voices in the living room. I would have turned and gone right back out again, but I wasn't sure where it would have been to. Instead of leaving, I stood in the stairway for long minutes until Mr. Rath walked down the steps from the kitchen and convinced me to talk to them.

Our little crisis group talked well into the night. The upshot of the sometimes intense discussion was that I would move back home, and my father and I would work very hard at reconciling our differences. I was reluctant to attempt a return, but Mr. Rath believed in the sanctity of family life and his arguments were a deciding factor. I said I'd be home the next evening. My mother tearfully hugged me, and I reluctantly shook my father's hand. An embrace with him was out of the question.

My father spent the next several weeks reminding me who he was and where his place was in the structure of the family. The entire family was operating with a wary acceptance. Although it had been an extremely difficult time for us financially, we'd scraped by and because of the struggle, had become a close-knit foursome. Our circle-the-wagons attitude had been disrupted by my father's return and his sudden materialization further strained the finances of our family. As soon as he walked in the door, everyone in the church, family, and support groups stopped contributing. Most people thought, "Jerry's back; everything's okay now." But my father thought his immediate job was to reclaim his rightful place as dominant male and he didn't look for work.

Grandma Phoebe was so mad she had Grandpa Teddy drive her down for a confrontation. Grandma had written out a repayment schedule for the money my father's absence cost her and Grandpa and she expected to be repaid. It wasn't pretty.

After I came home my father made sure to appear patient (but firm) when my mother was present and vigorously attempted to insert himself in the growing up of my brother and sister. I felt his concentration on Chip and Peg was due largely to his feeling there was something worthwhile to do where my siblings were concerned. With me, despite the discussion at Mr. Rath's, my father still felt the best way was through force. We continued to revolve around the central figure of my mother: two planets whose orbits were fixed and firm but never intersected. On several occasions, we approached physical violence but had to that point avoided anything so final.

Then one night at dinner, my father announced that he thought it would be best if I went away to another Baptist summer camp for two weeks. Summer was waning, and our relationship was worsening just as surely as the season's change. Where they came up with the money when we were so far behind financially I never knew, but somehow they'd scraped it together. Whatever gyrations they went through in order to send me, they thought my absence would benefit our family's reconciliations.

I thought so, too, but not for the same reasons.

I'd been dating a girl who lived in Detroit. Mitzi and I were introduced at some church function that I hadn't been able to avoid, and I'd been pleasantly surprised at the outcome. I met Mitzi and was instantly smitten despite the required church attendance. She was a bright light at the end of my life's tunnel. She was cute and lithe, clever, graceful, and friendly. I was quickly hooked.

Mitzi and I dated whenever circumstances allowed, wrote letters back and forth, and saw each other at every opportunity. We'd become quite close despite the intervening sixty miles. I hitchhiked when I had to and drove when I could afford the gas money, but much of our blossoming love was conducted long distance. Bible Camp meant Mitzi; I knew she was going to go but hadn't planned on doing so myself. Without appearing too eager, I secretly applauded my parents' decision that I would attend.

I made arrangements for a two week absence from the gas station. Of more concern to me than my job was Patch. She'd gotten so much older during the previous winter; a slight stroke and arthritis had taken a heavy toll on my once supreme companion. Although she and I didn't romp through the fields as we once had, she was still the one to greet me when I came in from school or work. While it was true that she wasn't as quick with her welcome, it was still just as heartfelt. I got promises from Phoebe and Chip for the extra care needed in her advancing age.

Our pastor drove a few of us into Detroit and dropped us off. We departed from Mitzi's church, a whole bus load of kids heading up to the Baptist Camp, ready for soul-saving, rededication to the Lord's work, or any other enlightening experience that afforded itself. In spite of pervious attempts at being alone together, this was Mitzi's and my first outing where some adult wasn't directly viewing our each and every move. We made the entire three hour drive seated tightly together holding hands and I wasn't tired of the pressure of her palm in mine when we arrived. I was in love.

Most Bible Camps are laid out with a military (or penal) precision and this one was no exception. It was (and probably still is) the God given duty of Christian adults to insure that there is absolutely no un-chaperoned contact between the sexes. The sleeping quarters, meeting rooms, and dining facilities were built with this foremost in mind.

The attitude of the camp counselors reinforced the philosophy. The people who met the arriving buses were armed with clipboards, pencils for the checklists and whistles loud enough to halt any unauthorized fraternization. As we got off the bus, boys and girls were separated immediately and marched off in opposite directions. I gazed sorrowfully as Mitzi disappeared into the distance.

The girls were bunked in cabins high on a hill while the boy's were situated down in the shallow valley below. A small stream further divided the two camps with a wooden bridge connecting the two sides. There were various trails leading to a small lake, or to the activities field, or to the dinner area. The counselor's accommodations were slightly down the side of the first slope, an intermediate listening post of sorts. The campsite was built into a thickly wooded area, and it was a pleasant place, cool despite the August heat. On another hill, higher up than the girls' accommodations, sat the community building of the camp. In the middle of the building was an actual tower with glass on four sides, and it had people stationed behind the windows. The building doubled as a meeting hall for the campers, but its real reason for being was to oversee the entire grounds.

The first day was spent with introduction to camp life and ascertaining where each boy or girl was positioned on the ladder rungs leading to God. Interviews were held in the respective cabins, and the group I was in underwent as thorough an investigation into Christian sincerity as I'd ever had. By this time, I'd become so adept at covert disbelief that I could have fooled anyone. I was pretty sure I'd convinced my keeper to think that I was on the right track.

There were endless camp rules and schedules (some even co-ed) that were covered; Bible study (by gender), meal times (co-ed) and activity periods (co-ed, but monitored by grim adults). There were scheduled reflection and prayer times (strictly gender oriented) and doctrine study classes (co-ed). Swimming, water-skiing, and boating were scheduled co-ed, but the boys were specifically warned about eyes lingering on the female form for too long a time. Horse back riding was an optional treat, and each and every teen was warned about straying off the clearly marked paths. New time frames were started with verification of attendance, and there were demerits for being late. Being absent was such a horrific a transgression that one would be sent home immediately if the cause was less than life-threatening. We were there to increase our Faith, and by God, we'd better do so. Everything else was secondary. We could have fun, but there were strict limits, and they weren't fooling.

Mitzi and I managed to shadow each other. We sat together during all co-ed activities, had meals together, and ended the first few days sitting side-by side at the evening's campfires. We'd even managed some longing looks while swimming was in session. I'd never seen anyone who looked quite as good as Mitzi did in a bathing suit. Every tuck was taut just right and every curve plumped perfectly. She had long legs and a slim waist. She looked good. Mitzi smiled generously when she saw me studying the terrain. If I hadn't been smitten before, I certainly was then.

One evening during some presentation, I made up a wildly imaginative tale about sneaking out the previous night. We whispered the fabricated story back and forth in French, a source of study for both of us in the eleventh grade (I secretly thought my teacher, Mrs. Lang, would have been proud). I recounted the snores that emanated from my cabin's overseer, and how his noise overwhelmed any evidence of my outing. Mitzi went along with the farce, and said her counselor wouldn't wake up for the last trumpet. I said things like how much I'd enjoyed our tryst, how her kisses were unbelievable, and how very much I looked forward to seeing her again after my counselor went to sleep that night. Mitzi made up a verse about the moon glow helping us find our way together after lights out. It was great fun and kept me from having to listen to some speaker extol the virtues of a Christian life. It was all a joke, a complete fabrication; two kids having fun, talking about secret things they wished they had courage or age enough to do.

It was also overheard by someone who spoke French.

By the time we walked back to our cabins after the gathering, some counselors were waiting for me. I found out later that there were more of them waiting for Mitzi as well.

I had to hand it to them. The pseudo wardens didn't tip their hand until they got me securely away. At first they told me there was a message for me in the main office. Unsuspecting, I followed along when they walked toward camp central. The two men who were waiting for me carried their subterfuge to great extent making pleasant small talk on the way. Maybe they thought I'd make an escape attempt and they wanted to make sure the sinner paid. Maybe those two didn't really know why I'd been summoned. I worried during our walk that something bad had happened at home. Maybe my father had left again. Maybe Patch had had a duplicate of her previous winter's stroke.

The camp director motioned me to a chair across from his desk. I figured it had to be something wrong at home. Once the door closed behind me their nice faces disappeared in a twinkling when the director started.

"What happened between you and that girl?"

At first I didn't connect the dots of Mitzi and me fabricating the make-believe assignation.

"Huh?"

"I asked what you and that girl did when you snuck out last night," he said.

I still didn't get it. I couldn't imagine that we'd been talking loud enough for anyone to overhear or that anyone would be interested enough to pay attention. It never dawned on me that anyone would be fluent in French or would eavesdrop on a private conversation. More importantly, I'd known for a long time to plead ignorance when confronted with any accusation. Unfortunately, I didn't take into account the heralded tenant of Christian leadership. Everybody is guilty and everybody sins.

"What?"

"Listen...we know you and that..."

He glanced at a sheet of paper on his desk.

"...Mitzi went out after everyone was asleep. We know you were necking and that you broke just about every rule we have. I want to know what went on before I call both your parents and have them come and get you."

"Nothing happened. We made it all up," I countered. "It was a game, a play act. It was just something fun to do during the skit."

"That's a lie! Someone heard all about your sneaking ways, how you two were kissing...and God only knows what else."

During my entire life, I'd dreaded facing accusations that I'd done something wrong. Many times the accuser was right. Some of the time I was innocent, but those times weren't frequent. I bore punishments, comeuppances, and restrictions with deliberate stoicism and a certain amount of acceptance when I couldn't avoid them completely. I knew that wrongs had to get put right and that vengeance belonged to the Lord (and my mother). I knew there was payback required for property and feelings damaged by me. I'd been spanked, whipped, swatted, switched, and twitched my entire life.

I also knew when to stand up tall when the accuser was wrong.

"I told you, it was all make believe," I repeated. "We didn't sneak out."

"Don't make it any worse by compounding the problem with lies. You and that girl did something bad..."

He didn't get to finish the rest. I was up out of the chair I'd been sitting in so fast I caught them all off guard. I stretched myself over the desk and made a grab at him. He scooted back in his chair.

"Don't say another word!" I shouted at him. "I told you what really happened! If you want to think it's a lie, then think so. Think whatever you want, but don't say another word about Mitzi!"

One of my escorts grabbed me from behind in a bear hug. He turned me loose as suddenly as he'd first grabbed but then made another attempt at physically controlling me and I struggled against him.

"All right," the director said. "That's enough."

"Yes, it is," I replied. "I'm not going to do anything. As long as you keep your mouth shut about Mitzi."

I went on to have an interrogation that would have done the Spanish Inquisition proud. The only things lacking were thumb screws and the rack. I was threatened with numerous punishments. He said he'd send me home in disgrace. Then he included Mitzi in the expulsion. Eventually the director figured out that I wasn't going to attack him and he dismissed the other two men, but that was only the beginning. In a calmer tone he went on to detail my responsibilities as a Christian youth, and the sanctity of physical love and the necessity of abstinence before marriage.

I put up with it for a couple of reasons. First was the scene I envisioned if I was sent back home. The ugliness of that in my mind convinced me to be as contrite as possible while not admitting anything. My other reason was Mitzi. I certainly didn't want to put her in harm's way, either from fact or fiction. The director and I talked well past lights out, and by the time he walked me back to my cabin, I was sure he believed my protestations of innocence.

During breakfast the next morning Mitzi recounted her experience. Four women counselors ganged up on her with the same suspicious allegations. They threatened her with a phone call to home and even went so far as to tell her that they were going to take her home that very night.

"We will not allow these things to happen."

"Think of your reputation."

"Think of what your parents will say."

"God loves a chaste woman."

Despite the intense questioning, Mitzi had also been able to convince her cross-examiners regarding the innocence of our game. She was very worried that some sort of report would reach her parents and I was as well. We wondered who it was that had listened in and why they'd felt it necessary to report their suspicions. We also wondered how something so simple could have turned into such a huge issue in so short a time.

"Yeah, well you know how these Baptists are," I teased.

"Yes, I do," Mitzi laughed. "Everybody is guilty until proven innocent."

"They will be watching us," she breathed in my ear.

And watch us they did. Furthermore, some of these God fearing and righteous people had seen fit to leak the story. By the end of the following day, there were enough Clark/Mitzi observers walking around the camp to insure that a timeline was developed for our bathroom breaks, intake of food, and numeric values assigned for piety expressed during prayer.

"If we're already guilty…" Mitzi murmured. "I won't put up with much more of them following me around."

I shrugged my shoulders. Nothing I could have said would have mattered.

"Do you think they're really worried about my reputation?" Mitzi asked. "Or theirs?"

The intense scrutiny provided results, but not the ones they expected. Maybe Mitzi and I would have found our way into an increased intimacy anyway.

Their accusations may have prompted us to find out what they were so concerned about. Our hand holding progressed to more personal caresses. I trembled to find that Mitzi was all smoother skin under her sweatshirt. Nights were cool in northern Michigan, and around the campfires at night Mitzi and I sometimes took a blanket for the extra warmth (and hidden motives). She voiced a small coo whenever she embraced my bare chest. Everything about her was perfect: her touch, her feel, her scent, and I hungered after more. Our petting was softly exquisite, tentative, and slow in development and mutually delightful. Each moment we were together blazed by with the speed of light and lasted forever.

Wherever we went, whatever we were doing, Mitzi and I searched for an opportunity to slip off. Despite the notoriety we'd gathered, in a camp of that size, with two or three hundred other kids running around, it was comparatively easy. With each successive tryst, it became easier and more important to do. Even the knowledge of the penalty that often comes with forbidden fruits didn't dampen our enthusiasm.

I'd been in love before, attracted to a pretty face or shapely form. This time love became real in more ways than I thought possible. For the first time in my life, I became psychologically and physically attracted in equal proportions.

Mitzi and I talked about everything. Her voice was music to me, and I was in love with the song. We discussed our increasing love. We talked at the breakfast table, during Bible study, and during the night activities. We pondered the passages in Psalms that sang the human form and wondered why they weren't used more in sermons. We wondered why babies died and if they went to heaven. We questioned how our physical caresses could be wrong if they felt that right. Our discussions were intense and for me were totally new; I'd spent my entire life having serious conversations only with Patch.

As far as I was concerned, this camp had done something for me like nothing before. By the time our two weeks were up and the church bus was ready to take us back to Detroit, I so strongly associated Bible Camp with the delight of Mitzi, I'd have moved there permanently. I was certainly a born again something.

We spent the trip home shamelessly hidden under a blanket, greedy for continued caresses. For all we cared, there might not have been another soul (lost or otherwise) riding along with us.

I'd never done anything more difficult than saying goodbye to Mitzi when the bus got back. I told her I'd call the next day.

With all the childhood indoctrination I'd received about punishment for sins, real or imagined, I should have known.

My father met me in the driveway when our pastor dropped me off. The glowing bubble I'd been wearing for the last two weeks vaporized.

Patch was dead, and my father was the assassin. He tried to explain, but I wanted no reasons for his act of abomination. I cursed him; cursed life in general; cursed myself, and ran away from the house to spend the night and the next day in the marsh retracing paths and trying to recapture memories. I failed miserably at both. I'd changed during my stay at the camp and so had the marsh. It was so much different I almost didn't recognize it. The quiet allure I'd experienced as a boy in my beloved sanctuary disappeared as surely as nightfall came over the reed beds. It was empty of noise. It was empty of life. It was empty of my dog.

It was the first time I'd ever been there without Patch by my side and it was the last time I ever went.

But God wasn't finished.

When I finally did go back home from the marsh, the first thing on my mind was Mitzi. I couldn't wait to share my father's treachery. I wanted someone to talk to. I needed some commiseration; someone to listen to me and assure me that everything would eventually work out. Mitzi was the perfect choice.

She was tearful when she came to the phone. I thought it odd because I hadn't begun to tell her my sad tale, but illumination was always a slow process for me. I launched into the sorrowful description of my homecoming, a candid but jaded ramble of words, a spitting and venting laced with enough curse words to fill a gunny sack. I was hurt, I was mad, I was…

Mitzi quietly interrupted my diatribe.

"I told my mother."

"Yeah, but my father killed…what?"

"I told my mother about our petting. I told her we loved each other, but my feelings about doing something that I knew was wrong…I had to talk to someone…I never wanted anything so much…I knew we shouldn't, but I wanted…"

"And you told…"

"My mom. I had to. I've never felt this way before."

"But you told your *mother*?"

I was incredulous. I'd only shared my inner feelings with Patch.

314

That was safe. Patch wouldn't tell anyone even if she could have. I did not talk to my parents about anything so personal (or delightful) as Mitzi. Thoughts bounced around in my head like a run amok ping-pong ball. The trouble with sharing private feelings was that they didn't remain private for long; it was sharing a secret. If two people know, a secret can remain a secret. If three people know, pretty soon it was front page news, the talk of the town. I envisioned her mother telling her father. I envisioned her mother calling my mother. I envisioned her father calling my father...I imagined her father loading the deer rifle he'd once shown me. All sorts of unhappy scenarios raced through my mind. There was going to be enormous penance for this.

"My mom said we can't see one another anymore. After talking with her, I think that's best, too."

"But, Mitzi...! No! You can't mean that! I love you! I'll tell your mother I'm sorry." I thought about that briefly. "Better yet, *you* tell your mother I'm sorry."

"I love you, too, so very, very much. But my mother said that we're only sixteen, and I can't let this continue."

"But, Mitzi..."

"I love you, Clark, but I can't see you anymore."

A buzzing filled my head, and it wasn't just the dial tone. I held the phone to my ear for some time after she hung up, wishing, hoping, pleading, that somehow the connection would be re-established. When the soft tone changed to a harsh breep-breep, breep-breep, I cradled the receiver.

The finality of our phone conversation settled darkly about me. I knew I didn't have enough integrity to plead my case before her parents. I was afraid they'd yell. I was afraid they'd scream, and I knew I had it coming. I'd never been good at facing up to problems I'd gotten myself into. This was no exception.

I actually prayed that night. It had been a long time and I was uncomfortable with bringing words to the Someone I'd hidden my thoughts from for so long. I prayed to ease the vacuum Patch's death left me in. I prayed to ease the hurt of losing Mitzi. I prayed long and hard in between the tears. Just before I went to sleep, I imagined I heard God speak to me. He paraphrased Numbers 32:23: "Be sure your sins will find you out..."

He sounded strangely like my mother.

I was so sluggish in high school I should have left a trail of slime.

My junior year had been noteworthy for such diverse accomplishments as changing the grades on my report cards to avoid the trouble for substandard results, skipping an inordinate amount of school, and generally making such a nuisance of myself that I spent equal amounts of time in class and in detention.

I was good for an occasional smart-assed remark and under duress, I handed in most assignments. I could frequently get myself mostly out of the trouble I'd gotten myself into with charm or extra credit. But for some reason, I just wasn't able to get motivated with school work. I handed in assignments late and incomplete. I sketched pictures in class, instead of doing lessons and pretty much ignored the necessity of preparing for an adult foray into life. I cut classes, cut school, and didn't pay attention. With the exception of eleventh grade English and the junior class play, I was in way over my head.

My final year of high school started out equally rife with problems.

I'd been forced to learn several hiding places safe enough to wait out any current Clark Crisis that reared its ugly head. Mrs. Vincent would give me occasional sanctuary in the library or Mr. Rath could be talked into a hall pass, and in a pinch, Mr. Zinner could be counted on to come through with a hiding place. Our custodian was pretty wary after the Mr. Daugherty episode, but every once in a while, he'd relent and let me through the door into the boiler room.

Left to their own devices, most teenage boys perpetually slide down, and I wasn't alone in this dissolute attitude. Whatever contaminated me must have been contagious, or maybe I caught it from someone else. In all likelihood I was the Typhoid Mary of the group. Similar to other sufferers, I sought the company of those I could relate to, and we were as easy to spot as a group of lepers. Fortunately, all of the afflicted lived within walking distance of the bus stop. Among Harley, Pete, Bernie and I, a reason not to go to school was easier to come up with than one to attend.

While other kids were planning their careers and deciding which college they would attend, we concentrated on such lofty ideals as right bower, left bower, and naming of trump. Of course, we had to find some den of iniquity in which to sharpen our card playing skills, but that was fairly easy.

Pete's parents both worked and left home early every morning. Because Pete had to take his younger sister Mary to school, his parents had given him the use of a car, a 1958 Chevrolet. Pete could often be encouraged to drop his sister off at the junior high building and come back to his house. Harley, Bernie, and I would be waiting behind a bush or sheltered from prying eyes in back of their breezeway. Or we'd all pile in the car, take Mary to school, and bypass the high school on Williams Road with no particular destination in mind. With our collective imaginations, we most often wound up at Pete's house. We didn't need much preparation to have all the makings of a day of truancy: a deck of cards and cigarettes.

Skipping school was for us initially, just a sometime thing. We'd cut a half day every other week or so, and it was easy to lay off some extra assignment as the reason for our failure to show up. As long as we kept abreast of work assignments (although this was where my cover eventually failed) most teachers really didn't notice which face was missing. In particular, I had the excuse of being on the yearbook committee and produced many authorized requests for me to be doing something other than attending scheduled classes. Many of my teachers had become so accustomed to my absence that they didn't ask for the signed permission slips.

Predictably, Bernie, Pete, Harley, and I gradually increased our euchre tournaments. Additionally, Pete's parents both smoked and the remnants of our smoking wouldn't be noticed as they would have been in my house. My mother could smell cigarette smoke at twenty paces. I was careful to rinse my mouth and sprinkle aftershave on my clothes whenever we skipped school.

If we didn't have any money to buy our own cigarettes, the ashtrays in Pete's house could always be counted on to supply our growing nicotine requirements since his folks left long portions of un-smoked cigarettes in the numerous ashtrays, and we weren't above smoking them.

Why we thought we'd get away with such blatant skipping isn't clear even now. Our thoughts of paying the piper for the day's absence weren't too logical if they ever existed in any form. The most we thought about was who would buy the next day's smokes.

Following the eventual depravity of every addict, we used and used and used our truancy until our prolonged and frequent absences couldn't be ignored.

We were called in for questioning. I don't recall what the others gave as a reason, but I concocted some wild tale about my mother being ill. We children were being tended by a grandmother, but she hadn't thought to write me a note explaining the positively, absolutely, undeniable reason that I must, had to, couldn't have done it another way but to stay at home and help Grandma take care of her. My poor ruse didn't last any longer than a phone call to my house.

The comeuppance party that was held in Mr. Kessler's small office was attended by everyone whether they had reason to be there or not. Bernie's folks, my folks, Harley's folks, Pete's folks, school secretaries and teachers and student helpers, all squashed and gaggled about in the office or at the door. The entire affair was over-laid by a distinct buzz of speculation, but the background noise did nothing to deafen the impending doom. Mr. Kessler laid it on heavy. He said that our behavior was inexcusable and that we'd made it all too clear that none of us were ready to graduate, as witnessed by our poor grades, our truancy, and our obvious immaturity.

He went on and on about our failures and how disappointed he was that we had squandered (I recall that word particularly) that which we would look back on in the future as our best years. He bemoaned the fact that we were products of a school over which he had responsibility; lamentations over lost trust, a requiem of issues he'd already overlooked on our part before this latest dishonesty, and a dire prediction that our current behavior would probably lead us further down the road of condemnation. Mr. Kessler could also be caustically sarcastic. He wasn't above assuring each and every parent that they could probably look forward to seeing our smiling faces on the cork boards of post offices in the near future.

The lecture and predictions went on for a long, long time. He further said that we were suspended for a week even though our grades were already in serious doubt due to our absences. He told us that if we didn't care about ourselves, there was certainly no reason for him to do so; he'd put up with us this long, he could put up with us again next year. With the jibe of post offices beating the four of us about the head and shoulders, he dismissed the group. After insuring each and every parent that we would surely NOT graduate, he stood by the door as we ushered out. I expected to see the executioner's tumbrel waiting in the parking lot.

My home sentencing was shockingly minimal. I was sure my parents didn't know what to do, and I didn't blame them. I didn't know what to do.

Mr. Kessler let us stew for two days.

He called all the parents back for another conference, but the guilty four weren't included. Whatever went on in his office, none of us ever found out, but I was told that I was going to go back to school before the week's suspension was up...on condition.

It should have been condition(s). There were plenty of them and each was inviolate. Grades would improve and continue to improve. Smart-assing in classes and halls was forbidden. Association among each of the Infamous Four was limited (in school) to nil. Our classes were rescheduled to eliminate taking classes with Bernie and Harley for fear of recurring contamination. Pete was a junior, so we didn't share any class time, but Bernie and Harley attended class sans Clark, and Clark attended classes sans Bernie and Harley. Our behavior, dress, demeanor, attitude, work habits, timeliness of assignments could and would be checked and re-checked by any and all teachers at any time. Our responses to this tight security must appropriately include the words, "Yes, Ma'am and Yes, Sir, or No, Ma'am and No, Sir." We were to report to Mr. Kessler's office at the beginning and ending of each day so that he could review homework assignments and check their completion.

I finally got the message...or at least part of it.

Although I'd been part of the college prep group, I had no intention of prolonging my formal schooling. I'd already been promised by one of my paper-route customers that he would sponsor me in an apprenticeship at Chrysler Corporation where he worked as a tool and die maker. As soon as my eighteenth birthday rolled around in the December after graduation, I was headed for the auto industry.

In the aftermath of the close watch on me, I tried to maintain the classes with which I'd begun the year, but reality found a way for me to be truthful about my ingrained indifference.

I started each school year with a stupid cheerfulness in a complete disregard of past accomplishment and my senior year was no different. I was always sure I'd do better this time before the reality of me set in.

As good as Mr. Bumbaugh was as a teacher, he was a better man.

He was Jefferson's chemistry teacher, and like all good college prep students, I'd been scheduled to take his class. I'd been great with my childhood chemistry sets; I knew how to make invisible ink, turn innocuous powders into gagging clouds of rotten eggs, and could produce a creditable splat of fake vomit on demand. I could fizz the contents of a test tube with the best of kids and knew about the test that proved the supposed gold nugget was a fool's wish. I thought I'd do well and who could tell what serious experiments we might find ourselves party to.

By November, I knew it was a futile if not lost undertaking. I spent much of my chemistry class time thinking up good reasons to drop it. There were so many people I'd have to convince: both parents now that my father had returned; Mr. Eaton, our school counselor; Mr. Bumbaugh, and, of course, Mr. Kessler. Although I'd done much, much better in the marking periods after the truancy episode, I was still on very shaky ground academically. Without chemistry it would be a near run race to graduate. With my impending grades in that class, there wouldn't even be a race.

The chemistry class that day in November began with an announcement of a pop quiz. How I dreaded them! It was always push and shove to get any chemical equations to take up even temporary residence in my head when I studied. Without pouring over the book at night, I had even less chance remembering anything past H_2O. I inwardly groaned at the thought of another "D" or "E" next to my name is the grade ledger. I was relieved when the loudspeaker interrupted Mr. Bumbaugh as he was handing out the quiz papers.

I welcomed anything that put off the inevitable.

The microphone screeched as someone in the office turned on the PA system. Mr. Kessler's voice strained over the static of the speaker but everyone heard what he said.

"This is Mr. Kessler and I have an announcement: John F. Kennedy, the President of the United States, has been shot. At this time details are sketchy, but the President has been shot as he toured Dallas, Texas. His condition is unknown. Further announcements will be made as information is updated. We will suspend classes for the remainder of the day. All teachers are instructed to keep their students in class until the buses arrive."

Mr. Bumbaugh had just been walking down the aisle that held my desk. I heard his sharp intake of breath. He uttered a moan, long and low, drawn out as if he was in agony. He dropped the quiz papers to the floor, as if his hands couldn't remember what to do. His shoulders slumped. It appeared that he shrunk in size, and great tears began coursing down his cheeks.

He walked to the front of the class and stood facing the blackboard for long minutes. Several students began to weep. The entire class could hear his stifled sobs as they gave way to hoarse groans of misery. I watched his shoulders shudder with the tragedy of loss. He pulled a handkerchief from his suit pocket and wiped his eyes before turning to face the class.

"You will never know another day like this, not if you live to be a hundred," he began.

He walked around his desk and sat on the edge. He wiped his eyes again and still his cheeks were wet with tears, unabated as he looked slowly from face to face to face in the classroom. Several more students began to cry as well. Many of the kids were uncomfortable with this display of emotion. Some softly laughed to allay the feeling.

"Of all the terrible things mankind does to one another, this is the worst. This…this…abomination, will change what we do, what we think, what we believe forever. We will never again be the same as we were five minutes ago."

He got up, once again overcome with the gravity of the announcement. He stood in front of us for more long moments before speaking again. His voice still quavered when he began again despite his obvious struggle to compose himself.

"Even though class is not in session, I'd like to talk to you while we wait for the buses. Maybe it will help you deal with this…maybe it will help me do so too. I don't know which…You are young people, just starting out, just finding out, really, what life is like. Despite what you think you know you know so little about the Outside…Most days the Outside is a fine place filled with people going to work, people taking care of their children, people doing the things that keep us together as a people…as a country…as human beings. But sometimes, the Outside isn't quite as beautiful as we'd like. Sometimes, like today, the Outside is downright ugly."

Someone in class asked to be excused to go to the bathroom, and Mr. Bumbaugh used the interruption to calm himself further. Many kids were crying openly now. I was one of them.

He intoned a litany: "The newspapers said the same thing in 1865 and 1881 and 1901, 'The President Has Been Shot.' John Fitzgerald Kennedy might make four. Whether you liked him or whether you didn't, whether you even knew who he was or what he stood for, I want you to know this; every time this has happened, America has changed for the worse. I'm not your history teacher, but what you've received today is a pivot on which we all must turn."

Mr. Bumbaugh's voice broke again.

"This country has already let someone kill three of our presidents. Hopefully, President Kennedy won't be the fourth. Some statesman or other philosopher once said that if we ignore history, then we are doomed to repeat it. Have we ignored something? I don't know, but someone shot our president today. Right now we don't even know how bad he is; he may be dying. I pray that's not the case. If this tragedy is not resolved, if this country can't fix this, this…whatever it is, then we are not doomed to repeat history, we are damned. Yours may be the generation upon which this burden will fall. The questions you must ask yourselves are these…Am I brave enough to fix the ailments of our country? Am I smart enough? Will I put forth the effort?"

His voice trailed off into silence. The loudspeaker interrupted and announced that students could go to their lockers and then board their respective buses. Everyone silently gathered up their sweaters and books or slung their jackets over their shoulders as we filed out. There was none of the usual chatter as we left the room. I turned to look back just before I left the classroom. Mr. Bumbaugh was hunched over, his face close to his knees, with his arms wrapped tightly around himself. He rocked back and forth several times, as if in supplication, and his body shook with silent grief. I'd never seen anyone so sad.

The halls were full of whispering kids. Teachers quietly stood by classroom doors as we walked by, and all of them looked like they'd been crying. Locker doors were closed quietly, reverently, as if some loud noise would interrupt an unspoken prayer. There was no jostling for seats on the bus, and there was no friendly greeting from the driver. The buses were silently filled with kids, and they eased away from the school in a long yellow line; it looked a great deal like a funeral procession.

By June of 1964, I finally found myself in a place I was moderately proud of.

Although I still had visions of Patch and me running through the marsh, they were more dim and less heart wrenching. I was reminded of Patch by her absence when I came through the door, but I'd moved on. I'd made something of a peace with my father and by mutual consent, we left one another alone. I still visited Mitzi in my dreams, but the dreams were less painful. I thought I could occasionally catch the scent of her, but the touch recollections had taken second place to work and school and life.

I'd also finally figured out that grades were more than a mark on a card and had applied myself during the last half of the school year. No one was more surprised than I was at the outcome. Teachers who had previously frowned to see my name on the class roster appeared, if not exactly happy, at least complacent about my being in their rooms. I'd re-established myself among the living in family and school. I was on the yearbook staff and enjoyed the intricacies of putting something together for publication. Mr. Rath and I had become fast friends, and I actually listened to him when he acted as an advisor. He continued to insist that I seek more formal education, but I was unsure.

Yet, I had made it that far.

Despite the indifference, absenteeism and poor grades, it looked as if I'd graduate. It was a near run race and the only reason I crossed the finish line may have been Mr. Kessler's distinct horror at the thought of having me to deal with for another year. He told me just before the end of the school year that I'd done admirably well despite a very shaky beginning. He also equated the shakiness to a magnitude 7.0 earthquake.

During my high school commencement ceremonies, our valedictorian spoke of the metaphorical path we were standing on. Susan said the trail beckoned us with promise; we were supposed to stride with strong, confident steps and lay claim the distant territory for our very own. She said we'd been given a map during high school, and with these directions in hand, the journey would be enjoyable and rewarding. The path she spoke of was lined with beautiful trees and flowers and strayed not from leading each of us to success.

To me the path appeared rutted and wandering, and was littered with sharp rocks and deep chasms which waited to impede the already weary me. Lining my path were shortcuts of questionable virtue and sirens of sweet and seductive voice. Although Susan could obviously see the promised wonderful end of her path, my path was shrouded in a dark and thickening mist. I had a hard time envisioning an easy hike.

I was pretty sure it was going to be an uphill climb.